EUROPEAN
BUSINESS
STRATEGIES

THE EUROPEAN AND GLOBAL STRATEGIES OF EUROPE'S TOP COMPANIES

SECOND EDITION

RICHARD LYNCH

KOGAN
PAGE

First published in 1990
This edition published in 1994

Apart from any fair dealing for the purposes of research or private study, or criticism or review, as permitted under the Copyright, Designs and Patents Act, 1988, this publication may only be reproduced, stored or transmitted, in any form or by any means, with the prior permission in writing of the publishers, or in the case of reprographic reproduction in accordance with the terms of licences issued by the Copyright Licensing Agency. Enquiries concerning reproduction outside those terms should be sent to the publishers at the undermentioned address:

Kogan Page Limited
120 Pentonville Road
London N1 9JN

© Aldersgate Consultancy Limited, 1990, 1994

British Library Cataloguing in Publication Data

A CIP record for this book is available from the British Library.

ISBN 0 7494 11724

Typeset by DP Photosetting, Aylesbury, Bucks
Printed and bound in Great Britain by Biddles Ltd, Guildford and King's Lynn

EUROPEAN BUSINESS STRATEGIES

Contents

This book is dedicated to my parents.

Acknowledgements

This second edition has benefited from feedback on the 1990 version; response from an extra 150 companies; global as well as European emphasis; more on the reasons behind the strategies employed; more on publicly-owned and private companies. As before, it has been an immensely complex book to put together. I thank you all for your comments. I would also like to thank the following for permission to reproduce extracts from the material cited: the Commission of the European Communities for 1989 data from *Panorama of EC Industry, Eurostats*, and *1992: The European Challenge*; the *Financial Times* for material from their 'Top 500 European Companies'; the A.C. Nielsen Company for *International Food and Drug Store Trends, 1988*; Professor J.A. Kay of the Centre for Business Strategy, London Business School for quotes from *1992: Myths and Realities*; Professor Peter Doyle of Warwick Business School, Professor J. Saunders of Loughborough University and L. Wright of Coventry University, for extracts from a joint paper; Landor Associates for brand image data from the *First Landor Image Power TM Study 1989*; Henderson Crosthwaite for market data.

In addition, I would like to thank the following organizations and individuals: all the European companies mentioned in the text which so freely make corporate data available to outsiders and thus contribute significantly to the development of international understanding; Bill Ramsey of Templeton College, Oxford for his help in contacting Nielsen and some helpful comments on business strategy; Charles Sproat, formerly Chief Executive of Leaf UK, for pointing me towards trends in European retailing; David Edelshain of City University, for his comments on an earlier draft and our many subsequent discussions on issues in the text; Colin Haslam and his colleagues at the University of East London; Roger Pudney of Ashridge Management College for prompting me to begin the process; Philip Mudd at Kogan Page for his unfailing help, advice and support.

Finally, my gratitude goes to my brothers and sister, Mike and Gerry Lynch and Anne Dobbing, for their suggestions, comments and encouragement. Our father died as this edition was being completed; this is a tribute to his memory.

While every effort has been made to ensure that all data and material in this book is accurate, neither myself nor the publisher accepts any responsibility for its accuracy. Nevertheless, if the reader sees something wrong or, more likely, capable of another interpretation, then I would welcome any comments.

Richard Lynch
March, 1994

Introduction

While Europe still represents a major strategy focus for many businesses, the single European market is no longer the only challenge: Eastern Europe and global opportunities are also opening up. The 1993 agreements on European Union and world trade (the Uruguay Round of the GATT) have removed some of the uncertainties in these areas and presented new growth areas. This second edition of *European Business Strategies* therefore reflects these new realities without losing sight of Europe itself.

For both European and North American companies the process of removing trade barriers, from whatever source, will also bring increased competition in European and world markets. The potential impact on profitability is significant. We live in demanding times. This second edition has therefore not just been updated, but has totally new case studies and an additional global approach to reflect these issues.

Although most business executives and business strategy students will want to undertake their own evaluations, many will also want to understand the *experience of other companies*. This book addresses this issue directly. It is based around a new study of Europe's top 400 companies and what they are doing about European and global issues; some are implementing profoundly new strategies, even if success so far has been variable.

Evidence on the activities of other companies demands a *European and global strategic framework* if it is to be useful – and one drawn from the reality of what is really happening in the new competitive marketplace, not just a 'shopping list' of possible options.

This second edition brings all this material together in an expanded framework. It still remains a unique sourcebook of European corporate strategy practices and of European and global industry structures.

Objectives and contents

Tackling European and global issues will involve exploring two key questions: how are other companies undertaking the task and what is the best strategic framework to meet the challenges?

The objectives of this book are to answer these questions, both for the large company looking for ways to exploit the new opportunities and for the smaller company seeking new ideas and contacts in the new wider markets. The structure of the book is outlined in the Figure on page 12 and explained later in this chapter.

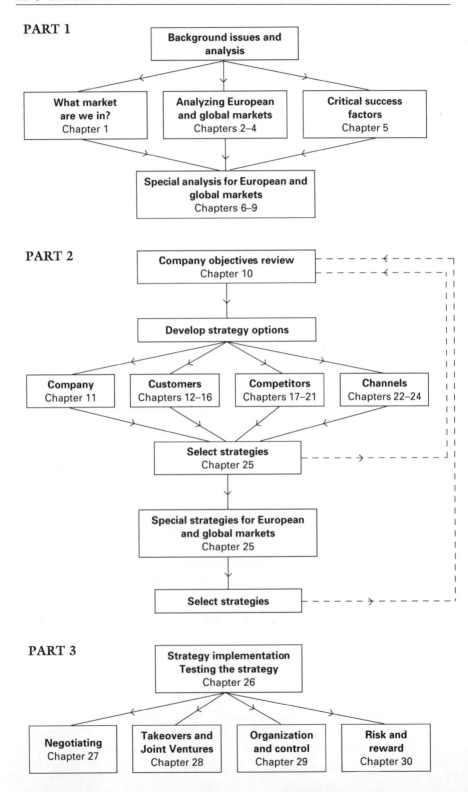

More generally, the book provides a framework to help companies:

- Examine European and global dimensions with factual data;
- Assess the most profitable course of action;
- Evaluate competition both within the existing 'home market' and in the new larger market arena;
- Develop the best ways to meet the challenge and opportunities;
- Protect existing profits and activities.

However it is no substitute for the work that individual companies or students will need to undertake. The book's continued strength is firstly its breadth of strategy and industry coverage. In addition, it continues to provide ideas, facts and a clear framework to develop the strategy process.

Business strategy guidelines have been especially developed to tackle European and global issues. These are illustrated with 100 case studies of how top European companies are facing the new opportunities and problems. Top US and Japanese company involvement is also covered, particularly where it may impact Europe.

In addition, there are 25 European market sector analyses of how top companies fit into main markets, outside basic commodities. These can be used as a starting point for more detailed, individual studies as well as being further examples of some major European and global strategies. They also provide a checklist for prospecting company sales and purchasing managers. Virtually all Europe's top 400 companies are used to demonstrate various key points covering the main market sectors. As I have discovered myself over the last five years, this range of information simply does not exist anywhere else in a usable format.

Because the book has also proved a highly popular student text, it is worth explaining that the strategy process used is totally consistent with many basic textbooks: background, then the development of strategy options, with selection of the optimal strategy and its implementation. However, I have left out most of the theory references, which are well covered elsewhere.

Structure and sources

The book is arranged in three parts: profitably analysing the current European and global situation; developing a successful business strategy; and implementing the strategy that has been developed. Each part is then divided into chapters that explore a particular topic with case studies to highlight the practicalities.

The company examples need a word of explanation. For reasons of space I have made no attempt to describe each company in great detail. (How can you describe Ford, Nestlé or Unilever adequately in 150 words?) That information is usually available from public sources. The cases therefore concentrate on information that is less readily accessible, and are directed solely at strategy issues.

Because our prime purpose is to explore strategy, the European companies in the book have been selected on the basis of turnover, rather than market capitalisation, except for banks and insurance companies where this is not feasible. This has the great additional advantage that companies in the public sector are included in the sample; essential when examining some European countries and markets. The reasoning is explored more fully in Appendix 1.

No study would be complete in some markets without North American and Japanese companies. These have therefore been added on a selective basis, again largely based on turnover.

Each case study of a European company is divided into three parts. First, there is a brief summary of the latest sales and market data, this is supplemented by four further statistics, especially calculated to give an indication of the company's strategic status in late 1992. These are:

1. *Return on capital* This is calculated before tax and interest and is used as measure of company profitability in relation to its asset base. The strengths and weaknesses of this ratio are well known and the detail of its definition is given in Appendix 2.
2. *Percentage of sales in the home country* This expressed as a percentage of the company's total sales. It is a useful indicator of the strategic task facing the company; some firms rely heavily on sales in their home territory. This means that there is a greater task if they are to expand elsewhere in Europe and the world. There is also greater reliance on the national economy and may also be the possibility of greater vulnerability to competitive threat.
3. *Percentage of sales in the rest of Europe* This indicates a company's experience of, and reliance on, Europe for its current business. It will therefore provide a measure of how it may need to move forward. 'Europe' throughout the book means all of Western Europe, principally the European Community (EC) and European Free Trade Area (EFTA) countries. Occasionally, it may include Eastern Europe. This is explained further in Appendix 2.
4. *Percentage of sales in the rest of the world* This will show global involvement beyond Europe. As we will explore later, this may be vital for strategy development in some markets.

The second part of each case study is devoted to European and global activity. Outlines are given of published actions by companies in these areas. This is a general review and bears no particular relationship to the context of the chapter of the case study.

Finally, 'keypoint on strategy' sets out how the case study addresses a specific aspect of strategy development.

Most of the material used in the book is from published data sources. However, for a variety of reasons, some European, North American and Japanese companies publish only limited European and global data. In order to ensure that the text summarises the strategy issues adequately, some estimates have been used where necessary. This has been recorded in the text and is explored more fully in Appendix 1.

How has the strategy structure been developed?

One of the problems of business strategy is that there is sometimes too much of it. Another is that some of it has only limited connection to the special issues of pan-Europe and global strategy development.

What I have chosen to do is to follow a conventional path but without the use of technical terms where possible. Thus I have left out some of the theory and concentrated on the end result. I have also included some modern thinking that still only appears occasionally in strategic texts, for example, quality management and technical development should, in my view, be part of the fundamental strategy of the company.

As well as the normal strategic analysis, I have identified and focused on four specific areas that every company needs to explore in European and global markets:

1. Defending the home market;
2. Tackling production overcapacity as a result of the single Europe or global competition;
3. Seeking lower costs from economies of scale and innovation;
4. Achieving larger sales from Europe and global markets.

For most companies, if they can devise optimal strategies in these areas then the rest should follow. Aspects of these areas are tackled throughout the book and then they are brought together at the end of Part II.

Because the four areas are at the nub of European and global strategy development, let us also introduce them now and assess their significance for the strategy development process.

With regard to defending the home market as trade barriers come down, strategy development is a two-way process; not only will the home industry be able to expand into other markets but, potentially, other companies can invade the home territory. But will this apply to all markets and all companies? Probably not, but what will make the difference and how can a company protect itself? We will look at the strategies some companies have undertaken.

As barriers come down in Europe and around the world, production overcapacity has already led to leading European companies going out of business, for example in the European steel industry and computer manufacturing. Excess capacity in some areas across Europe and the world will only lead to greater efficiency and the savings projected for national economies, if some companies are closed down. How do companies tackle these issues? What strategies can be found to minimise the damage?

With lower trade barriers from the single Europe and the GATT Round, it may be possible to obtain economies of scale, for example through the concentration of production into fewer countries, and the significant cost savings in transport and logistics now being implemented by some European companies. What are the benefits and will they outweigh the costs? We will look at the activities of top European and global companies.

Examining the scope for sales development from the new Europe it will be evident that there are opportunities. In addition, there are some cases where European scale has provided the basis for companies to expand globally. Some immediate questions include:

■ what is the size of the opportunity?
■ what are the barriers and constraints?

- what will it cost to overcome them?
- will it be profitable?

But it is not just a matter of 'barriers and constraints'.

What will persuade customers to switch from their existing supplier and can this be achieved profitably? How do we develop a strategy to exploit the European and global opportunities? We will tackle these fundamental matters using examples from Europe's top companies.

Ultimately each company will produce and implement strategies that are unique to itself; there is no such creature as the 'all-embracing European and global strategy' valid in all circumstances. Indeed, it is fundamental to competitive strategy to devise a series of unique long-term actions, or there will be no sustainable company advantage.

But most company strategies will have a common industry or market base. One of the major difficulties in tackling the single Europe and global markets is that the *pan-European* industry background may be difficult to establish. This is the reason for the 25 European market sector analyses; they provide a starting point for strategy development. Equally, although the final strategies will be unique to each company, the analytical steps are common to all. Thus, this book consists of a series of chapters for strategy development.

PART I

Profitably Analyzing the Current European and Global Situation

Before looking in detail at the current situation, it is right that companies satisfy themselves that European and global markets have real relevance to their future plans. Correct assessment is vital to future profitability and Chapters 1–5 therefore examine the current position. It is particularly important for profits not just to gather facts in a general way but, at this early stage, to probe real issues for their possible impact on profits.

We then complete our examination of the current circumstances by looking (in Chapters 6–8) at three areas which, unless companies take care, can result in them losing a great deal of money. Two of these concern matters outlined previously: production overcapacity and protecting the home market. The third covers entry barriers.

Finally in this part of the book, we will connect the background analysis to the profitability of European industries.

CHAPTER 1

European and Global Markets: Opportunity or Irrelevance?

We will start with the fundamental question that every company must consider: whether there is a real opportunity or threat from European and global competitors or whether the whole issue is largely irrelevant.

For some companies, the single European market itself may be too small. There is little point in debating the merits of Europe if the company operates essentially in world markets. However, Europe may be a stepping stone to achieving world scale if this is a profitable long-term objective. Equally, a firm whose skills lie largely in local service may benefit little from consideration of Europe for its growth opportunities, let alone global markets. The same company will face only a very limited competitive threat from other European or global firms attempting to enter the local market.

Now, it might be argued that a company can turn its hand to anything. Given enough time and money for example, a company's canteen staff can be taught to play the piano. But it may not be the best use of their cooking skills. Companies need to apply the same thinking to Europe.

It is more efficient for companies to find the right market size in which to operate than to leap beyond their national boundaries as if it was the solution to everything. So what are the choices and how does a company judge whether European and global markets are an opportunity or an irrelevance? The company needs to assess what type of *market scale* it operates in. There are four main types: local; regional; European; and world.

A local-scale company's resources, markets and expertise are essentially suited to operation within an existing national boundary. Growth will come nationally or locally. This category may tread on the toes of those politicians who have been trumpeting the single Europe as if there was no survival without it. We will look at the evidence shortly.

A regional-scale company operates across national boundaries but is largely confined to regional areas of Europe. Depending on opportunity and potential, this could become a larger-scale operation later. It is really a sub-set of the European-scale company category but could have lower business risks.

A European-scale company, either actually or potentially, operates across Europe. Growth opportunities and scale will emerge with the single Europe and competitive threats will also appear.

World-scale companies operate in world markets.

Let us take each of these categories separately and examine, with examples, the criteria that define them.

LOCAL-SCALE COMPANIES

We need to distinguish two types of company under this heading: companies that are truly local or national and will remain so (the local-market companies of our categories); and companies which are national now but which will be open to European competition as the barriers continue to come down. These are not local-market operations.

Truly local-scale companies

These companies essentially operate within national boundaries. While they could expand beyond these, there may be legal and operational constraints making this difficult, if not impossible. For them, the single Europe is largely irrelevant: there are few future growth opportunities, scale benefits or competitive threats from Europe.

Companies falling into this category include some, but not all, small businesses in the service industries. For example:

- Local garages;
- Local building companies;
- Local office services; and
- Local bus services.

All essentially rely on local resource, knowledge and skills. Now, there may be some obscure saving by combining window cleaning in London, with a similar company in Reggio Emilia in northern Italy, but there would also be heavy co-ordination costs. The single Europe does not hold out any clear attraction and the competitive threat is minimal for the foreseeable future.

There is another way to test this: examine the United States of America where a single market has existed for some time. Local-scale companies thrive there very well. The same will continue in Europe.

There are some existing national operations that may also basically fall into this local category. Let us explore three companies: Migros, Switzerland; Deutsche Bundesbahn, West Germany; and British Telecom plc, UK. What makes these three large companies essentially local is a combination of their shareholdings, local expertise, local customers, local contacts and, fundamentally, *local service*. Will 'Europe' make any difference?

Case Study: Migros, Switzerland

Data
Europe's eighth largest general retail chain.
1992 turnover: SFr15,125 million
1992 net income: Sfr79 million
Return on capital: 2.7%
% sales in home country: over 95

% *sales in rest of Europe:* 100
% *sales in rest of world:* 0

European and global activity
The 12 Migros co-operatives accounted for around 90% of total sales in 1992. Migros dominates Swiss retailing with a 23.4% share of food sales and 8.9% of non-food sales.

It operates mostly in Switzerland with many local subsidiaries in farming, travel, food processing, banking, etc. It has a strong non-profit but professional service objectives.

The company pleaded for a 'yes' vote by the Swiss in the 1992 referendum to approve the European Economic Area Treaty. It was so concerned about being isolated when the Swiss voted 'no' that it purchased 112 Familia supermarkets in Austria for £88m in 1993. It also formed a joint venture with Austria's largest supermarket chain, Konsum. Both of these moves assumed Austria would join the EU in the mid-1990s.

Keypoint on local scale
Although Migros has an international travel company, Hotelplan GmbH (operating as Inghams Ltd., UK) trading throughout Europe, most of its operations are in businesses with *local* connections. Outside travel, corporate ownership and ambitions lie largely in Switzerland. The company has the market share and resources to remain successful in Switzerland.

Migros is a local-scale operation, but with some limited Austrian/European ambitions.

Such a conclusion might also be taken to apply to the other national retail co-operative institutions that are so prominent in retailing throughout Europe. The only doubt stems from the sheer inefficiency in some of them leading to a competitive threat from other retailers.

As we shall see later, Europe is not an expansion opportunity for some retailers. We will examine one that has found regional expansion possibilities, but retailing is essentially a mature market in Europe for the large companies. The sector is reviewed across Europe in chapter 13.

Case Study: Deutsche Bundesbahn, West Germany

Data
Europe's largest rail company.
1991 turnover (DM million)

Passenger	6239
Freight	9264
Other	896
Total	16399

1991 return on capital: (4.6%) loss
% *sales in home country:* over 90 estimated
% *sales in rest of Europe:* 100
% *sales rest of world:* 0

European and global activity
The company operates within Germany. Losses in 1991 were despite price

increases; the German downturn in economic activity on freight transport was already having an effect through declining traffic volumes.

Outside the long-term possibility of a trans-Europe high-speed network, DBB is essentially involved in Germany alone: the single Europe is not of major significance. Indeed, its version of the European high speed train (the ICE) does not operate on the same track as the French train (the TGV).

Keypoint on local scale
This company is essentially a local scale operation. Europe is irrelevant to the major service areas of the company. Other companies with national monopolies, such as SNCF (France) and British Rail, also have limited opportunities for expansion outside the home country.

Another national large company, British Telecom plc., also faces the question of examining Europe for its growth, scale benefits and competitive threat. Here, the local scale argument is much less clear.

Case Study: British Telecom plc

Data
Europe's second largest telephone company.
1993 turnover (£ million)
13,242
1993 trading profit (£ million)
2449
Return on capital: 14.6%
% sales in home country: 86
% sales in rest of Europe: 5 estimate
% sales in rest of world: 9 estimate

European and global activity
After privatization, the company has been engaged principally in modernizing its network and improving its service levels. It has strong profitability and cash flow and still retains around 85% of the UK market.

The company operates in the most liberal telecommunications market in Europe. Put another way, it is difficult for BT to expand into other parts of Europe at present because of regulatory restrictions in Europe.

Beyond Europe where it can do little, BT has suffered from a rather muddled business strategy over the last few years. In 1986 it bought the Canadian telecommunications equipment company Mitel for £150 million. It sold the company for £135 million loss in 1992. In 1989, it acquired 20% of McCaw, the US mobile telephone group for £903 million. It sold McCaw to the leading US telephone company AT&T in 1992 for £1200 million. Each time it acquired companies BT made weighty statements about its global telecommunications strategy.

In 1993, BT acquired 20% of MCI, the second largest long distance telephone carrier in the USA. It paid £2,800 million and again made important statements about global strategy. BT also invested £450 million for a 75% shareholding in a separate joint venture with MCI, to develop a global telecommunications service for multinational companies.

> *Keypoint on local scale*
> BT has been seeking to move from local to global scale for over ten years. So far it has not succeeded, but has substantial profits and cash flow from its UK national operations to fuel its ambitions. The opening up of European telecommunications services markets in 1998 may also provide a further opportunity. At the same time the company will also need to protect its national market, which is the least regulated in Europe. North American and domestic competitors are beginning to take some of BT's most profitable customers – local scale still matters.

Thus, even for some large companies, the single Europe holds limited opportunities and scale benefits. Also, there is very limited competition in some cases: to regard Deutsche Bundesbahn as competing with British Rail is not realistic in the current environment. Large local-scale companies exist.

National companies for which 'Europe' is relevant

There are some companies which still operate mainly inside their national boundaries because of history and barriers to entry (see Table 1.1). In the new single Europe, they are having to face new competition. Such firms cannot be classified as local-market companies and Europe is highly relevant. In some markets, global and Eastern European competition will increase over the next five years.

Table 1.1   Selected top European companies with at least half their sales from the national home market (home sales as % of total sales)

Iron & Steel	Thyssen	Ger	56%
	Krupp	Ger	79%
	British Steel	UK	51% (and declining)
Oil & Petrol	ENI	Ita	65%
	Elf	Fra	61%
	Repsol	Spa	77%
Cars & trucks	Fiat	Ita	51%
	Renault	Fra	50%

All the companies in Table 1.1 are no doubt aware of the situation. In fairness, the figures look back not forwards, but they are taken from the latest company annual report available at the time of writing, either for 1991 or 1992. (Top European retailing companies virtually without exception have over 50% sales in the home country. This does not pose the same strategic problem because markets are essentially localized, as we discussed with Migros in the previous section.)

We will come back to these issues as we progress through our analysis of market sectors in this book. But let us briefly characterize the markets in which the Table 1.1 companies operate. The strategic implications are significant:

Iron and Steel   Essentially more than a national market, but there are good reasons associated with national government and EC subsidies, which may help to explain why the situation will only

	change slowly. The sector is discussed in Part II 'Channel strategy'. 1993 brought a new threat from cheap Eastern European steel.
Oil and petrol	Many years ago John D. Rockefeller realized that owning oil production was not enough. Retail petrol sites were an important leverage point in defining market strength: all the Table 1.1 companies certainly have such locations nationally. Since the earlier years, oil companies have become involved in a wider range of products so the situation is more complex. Company nationalized ownership is also important but Europe and global markets are certainly relevant.
Cars and trucks	National protection has operated with these companies. This is changing: Europe is relevant.

Having recognized that these companies are not local-scale operations, we will consider what action they are taking and the scope they have later in this book.

Conclusions on local scale operation

Characteristics of a local scale operation are summarized in Table 1.3 at the end of this chapter. For companies operating in such an area, Europe and global markets are largely irrelevant.

This does not mean that it is impossible to move into Europe or beyond but rather that for these companies the way to sales growth using existing resources and skills does not lie with these markets. Local scale companies can continue to make attractive returns on their capital without worrying about the single Europe or global initiatives.

REGIONAL-SCALE COMPANIES

It is not at all clear how many companies currently operate on this scale. It is highlighted in this book because it may be a prudent way for some large national companies to expand beyond their existing boundaries, possibly as a starting point for pan-European expansion. By 'regional-scale', I mean operating within a region of Europe, eg Scandinavia.

Even some local companies have made a move to expand into neighbouring geographical countries: regional-scale markets. While there may never be full European expansion, it does show both practicality and an ability to seize opportunities.

Possibly a good regional example is the linking of trading across the geographical area of northern Germany with neighbouring parts of Holland and Belgium. For many years there has been activity across these borders in certain types of businesses. This will continue and expand in the 1990s as the remaining border restrictions are dismantled. Here, local services will benefit.

But the important aspect of this category is the scope it offers for current national companies to move beyond their national boundaries. Let us look at two examples.

Case Study: Promodes SA, France

Data
1992 turnover (Fr million)

France	62137	Hypermarkets	43540
USA	3287	Supermarkets	12800
Spain	23627	Wholesale, etc.	41552
Italy	8274	Intergroup	(13692)
Germany	567		
Intergroup	(13692)		
Total	84200		84200

Return on capital
% sales in home country: 63 estimate
% sales in rest of Europe: 33 estimate
% sales in rest of world: 4 estimate
Note: Sales data above includes franchise associates.

European and global activity
Promodes is involved in hypermarkets and supermarkets. It also has nationwide wholesaling and retailing through franchises and affiliates. It has five stores in Germany and more in Italy and Portugal; it is using joint ventures in Portugal as its strategy for expansion. In 1993 it opened two hypermarkets in Greece, which it described as a 'genuine commercial innovation', because there were none previously. Its earlier 1980s expansion into the USA has stopped, probably because of the geographical distance and mature US market.

Keypoint on regional scale
The company has not found pan-European growth opportunities, but has expanded regionally.

Case Study: Dalgety plc, UK

Data
One of Europe's largest food companies.
1993 turnover (£ million)

UK	1693	Food	594
Other Europe	170	Food ingredients	278
USA	2330	Food distribution	2545
Canada	277	Agribusiness	1110
		Intergroup	57
Total	4470	Total	4470

Return on capital: 27.2%
% sales in home country: 38
% sales in rest of Europe: 4
% sales in rest of world: 58

European and global activity
Over the last few years Dalgety has largely withdrawn from its southern-hemisphere sheep rearing and lumber operations. It has concentrated on the US,

UK and, to a lesser extent, continental Europe. It has also pulled out of its global trading in cocoa and other food commodities, which were conducted through the company Gill & Duffus. The prime strategy reasons would appear to be a desire to focus on higher added value products and away from basic commodity businesses, where the markets are so large that it is difficult to build significant market share.

Up to 1988, its European turnover was largely confined to its UK businesses in Spillers petfoods, Golden Wonder snackfoods, Lucas food ingredients and agricultural feed products. Since this time it has used its UK experience to acquire several small continental European businesses in similar product areas: Nibb-its branded snacks in the Netherlands and food ingredients companies in France and Germany. It has been carefully adding to its existing areas in a programme of controlled expansion.

Keypoint on regional scale
The company has acquired small companies relative to its current size, consistent with its existing product range. They will allow it to expand into Europe whilst still testing the market: a regional expansion policy in Europe.

Conclusions on regional scale

Certainly for some companies, it has provided the right scale of expansion and a path to profitable growth opportunities at relatively low risk. The main areas are summarized in Table 1.2 at the end of this chapter.

The USA experience of local-market companies can also be extended to regional companies. There are whole areas of the US economy with strong and viable regional companies (for example, brewing, delivery companies, newspapers and television). Clearly, the *cultural influence* sustaining such regional US companies will operate just as strongly, in Europe. For example, Europe will still have during the 1990s strong regional brewers, food companies making regional food and strong regional newspapers, radio and TV.

The key to survival and growth for such companies will lie in their ability to continue their specialization. We will explore this in more depth later.

EUROPEAN-SCALE COMPANIES

These are the companies that above all should benefit as barriers come down and cross-Europe activity increases in the 1990s. For some firms, the process has already begun with the year 1992 being merely a milepost on the road. For others, there is still much to resolve depending, for example, on how alliances are built, how EC legislation develops and to what extent non-EC companies establish manufacturing inside the Community. We will examine these issues as the book progresses. Let us, for now, take two examples and see what is happening.

Case Study: Siemens AG, Germany

One of Europe's largest mechanical, electrical and power engineering companies but without clear market leadership in many markets.

Data
1992 turnover (DM million)

Germany	56339*	Public comms. networks	13165
Other Europe	23485	Private comms. systems	5383
North America	8716	Automation	5811
Latin America	1417	Power generation	6570
Asia	2582	Industrial building systems	8717
Other	1178	Drives and standard products	6686
Other	1178	Defence electronics	1460
Intersegement	(15208)	Automotive systems	2540
		Transportation systems	2718
		Medical engineering	7887
		Semiconductors	1881
* of which 19864 exports		Electronics	2343
		Siemens Nixdorf Computers	13010
		Lamps	3119
		Other	1512
		Intersegment	(9861)
Total	78509	Total	78509

Return on capital: 2.2%
% sales in home country: 39 estimated
% sales in rest of Europe: 36 estimated
% sales in rest of world: 25 estimated

European and global activity
Siemens has traditionally used its proximity to other German companies and institutions to act as their main supplier: hence its reliance on German sales. However, it also operates in European and world markets but does not have clear market leadership. [Siemens' acquisition of Nixdorf is discussed in Chapter 14]

For example, amongst telecom equipment manufacturers, here is the ranking of the top *world* companies for 1987 and 1991:

		Telecom sales (ECU million)	
		1987	1991
AT&T	US	9000	8337
Alcatel	France	6800	14454
Siemens	Germany	5400	7984
NEC	Japan	4400	6010
Northern Telecom	Canada	4100	6596

Similarly, taking the example of world power turbine markets, Siemens is a significant player but is in competition with US and other European companies. In some markets, where scale matters, it is a very small player, for example semiconductors.

Siemens has been actively seeking partners in Europe to produce the scale to act in *world markets*. Thus, in telecommunications, it made a successful bid with GEC (UK) to acquire Plessey plc, the UK electronics, aerospace and telecommunications company. This involves joint ownership of some operations and outright acquisition of others by GEC. Similarly, in power and turbine engineering, a joint venture has been set up with Framatome SA, France, the French nuclear power plant company. This has produced world scale to compete against GEC of the UK, who have combined this part of their operations with Westinghouse (US) and Thomson (France).

Keypoint on European scale
Siemens has set up *European-scale* joint ventures to enable it to operate on a world scale. The company has been seeking European partners not just for the single market but for *world* markets: the single Europe has provided the opportunity for world-scale production.

We will explore other joint ventures in later chapters and their implementation, which is not so straightforward. There can be some difficult choices. At this point, let us look at another company, which lies outside the European Community but which has seen the trend and acted accordingly.

Case Study: Ericsson AB, Sweden

Data
Europe's third largest telecommunications company.
1992 turnover (Skr million)

Telecomms. systems	38681
Cables and networks	6407
Defence systems	1659
Other	273
Total	47020

Return on capital: 5.7%
% sales in home country: 13
% sales in rest of Europe: 47
% sales in rest of world: 40

European and global activity
Ericsson is heavily reliant on European sales and has had to build competitive advantage. For example in telecommunications, it is smaller than the EC telecomms company Alcatel NV, so it has built a more integrated range of products. This is advantageous to Ericsson's customers because it allows the company to produce integrated developments more quickly – i.e. the complete solution with minimum negotiation with other suppliers. It has also concentrated its efforts in growth segments, such as telecommunications systems (see above).

The background to Ericsson's product range is that it took a hard look at its businesses some ten years ago. It decided that it needed to concentrate in certain areas. Thus, it sold its computer business to Nokia, Finland and made other divestments. Equally, it acquired some businesses in the telecommunications area. The effect was to concentrate its activities internationally: this can work well if the 'right' product area is chosen: the difficult part is making the right choice.

Keypoint on European scale
Ericsson is already a significant world player but has had to forge links inside Europe. Thus, over the last few years it has acquired Intelsa (Spain), CGCT (France) with Matra SA and, Thorn-EMI telecom interests (UK). Conclusion on Ericsson: operating on at least European scale within Europe.

Conclusions on European scale

Companies in key areas have reorganized through sales initiatives, acquisitions and joint ventures to take advantage of the new situation. We will come back to these topics in later chapters. The main areas are summarized in Table 1.2 at the end of this chapter.

Some of the companies now seeking new European markets are truly engaged in world-scale markets. Others are expanding just to achieve European-scale sales growth. Both are legitimate reasons for seeking European-scale operation. Europe is highly relevant to these companies.

WORLD-SCALE COMPANIES

There are some companies which have been engaged for years in world-scale activities. What difference will the single European market make? Are any additional activities being undertaken? We will take three examples to probe these questions: Grand Metropolitan plc, Unilever plc and NV and the European pharmaceutical industry.

Case Study: Grand Metropolitan plc, UK

Data
One of Europe's largest alcoholic beverages and food companies.

1988 and 1992 turnover (£ million)

	1988	1992		1988	1992
Food	1253	3149	UK	3835	1747
Drink	2581	2858	Continental Europe	221	1345
Retailing	1671	1906	USA	1758	4127
Discontinued:			Rest of North America	54	218
Hotels	338	–	Africa & Middle East	127	181
Other	186	–	Rest of world	34	295
Total	6029	7913	Total	6029	7913

	1988	1992
Return on capital:	19.2%	13.8%
% sales in home country:	64	22
% sales in rest of Europe:	4	17
% sales in rest of world:	32	61

European and global activity
In 1988, Grand Met had extensive food brands in the UK centred around its dairy products. The company also had major UK brewing interests together with public houses and licensed restaurants. The latter ventures are discussed in the later analysis of European brewing. Grand Met also had a stable of international spirits brands: J&B Rare scotch and Gilbey's Gin are world no. 2 brands.

Importantly in 1988, Grand Met decided to expand globally. It sold its international hotel chain, Intercontinental Hotels, shown as 'discontinued business' in the figures. In 1989, it also sold its chains of betting shops which included some in Belgium and Holland and which were included under 'retailing' above, along with restaurants, etc.

In 1989, the company bought the Greek company, Metaxa Distilleries to join its stable of international spirits brands. It chose this product area as being particularly suited to global expansion. It now owns 11 of the top 100 global spirits brands.

With finance from its hotel sale and other, Grand Met purchased Pillsbury Inc, USA in 1989. This brought a range of food products which it has expanded globally: Burger King fast food, Häagen–Dazs premium ice cream, Pillsbury chilled and frozen dough. The company actually sold UK food operations, such as its dairy interests, that were inconsistent with this clear vision. In 1991 and 1992 it acquired European companies in its selected areas of global expansion, eg German, French and Italian frozen baking companies.

Keypoint on world scale
Without any doubt, it is a world-scale company, not a European-scale company. Its radical restructuring will take time and vision for completion.

Case Study: Unilever plc and NV, UK and The Netherlands

Data
Europe's second largest branded consumer goods company.
1992 turnover (£ million)

Europe	14516	Food	12731
North America	4846	Detergents	5877
Rest of world	5338	Personal products	3200
		Speciality chemicals	1962
		Other	930
Total	24700		24700

Return on capital: 22.6%
% sales in home country: irrelevant
% sales in rest of Europe: 59
% sales in rest of world: 41

European and global activity
The company is truly one of the world's largest branded goods companies and is highly profitable. It has extensive European interests and a vigorous acquisition policy over the last few years. During the period 1989–92, it has acquired a series of medium-sized companies in France, Portugal, Germany and Italy. It has also bought companies in Hungary, Poland and the Czech Republic. In each case they consolidate its existing areas, eg fats and oils, ice cream and detergents. It is building on its strengths. However, it is weaker than its rivals; P & G (USA) and Nestlé (Switzerland), in developing global brands.

Every European country already has substantial activity by Unilever companies. The single European market has prompted some further concentration in production facilities to obtain extra scale. But it will not make any fundamental difference.

Keypoint on world scale
In 1989, Unilever acquired Fabergé and Elizabeth Arden, making the company the second largest cosmetics company in the world. This followed the purchases of Rimmel and Calvin Klein in the same general product area earlier in the same year.

The Fabergé cost was $1.55 billion. This is a world-scale move and Europe itself was not a major reason for the purchase. This company is a true world-scale company and Europe is only one consideration in its global strategy.

In considering world scale, let us finally look at European pharmaceutical companies. Will the single European market have any significant impact in this area?

Case Study: The world's top pharmaceutical companies

		Turnover (US$ million)	
		1991	1992
Merck	USA	8603	9662
Glaxo	UK	6004	6767
Ciba	Swi	5471	6581
Hoechst	Ger	5428	6350
Bristol Myers Squibb	USA	5908	6313
Rhone–Poulenc	Fra	5187	6046
Bayer	Ger	5305	6008
Pfizer	USA	4998	5614
Roche	Swi	4131	5220
Sandoz	Swi	4390	5208
SmithKline Beecham	UK/USA	4396	5056
ICI/Zeneca	UK	5220	4921
Lilly	USA	4609	4872
American Home Products	USA	4018	4589
Johnson & Johnson	USA	3795	4340
Schering-Plough	USA	2895	3359
Marion-Merrill Dow	USA	2851	3320
Upjohn	USA	2740	2935
Wellcome	UK	2838	2810
Schering	Ger	3831	2800

Note: some companies such as Johnson & Johnson have even greater involvement in the health market through sales in related areas, eg dressings and surgical equipment. These are not included in the above table.

European and global activity
Over the last few years, several mergers and acquisitions have taken place in order that companies might build global scale. They include Beecham (UK) merger with Smith Klein (US); Rhone Poulenc (France) acquisition of Rohrer (US); Bristol Myers (US) merger with Squibb (US). More specifically, the main reasons given for this activity are:

- high research costs in pharmaceuticals which need global scale to be recovered;
- high marketing and sales costs which benefit from being shared across a range of products;
- need for US market presence as this country accounts for around 40 per cent of the world market.

In spite of its global nature, the drug market is characterised by fragmented market share: Merck, the world's largest, has only around 4 per cent market share. To complicate matters there are a series of product segments, eg heart drugs, anti-ulcer drugs, each of which has its leading companies with a rather larger share of the segment. Moreover, there are other factors that make a simple global description more complex:

- disease patterns vary worldwide;
- salesforces are stronger in some countries than others;
- pharmaceutical distribution structures vary between countries;

- national healthcare schemes are the biggest customers of the drug customers, yet provision and regulations differ across the world.

Global pressures therefore need to be balanced by national knowledge. Hence, alliances and joint ventures continue also to be a major aspect of business strategies, for example in 1993, the three companies, Glaxo (UK), Warner-Lambert (USA) and Wellcome (UK) announced a new alliance in over-the-counter (OTC) medicines.

European activity is only one part of this picture. There has been some attempt to harmonise single Europe new drug acceptances. However, the prime coordinating body, the European Medicines Evaluation Agency, is still unlikely to be set up before 1995.

Keypoint on world-scale in pharmaceuticals
The major companies are already operating on a world scale. Perhaps surprisingly, there are no Japanese drug makers in the leading group. The biggest single threat to profits is probably the *world trend* for public health authorities to seek lower drug prices. Because they are the largest customers, this is an important strategy issue for the drug companies. Some are countering by extending from public health into the branded, over-the-counter market, where profit margins are higher. However, OTC is a smaller market with only US$ 29 billion sales worldwide versus US$ 132 billion in the prescription market.

Conclusions on world scale

Europe's largest company is Royal Dutch/Shell (Netherlands and UK). The company has massive world-wide resources and substantial European involvement. No doubt there have been some cost savings from the new Europe as production has moved across national EC barriers. But, outside these relatively straightforward matters, the fundamentals of the company will remain global, not European.

What is so striking for world scale companies is the complete absence of any obvious European dimension to their thinking. This does not mean that European expansion is excluded, nor that opportunities presented by the single Europe will not be seized, just that it is not the starting point for consideration of growth, defence and other aspects of company strategy.

CONCLUSIONS

Defining what market a company operates in is at once both a difficult and fundamental strategic task. What we have been doing in this chapter is to raise the question in the context of European and global markets. There are no simple answers: many companies will quite rightly take some months to resolve the matter. But it is an issue that must be resolved.

This chapter is a means of setting out some of the ground rules but it will not resolve the issues instantly. Many readers may therefore wish to read further through this book and then return to the question of geography at the end.

It is important to recognize that, apart from those companies purely involved in local-scale operations, the distinctions are only matters of degree. To operate on a pan-European scale may be to exploit some of the markets of the single Europe or to use it as the basis for world-scale opportunities. Regional-scale may only be a step on the road to European-scale. To assist the analysis, let us therefore (in Table 1.2) set out some of the characteristics of the different operating scales and their implications for action in the single Europe.

Table 1.2 Scale selection characteristics and action required

Characteristics	Action
Local-scale	
National monopolies or semi-monopolies	Monitor Europe for any
Small-scale local companies	changes in laws
Companies offering strictly local service in the community	Single Europe largely irrelevant
Largely within national boundaries	
Little advantage from the new Europe	
Regional-scale	
At present, national & local companies	Develop European strategy
Specialize in area relevant to the region	Will be hit by single market
Face threat from across Europe	But not necessarily pan-European
Neither barriers nor scale economies debar entry	Resolve matters deriving* from the new Europe
European scale	
Major European traders but perhaps strong national presence	Identify opportunities
Involved in markets without obvious national boundaries	Develop European strategies
	Monitor barriers closely
	Possibly build alliances
Pan-European opportunities now or soon.	Resolve matters deriving from the new Europe*
World scale	
Engaged for last few years globally	Monitor specific developments
Aware of special opportunities in European markets	Build limited strategy to secure any additional benefits
European scale may provide base on which to build world scale	Exploit any single Europe benefits

* These are set out at the end of Part II.

For companies concluding that Europe is relevant, the categories focus on where companies are now, rather than where they will be by the year 2000. But that is a perfectly reasonable basis to plan business strategy in the early 1990s.

What we need to do now is to set up a process to examine the current European scene. That is what we will start in Chapter 2.

CHAPTER 2

Preparing Background Material

Sourcing and organizing European and global data to bring out the real issues are the next tasks. There are two principal problems:

1. Organizing the vast amount of data available on Europe's 12 national markets can be a mammoth undertaking, let alone world markets; and
2. It is not enough just to classify the material – it needs to be prepared so that it can identify *profit* opportunities and threats.

Now, there is no point in denying that this will take some considerable effort.

For those keen to know more, there are three major steps to preparing good background data. We will take them in turn: shortcuts to data gathering; sourcing the data; and preparing the material, once it has been acquired.

SHORTCUTS TO EUROPEAN AND GLOBAL DATA GATHERING

For those prepared to spend the time, there are ways of cutting down the analysis to reasonable amounts. This book will provide pointers in many markets because of its breadth of coverage but the evidence, taken as a whole, also suggests six ways of honing down to the essentials.

Concentrate on the main industrialized countries
For Europe, these are West Germany, France, the United Kingdom, Italy, Belgium, The Netherlands, Spain and possibly Denmark. Naturally, if you know that the prime customers will be an obvious target group across *all* countries (eg the EC's large electricity producers), then you will ignore this. Beyond Europe, the USA, Canada and Japan represent clear targets.

The concentration, at least at first, on the main industrial countries is not meant as a mark of disrespect to other countries. Simply that, to answer the fundamental question of EC expansion, it is essential to look at potential in Germany whereas Greece may be a luxury. Doing it this way also has another advantage: it is rather easier to prepare background on France than, say, on Portugal, because there is more data readily available. Spain is the only real problem country in the list.

Select the growth opportunities
For Europe, these might be Greece, Portugal, Spain and Ireland. They might include Eastern Europe, though again reliable data is difficult.

Beyond Europe, South East Asian countries have had a strong growth record in the early 1990s.

Base analyses on a checklist developed for the 'home' country

Most companies will have a fair idea of what is important in their own markets. Other countries certainly have different languages and cultures but are, in many respects, much the same: goods are produced in factories, distributed by carriers and sold to customers.

Certainly, it would be unwise to reject the experience gained in one country when moving elsewhere. The danger comes if this is taken too far and 'foreign' methods are imposed on another country. Using experience from one country must be the starting point for action, not an excuse to shorten the analysis.

Recognize that outcomes could be a niche within a market

The Japanese success has come partially from the recognition, even in large markets, that it is easier to gain a foothold by strength in a sub-sector. The search that recognizes this from the start is more likely to be successful because it knows what it is seeking.

Even when takeovers are being considered, it is important to consider this issue. Some will question whether this is wise because it assumes that a segmentation strategy is to be developed, which may not be the case. We will look at this shortly: at present the aim is to save ourselves the need to go back over all the data again later. If we do not pose the question early on, then we could waste a great deal of time.

Analyze one country properly rather than four badly

The temptation with many new opportunities will be to analyze them all. If the resources are present or can be bought in, then comprehensive analysis is fine. But for many companies, including large ones, the senior management attention that needs to be devoted to develop an opportunity successfully is better concentrated on a limited shortlist.

Gather views from all around the company

Major surveys of this kind are not the exclusive preserve of 'marketing' or 'planning'. Company financial managers, purchasing officers and personnel executives will have an important knowledge of other countries that needs to be tapped. The preparation must not just be viewed as a sales or marketing opportunity, but rather as a *company opportunity*.

Nevertheless, there needs to be a focus for activity: it might be better to operate this as a *multi-disciplinary team* under a general rather than a functional manager.

Overall none of the above points is infallible: they should all be treated as aids to obtaining useable data.

SOURCING THE DATA ON EUROPEAN AND GLOBAL MARKETS

We discussed in the Introduction the necessity to have certain data on competitors (ie return on capital, home sales as a percentage of total sales and

European sales as a percentage of total sales). This material will come from the company's annual accounts. But what other data is required and available to analyze the single market opportunity?

Table 2.1 shows some basic European data sources. In addition, there is a further list of market research and other sources in Appendix 3.

Table 2.1   Selected sources of European and global market data

Source	Publisher	Content	Availability
Eurostats	EC Commission	Basic economic data	Libraries and for sale through HMSO Bookshops
Panorama of EC Industry 1989	EC Commission	Data on 125 EC markets	As above plus sale through other bookshops
Facts on the EC	EC Commission	Summary economic data	As above
Extel Financial service	Extel	Financial data on top European companies	Libraries (but no photocopying) & from Extel
McCarthy newspaper & magazine cuttings service	McCarthy	Recent stories on companies & markets	Libraries (but no photocopying) & from McCarthy
Company annual reports	Individual companies	Extensive details often in more than one language	Individual companies and libraries
Economic Outlook	Organisation for Economic Cooperation and Development	Bi-annual economic forecasts	Libraries
Handbook of International Trade and Development Statistics	UN	International trade data	Libraries

As a starting point for many companies, I would recommend *Panorama of EC Industry* mentioned in the table. The content detail is variable but it is useful for its breadth of coverage and its listing of European trade association contacts.

The current book covers the activity of companies in relation to markets, but if you want more detail than is possible here, then many of Europe's top companies publish multi-lingual versions of their reports, often more informative than for US companies. Even for smaller companies in the same or similar industries, they do shed light on trends, investments and opportunities. The addresses and telephone numbers of these companies are available from public libraries.

To be more specific, let us take two related industries and review what is available in the context of tackling European opportunities. We will look at the electricity generating and gas distribution industries: both are prime energy suppliers in the single Europe.

Case Study: Electricity and gas generating and distribution in the EC

Data
In the UK, France and Italy, both electricity and gas are currently dominated by large nationalized companies. Belgium, Spain and Germany are structured with more regional and specialized companies. The following data covers selected European electricity and gas suppliers.

Electricity suppliers		*1991 Turnover (US$m)*	*Return on capital (%)*
Electricité de France	Fra	30448	4.6
ENEL	Ita	21756	na
RWE	Ger	10078	5.4*
National Power	UK	8310	16.3
VEBA	Ger	7183	6.9*
Tractabel	Bel	6912	na
CEA	Fra	6904	na
Endesa	Spa	6604	na
Preussen Elektra	Ger	5760	na
Electrabel	Bel	5585	0.0
Powergen	UK	5319	15.1
Iberdroia	Spa	5160	5.8
Bayernwerk	Ger	3734	na
Vettenfall	Swe	3563	12.3
VEW	Ger	3232	na
Electrowatt	Swi	3171	5.4
Fenosa	Spa	2794	8.9
Scottish Power	UK	2439	na
Sevillana Elec	Spa	2299	6.4
Fecsa	Spa/ Cat	2091	8.0
Badenwerk	Ger	1709	0.0
Berliner K&L	Ger	1645	na

* Return includes non-electricity profits and assets
Note: SPE Netherlands is also a large electricity supplier but data is not available. The 1992 company annual report for Vattenfall has further useful information on Europe's top electricity companies, including Eastern Europe.

Gas suppliers		*1991 Turnover (US$m)*	*Return on capital (%)*
British Gas	UK	18126	8.0
Nederlands GasUnie	Net	10137	11.6
Gaz de France	Fra	8767	8.4
Ruhr Gas	Ger	9201	23.7
Italgas	Ita	2452	5.2
AGA	Swe	2109	16.7

Gas Natural	Spa	1934	na
Repsol	Spa	1679	na
Electrabel Gas	Bel	1126	na
VEW Gas	Ger	683	na

Note: The above electricity and gas companies do not have significant sales outside Europe, except for British Gas.

Both the electricity and gas industries are characterized by large national or regional institutions. Ownership has been invested mostly in governments and other public bodies with all their specialist business policies. Some countries, such as the UK, have pursued a rigorous policy of privatization. But the majority of ownership still rests with national and regional governments.

European activity: the gas industry
Long before the EC single market, the industry had developed a system of pipelines to carry gas feedstock from the North Sea, Mediterranean and from Russia to the EC's industrialized users. This included agreements on pricing, tariffs, supplies, standarization, etc.

It is a model of its kind in terms of cross-European co-operation and probably stems, as much as anything, from the nature of the industry: a few large suppliers with sufficient power and control of their own markets to make international agreement attainable.

European activity: the electricity industry
This industry has operated more on a national basis over the last few years, probably for strategic reasons but also because of the mechanics of electricity generation.

More recently, there has been some cross-border supply, for example between the UK and France, but the published data shows this to be a relatively small share of total turnover. Whilst some further power sharing is possible, there has been no move in the EC to establish pan-European activity. The main trend is currently against this with increasing divergence of supply sources (eg the UK electricity privatization).

Key point on data sources for the above
Gas pipeline data: company reports (some useful maps).
Gas production data: *Eurostats*.
Gas consumption data: *Eurostats*.
Gas pricing data: Bulletin on EC prices.
Electricity production data: *Eurostats*.
Electricity national consumption data [including by user type]: *Eurostats*.
Electricity pricing data: Bulletin on EC prices.
National data by type of user: some company annual reports.

More data is available, but the above illustrates the material for a study of these market sectors.

PREPARING THE DATA

Having considered the general issues of organizing the collection of data, let us now turn to how it is actually prepared.

There are 4 basic stages in sorting the material on European and global markets. They interconnect and overlap but can be summarized as shown in Figure 2.1.

Background covers all those outside factors having a significant impact on a

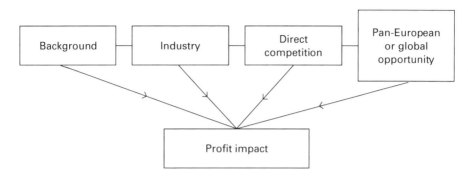

company and its opportunities. *Industry* means businesses in related areas having an effect on the company but not necessarily forming immediate competition.

Direct competition concerns those organizations offering a product or service that potential customers would consider as an alternative in making their immediate choice. Finally, *Pan-European and global opportunity* relates to those markets where a significant sales opportunity will emerge as a result of the lowering of trade barriers in the 1990s.

At every stage, the main focus is on *profit impact*. This needs to be produced unambiguously, rather than the highly elegant but esoteric analyses far removed from reality that occasionally emerge from some parts of European companies.

Because industries vary so widely, it is better to establish and adapt the guidelines governing each of the above sections rather than to be dogmatic on content. With this caveat, we can work our way through each part of the sequence and explore the key elements in more detail.

Stage 1: Background

Covering all the outside factors affecting the industry, the market and the company. They might include, for example:

- Country growth, wages, employment, prices, investment policies, environmental issues;
- Customer profiles, e.g. demographics;
- Distribution channels, costs and benefits;
- Communications channels for reaching customers, e.g. advertising and promotion.

It should be emphasized that the above does not pretend to be a comprehensive list of factors. They must be constructed to suit the industry concerned.

To put some flesh on the bones, let us take the example of British gas.

Case Study: British Gas, UK

Data
Europe's largest gas supplier.
1992 turnover: £10,254 million
1992 trading profit: £1685 million

Return on capital: 8.0%
% sales in home country: 90 estimated
% sales in rest of Europe and rest of world: 10 estimated

European and global activity
British Gas has been the monopoly supplier in the UK for many years to both industrial and domestic customers. However, this is changing in the 1990s with the UK gas market being opened up to alternative suppliers. Plentiful and relatively cheap North Sea gas supplies will assist this process. Turnover at British Gas will inevitably decline unless it can supply and sell gas elsewhere. Many other European countries still operate a system of monopoly sale. Continental European customers for the company may therefore be strictly limited. For this reason, British Gas has spent around £1 billion over the years 1988–92 purchasing oil and gas interests in North America.

British Gas strategy could change if Continental European markets are opened up during the 1990s. The barriers here are totally contrary to the spirit of the Treaty of Rome. The European Commission has been examining the free sale of gas across Europe and has some plans in this direction. But there are powerful national interests against this and their business strategy is one of inertia: do nothing and block all attempts at change.

The policy of making no change can be an important part of business strategy: why encourage competition? British Gas had the same strategy in its national market until 1993 when the British government began the process of allowing competitors to supply gas. The key determinant in strategy here is clearly action at government and inter-government European level: background factor analysis (stage 1 above) is therefore a crucial issue.

In practical business strategy terms, an important action for national gas suppliers in this situation (after stage 1 analysis) would be to keep close contact with and lobby national governments and the European Commission.

Keypoint on background analysis
This would include:

- Country: political desire to continue national gas monopolies; size and buoyancy of each economy; source and use of all energy sources; current import/export of all energy sources; pricing of all energy sources (not just gas).
- Customer: leading energy users with a definition of their usage by nature and size.

(Both 'distribution channels' and 'communications' in the checklist above are relevant, but are here better covered separately rather than in a background section.)

Profit impact: if alternative gas supplies are being brought more cheaply than those from British Gas, then the opportunity is a non-starter.

Stage 2: Industry

These are the broad factors affecting businesses in related industries but not necessarily in direct competition. Naturally, it is important to define here correctly what market we are in: this is covered in Part II. Here are some examples of relevant industry factors related to common customers, competitors and suppliers:

- Biscuits from one of Europe's leaders BSN SA (France) can be bought instead of chocolate confectionery products from, for example, Nestlé/ Rowntree SA (Switzerland): common customers

- Whisky products from Guinness plc (UK) compete not only with other whiskies but may also be consumed in place of other spirits from, for example, Heineken NV (Netherlands): common competitors
- Unilever plc (UK) dishwasher products under the Lever *Sun* product label will be an alternative in some circumstances to Procter & Gamble's (UK) washing-up liquid brand *Fairy*: common suppliers

Stage 3: Direct competition

Most companies will find this the easiest to define, since they live with it all the time especially in the sales force. Let us look at some competitors in the European Coal industry.

Case Study: Some Top European Coal Companies

Data

		1991 turnover (US$m)	Return on capital (%)
RuhrKohle	Ger	14879	(1.7) loss
British Coal	UK	6982	na
Saarbergwerke	Ger	3005	0.0
Charbonnage de France	Fra	1742	(42.5) loss

European and global activity
Scandinavian countries, Switzerland and Spain rely heavily on hydroelectric power. France and Belgium use atomic power extensively. Hence, one of the main uses of coal – as an energy feedstock – is confined to a few countries in western Europe; Germany and the UK in particular. Traditionally, those countries have been supplied by their national mines. As markets have become global, coal supplies have come increasingly from countries as far apart as Poland and Chile. The European national companies have found it increasingly difficult to compete in a market where price is the chief factor for customers.

There is low value-added in coal production with one of the chief determinants of company cost being wage costs: Europe's relatively high labour costs compared to other global coal producers are disadvantageous in this industry.

Keypoint on background factors (stage 1) and direct competition (stage 3)
The chief *background factor* (stage 1), the reduction in protection for European national coal companies, needs to be handled at the national political level as with the gas companies outlined above.

Direct competition (stage 3) has moved to global scale with the main competitive factors being price and quality. It is difficult to identify and maintain sustainable competitive advantage in such commodity markets.

Stage 4: Pan-European or global opportunity

For some specific industries, there are real opportunities to come together right across Europe after 1992: the whole will be more than the sum of the parts. It is essential to explore this area early in any consideration of the new Europe or much of the analysis will be misdirected.

Two examples of pan-Europe thinking are the new European digital mobile telephone network now being set up across Europe. This is explored further later. Secondly, the UK financial newspaper, the *Financial Times* (part of Pearson Group plc.) has started a European edition based in Frankfurt.

Finally in this consideration of preparation of background material on Europe, let us take two more examples and explore them across the stages outlined above: the US company that is heavily involved in Europe, Philip Morris, and the European transport industry.

Case Study: Philip Morris Inc., USA

'Our mission is to be the most successful consumer packaged goods company in the world.' *Annual Report 1992*

Data

	1992 turnover (US$ m)	Brands include:
Tobacco	25677*	Marlboro, Chesterfield
Food	29048	Post Cereals, Gains petfood, Jell-O and Birds desserts, Kraft dairy, Maxwell House and Jacobs coffee
Beer	3976	Miller Beers
Financial services	430	
Total	59131	

*before deducting US$ 9036 million excise taxes

Return on capital: 27.3% Tobacco has been particularly profitable but a price war began in 1993 in North America
% sales in home country, ie USA: 60
% sales in Europe: 29
% sales in rest of world (outside above): 11

European and global activity
Philip Morris is the world's leading tobacco company with its Marlboro brand and an especially strong franchise in North America: it has a lower market share in Europe. The company has used its tobacco profitability to acquire a series of US and European companies over the last ten years, including the major international food companies, General Foods and Kraft.

For our case study, we will concentrate on *European confectionery markets*. Philip Morris acquired the Jacobs-Suchard SA (Switzerland) coffee and confectionery company in 1990. It followed this with Marabou (Scandinavia), including its chocolate confectionery interests, in 1992, and Terry's Chocolates (UK subsidiary of United Biscuits plc) in 1993. It has begun to build a European base. By early 1994, it possessed a mixture of useful but disparate European brands. It therefore had the task of devising a coherent business strategy for its acquisitions in European confectionery. How might it structure this analysis?

Stage 1: Background: increased concentration in European grocery and confectionery distribution; changes in European label-scanning in retail outlets; growth in private label products; and environmental health factors – sugar and fat content in chocolate.

Stage 2: Industry: relative pricing versus other snack products such as biscuits and savoury snacks; new packaging; and raw material price variations.
Stage 3: direct competition

Confectionery market shares (%) 1992

	UK	Germany	France	Italy	Spain	Benelux	Scandinavia
Nestlé	26	13	27	24	35	10	2
Mars	26	16	11	2	2	14	2
Philip Morris	7	19	15	2	10	27	34
Cadbury	31	1	8		15		
Ferrero	2	18	6	32	4		
Other	8	33	33	40	31	49	62
Value (US$ Bn)	3.3	4.1	2.0	1.0	0.3	0.7	1.0

Source: Courtesy of Henderson Crosthwaite, London

Stage 4: pan-European and global opportunity: There is clearly the possibility of building a European product base. However, an important area of global expansion, North America, may be limited. The US and Canadian markets are dominated by Hershey and Mars: acquiring the former would be expensive and the latter is a family company and probably not for sale.

Conclusions: Philip Morris will need to carefully examine its strategies based on the above data: should it concentrate on its areas of strength, eg Germany and Scandinavia, or should it start activities in countries where its market share is weak, eg the UK and Italy? Does it have the resources and organization to do both? Should it develop a series of national strategies rather than a pan-European strategy or would this reduce the scale benefits to be derived from the single Europe?

We will return to this case later in the book. For now, we register the importance of establishing and analyzing the background data.

In the Philip Morris example, it has not been possible to be precise about the profit impact of each item identified. In practice, this would be possible for the company to estimate with some precision.

Case Study: European transport industries

Data
The *road transport* part of the European transport industry is highly fragmented with many small- and medium-sized companies. *Rail transport* is highly concentrated with a series of national rail companies, mainly operating inside their national boundaries. *Air transport* is national, European and global in terms of market demand and competition. More detail is given below.

To focus our analysis and keep it manageable, we will concentrate on the largest of the European companies involved in transport.

Road transport companies

		1991 turnover (US$ Bn)	*Return on capital (%)*	*Destination of 1991 sales % in Europe and rest of world*	
Danzas	Swi	6752	na	89	11
NedLloyd	Net	4018	4.3	68	32

P&O	UK	3341**	15.2	na	na
Hapag Lloyd	Ger	2203	9.9	46	54
Haniel	Ger	1747	na	49	51
Veba*	Ger	1434**	not available but mainly Europe		
Preussag	Ger	480**	na	86	14

*Veba trades mainly through its subsidiary Raab Karcher
**Transport element of turnover only

Rail transport companies

SNCF	Fra	12970	2.8	100	0
Deutsche Bundesbahn	Ger	9879	(2.6)	100	0
British Rail	UK	5570	(4.4)	100	0

Air transport companies

British Airways	UK	15185	18.0	39	61
Air France	Fra	10238	0.5	na	na
Lufthansa	Ger	8593	(2.3)	42	58
SAS	Sca	5706	4.1	50	50
KLM	Net	5504	6.8	na	na
Alitalia	Ita	4742	na	na	
Swissair	Swi	3715	0.5	44	56

European and global activity
The three distinctive groups in the above compete with each other for some turnover: for example, in some passenger transport services. However, some of the fiercest competition comes from rivalry within a group: for example, bidding for a road freight contract, where air transport may be faster but will be ruled out for reasons of price, takes place mainly between road transport companies.

Road
The road transport companies have now largely reorganized to meet the immediate challenge of the single Europe without frontiers: in its 1992 Annual Report, Danzas described the 'revolutionary changes' that have led to the end of customs brokerage and the conversion to pure freight forwarding. The company has been making a real effort to build a European communications network using computer technology to enhance its European operations. Interestingly, it has now extended this operation to Asia/Pacific and North America. But it does not yet have the global spread of Haniel or Hapag Lloyd.

Veba, operating through its subsidiary Raab Karcher, merged and extended its transport network in 1992 with the integration of the Stinnes network. It has also been developing in the former Eastern Germany and elsewhere in Eastern Europe, where the poor transport infrastructure presents major opportunities for those companies with deep pockets and some persistence.

P&O has passenger-carrying activities beyond Europe through its cruise ships.

Outside Europe's top companies, several leading UK freight companies purchased German freight carriers in early 1990. The objective appeared to be to offer local service in Germany for UK national manufacturers selling into Germany. The prediction was that cross-border trade would grow grapidly. This has not happened and several have made large losses and are pulling out.

Equally, several of the leading North American overnight courier companies, such as Federal Express, have built pan-European networks only to see them remain under-used. As it pulled out in 1993, the company commented that the single Europe had still not generated anything like the same level of cross-border trade as in North America.

Up to 1989, freight transport across Europe was made more difficult by restrictions on the ability of lorries delivering across Europe to pick up a return load. To have to return empty is evidently less profitable. The process is called 'cabotage'. Even in this area, restrictions have continued to operate across Europe but barriers are now coming down.

The Channel Tunnel may have some impact beyond 1994 but it is only one small part of the European transport network.

Rail

The national monopolies are still largely protected and subsidized in their home countries. For some nations such as France, the Netherlands and Germany, there are social policy reasons associated with the provision of public transport services for this approach. In the UK, privatisation is under way with largely unpredictable results and a different view on public policy issues.

More generally, the national railway companies are under attack from cheaper and more flexible road transport. Freight has been moving from rail to road across Europe for some years now (see 'Panorama of EC Industry 1991/2, section 25' for data).

The opportunity for a high-speed European rail network is still bedevilled by national considerations: for example, the German ICE and French TGV versions are incompatible with each other. Many of these pan-European rail network ideas remain merely speculative lines drawn on a map of Europe.

Air

Europe's national airlines operate a series of price-fixing cartels across Europe which the European Commission has been slowly dismantling. Moreover, some airlines are heavily subsidized by their national governments: in 1992 alone, a total of US$ 3 billion was given to Air France, Sabena and Iberia of Spain.

Outside Europe, the airlines compete in increasingly global markets where alliances and joint ventures may be important. There have been several attempts to form alliances across Europe: for example, in 1989 British Airways tried unsuccessfully to link with Sabena (Belgium) and KLM. In late 1993, SAS was also unsuccessful in a four-way deal with KLM, Swissair and Austrian Airlines. Previous experiences and national interests were too strong.

The most enduring links of the 1990s are taking place on a global, not European, basis: British Airways with US Air, Quantas and Air Russia; Lufthansa with American Airlines; KLM with NorthWest (USA); Singapore International Airlines with Swissair and Delta (USA). Such links may involve joint shareholdings, minority stakes and trading alliances. There have been five driving forces:

- world recession and excess airline capacity;
- increased competition as capacity and price-fixing cartels weaken;
- European airline deregulation;
- need for airport 'hub and spoke' strategy;
- new computer reservations systems.

World recession has meant that the increased availability of airline seats has not been fully utilized. Since half-empty aircraft still have to fly routes, part of the strategy has been to fill the seats at lower prices, some of which may be obtained through links with other airlines.

This process has been exacerbated by increased competition through the deregulation of some routes: between 1991 and 1992, Air France increased its capacity on its key Atlantic routes by +8 per cent whereas US airlines capacity went up by +30 per cent. This could only take place in a market where agreement on the total number of available seats was weakening.

It has been assisted further by European airline deregulation in 1992–93 which gave airlines the possibility of operating in other European countries. Couple this with some European airlines operating at lower wage costs and there is the likelihood of real competition. British Airways has much higher productivity figures, measured as sales per employee, than Air France for example. In October 1993, the French airline attempted to impose a restructuring involving 4,000 job losses that would have redressed this issue but the resulting transport chaos in France made it impossible to implement.

A longer term issue has been the need for a 'hub and spoke' strategy. Some airports, such as Schipol in the Netherlands, are used as the main international terminals with other airports acting as regional feeders. Hubbing not only impacts on the immediate economics of air flights but has other effects: priority airline service and takeoff and landing slots are awarded to those controlling the airport. This can keep out competitors and thus raise profits. European airlines are following the lead of American air practice in this respect.

Cross-linking of European airlines goes further than airport capacity considerations. New and incompatible computer reservation systems were set up in the early 1990s: for example, 'Amadeus' by Air France/Lufthansa and 'Gallileo' by British Airways/KLM/Sabena. These systems first showed to agents seeking seat reservations the details for their own national airlines. There were complaints that this distorted the free market in tickets and there has now been an agreement to make them transparent to each other. But this has not yet been tested in practice.

Overall, the single Europe has only been part of the driving force in the development of business strategy for Europe's leading airlines. Global issues have also been relevant and are reflected in the turnover generated outside Europe by the leading companies, as shown in the data above.

Keypoint on analysis
Let us use the analysis to set out some of the key issues for European transport, since at one level each form of transport may substitute with another (back again to the question 'What market are we in?')

Background: Cross-Europe motorway development, including the Channel Tunnel; changes in fuel costs; environmental pressures to reduce fuel emissions, protect the countryside and use public transport; rate of increase in cross-border trading; European recession or growth.

Industry: Pan-European high-speed rail link; emergence of Euro-freight market as harmonization takes place; price/service balance between rail/road/air as cross-border journeys are speeded up; the impact of deregulation on price-fixing of European air fares.

Direct competition: Increased air price competition; substantial price considerations outlined above.

Pan-European and global opportunities: Global and pan-European alliances and joint ventures; new structural projects that will enhance cross-European links; deregulation of fare structures; rebuilding Eastern Europe.

This sets out our basic analysis format, though it hardly does justice to the many complex issues involved. In practice, these would need to be explored in much greater detail.

CHAPTER 3

Profiting From Country and Company Specialization

In building up a picture of the current situation, it is vital in assessing profits to evaluate the possibilities for *specializing in some European or global markets*, i.e. selling a product or service that is especially tailored to meet the needs of some customers particularly well, rather than all potential buyers in a general way. Thus, for example, there are Porsche high-performance cars at premium prices with limited volume and Ford cars at value-for-money prices selling in volume.

Indeed, it has been argued that in the new world order the only two possible strategies are to grow larger or specialize. While this is grossly oversimplified, it does have a grain of truth. We are not concerned to pick the best strategy at this point (we will do that in Part II). However, in gathering the data we must examine the possibilities for market specialization because it can be more profitable.

There are two types of specialization, country and company, and we need to consider them both in examining our European and global options.

COUNTRY SPECIALIZATION

Some countries have developed special expertise in certain product or service markets. This does not mean that other countries have no skills or resources but rather that, in the new situation, it may be better to accept that some countries can do certain things better than others. For companies outside the country with the skills, the most profitable way to get around this will be to avoid hitting these areas head-on. But to do this, they need to be identified.

The real advantages these country industries will have when it comes to expansion include, for example more managers and workers with expertise, more familiarity with sources of supply for raw materials and service, cheaper labour costs and highly specialized market experience. New companies outside these countries have to be brave to tackle this head-on and must expect profits to be hit.

Let us look at four examples: German engineering; Italian and Spanish ceramic tiles; French private-sector service companies; and British brewing and leisure companies.

German engineering

Germany is strong in the engineering industries and has been so for some years.

Table 3.1 Share of total EC value added by member states (1991)

	Machine tools	Insulated wires and cables
Germany	52%	33%
Italy	22%	17%
UK	9%	14%
France	7%	17%

Source: Panorama of EC Industry 1993, pages 8–13 and 9–8.

This is matched by the companies involved: Germany has more engineering companies in the Top 250 than any other country. The following German firms are in engineering and all these are in Europe's first 50 largest companies: Daimler Benz/AEG; Siemens; Thyssen; Bosch; Mannesmann; and Krupp.

The industry skills and contacts generated by this concentration of market power are formidable. They are now being used to start the re-equipment of East German industry. With the accession of East Germany into the EC, this has made Europe (and Germany) a powerful world competitor in many engineering markets, where its relatively high wage costs are unimportant.

Conclusion for specialization

To fight this would be to waste company resources. It is better to find the specialist gaps. The European Commission and the German companies will no doubt want to ensure that the opportunities from this activity spread through the Community: specialist services and niche markets are the best route forward for other companies.

Italian and Spanish ceramic tiles

Table 3.2 shows an example taken from companies that are outside the European Top 250 to show that there is nothing especially unique to the largest companies.

Other examples of concentrated European industries include shoes where three Mediterranean countries account for 62 per cent of production, and leather tanning/production where 90 per cent of production is concentrated in the Mediterranean. Importantly for profitability, Italy's shoe production is reported to be in up-market sophisticated products. This puts Italian companies into the position of being better protected against cheap imports and more easily able to obtain high profit margins.

Table 3.2 Share of total EC output by member states (1989)

	Ceramic tiles
Italy	54%
Spain	27%

Source: Panorama of EC Industry 1991/92, Page 7.

Conclusion for specialization

Companies outside these countries aiming to build a dominant position in these industries need to have very clear reasons, e.g. a major product breakthrough. More likely, they will be looking to more limited market specialization opportunities.

French private-sector service companies

Within Europe's Top 250 companies, there are only three that have significant operations in the local service industries, i.e. water supply, cleaning, maintenance, etc. (see Table 3.3). Two of them are French. As Europe has privatized its local services, these two companies have made advances in the UK, Spain and elsewhere.

Table 3.3 Local service companies from Europe's Top 250

	1992 sales (US$m)	*home country*	*1992 % sales** rest of Europe*	*rest of world*
Compagnie Générale des Eaux	18774*	73	27	
Lyonnaise des Eaux Dumez	6528*	57	18	25
BET	3875	57	18	25

*Services only
**Total company.

Conclusion for specialization

It would take a carefully devised strategy to take on these companies in their home territories and expect to have even limited success. Such a task is most likely to involve market specialization of some kind. The French companies have now bought UK privatized water and waste management companies to sell their local service expertise in the UK. Competition on home territory is also an issue for the UK.

British brewing, spirits and leisure companies

Amongst the Top 250 European companies, the accompanying case study includes a list of all those involved in brewing, wines and spirits and leisure: the majority are British.

Case Study: Europe's top brewing, spirits and leisure companies

	Country	*1992 sales (US$m)*	*Destination of sales home country (%)*	*rest of Europe (%)*	*rest of world (%)*
Drinks: brewing and spirits					
Guinness	UK	7164	24	36	40
Allied Lyons	UK	5280	50		50

Grand Metropolitan	UK	4723*	18	19		53
Heineken	Neth	4670	25	50	12	25
Bass	UK	2600*	88		12	
LVMH	Fra	2143*		na		
Carlsberg	Den	1911		na		
Pernod Ricard	Fra	1576*	46		54	
Whitbread	UK	1481*	95		5	
Scottish & Newcastle	UK	1454*		na		
BSN	Fra	1300*		na		

*Data refers to sales in brewing, wines and spirits only. Food and restaurant sales are excluded.

Pub retailing, restaurants and leisure

Ladbroke	UK	3984*		Betting & leisure	
Rank Leisure	UK	3736	68	3	29
Whitbread	UK	3239*		na	
Bass	UK	3373*		na	
Grand Metropolitan	UK	1653*		na	
Scottish & Newcastle	UK	1003*		na	

Hotels

Accor	Fra	6064	39	51	10
Forte	UK	4400	78	12	10
Ladbroke	UK	1491*		Hilton International	
Bass	UK	826*		Holiday Inn franchises	

*Only part of total sales

European and global strategies

Business strategies differ within this category. *Brewing* benefits from economies of scale, branding and tied outlets, ie only selling beers from a particular brewery. But with varying regional tastes and low unit prices, the industry has tended to operate on a national or European basis. More recently, the trend to premium-priced and unusual beers has stimulated global activity, eg the world's largest brewers, Kirin (Japan) and Budweiser (US) have now made a European entry on a modest scale. By contrast, substantial branding investment and common tastes have enabled *Spirits* to operate globally: whisky and gin know few boundaries.

Some *hotel chains*, such as Hilton International, also operated regionally or globally usually by moving up-market. But some of the largest, such as Forte, had only limited European activity up to 1994. Many *leisure* companies, which include betting, have been constrained by national laws or national betting monopolies that limit their operation across Europe. Only Burger King (Grand Met, UK) and McDonalds (US) operate significant cross-border *restaurant* operations: markets and tastes are too fragmented.

The UK brewers within this category developed their strong positions over many years through a complex oligopoly. Although the UK Monopolies and Mergers Commission attempted to reduce their dominance in 1989, the leading companies have adopted new strategies to retain their strengths with some success. New entrants to the UK market have built their strategies on the basis of links with these powerful market players. Although the German beer industry is more fragmented, it has strong regional brewers. Strategy here might also benefit from a similar approach.

Grand Met
Described elsewhere.

Bass
One of the UK's largest brewers. It has a major range of UK beers and public houses

and has divested 2500 out of 7000. It is also separating its brewing from other retailing, possibly for a public flotation of shares. It has no international drinks business.

In a major departure, it bought Holiday Inns International for US$2 billion to become a major world hotelier in 1989.

Allied Lyons
The company acquired Hiram Walker's international drinks business to add to its own and build a powerful world position (e.g. Harvey's Sherries, Courvoisier and Cockburn's Port). It has been involved in distribution via acquisitions in Europe, Asia and South America. In brewing, its Tetley subsidiary is involved largely in the UK, where it has set up a joint venture with Carlsberg. In early 1994, it acquired the Spanish sherry and spirits business from the Domecq family for £739 million.

Among its important food interests, it owns the Donut Corporation of America and Baskin Robbins. It is also buying companies in this area.

Guinness
The company does not own UK retail outlets but is a major world branded spirits and drinks business (e.g. Johnnie Walker scotch, Gordon's Gin) and many of its brands are No. 1 in the world.

It has a share cross-holding of around 22% with LMVH drinks business outlined below.

LVMH
Surely the world's leading luxury goods company. It holds some 25% of Guinness' shares as the result of a 1988 share swap. Brands include Hennessy cognac and Moët et Chandon champagne. Its ownership of luxury producers beyond drinks suffered as global markets declined in the early 1990s.

Heineken
Described elsewhere.

Forte (Formerly Trust House Forte)
A major European/US hotelier and caterer. It has recently had good steady growth, extending its European interests by individual hotel acquisitions rather than hotel chains.

Ladbroke
Owns the world's largest off-track betting organization with interests in Belgium, Holland and the USA as well as in the UK. It also has a major UK DIY retailing chain (excluded from the above figures) and the Hilton International hotel chain which it bought for a bargain price in 1987 (142 high-class hotels world-wide).

Whitbread
Another of the UK's major brewers. It has divested some 2000 of its 6000 pubs over the years to 1992. It is staying in brewing manufacture and has purchased a regional UK brewer, Boddingtons, but sold its international drinks business because it did not believe it could be sufficiently large in this area.

Pernod Ricard
In addition to its traditional spirits, it acquired Irish Distillers in 1990. It is also the world's leading producer of fruit preparations for the food industry and owns the Orangina brand.

BSN
Described elsewhere.

Carlsberg
Denmark's pan-European brewer. Also owns Tuborg.
Overall, there has been much change in the UK brewing industry. There is no sign of any particular interest in the single Europe, but it would not be surprising if some continental or US brewers were not assessing the prospect of a UK purchase or at least further joint ventures. Many companies are moving globally, eg Guinness into China and Carlsberg into Thailand.

Keypoint on specialization
The remarkable number of UK companies in the Top 400 is only partially explained by the complex monopoly that these companies enjoyed in the UK. Some of them at least have major businesses internationally.
Arguably, there is real expertise in the UK in these areas that is not matched elsewhere in much of Europe: for example, skills in catering, hotel management and branding of alcoholic drinks. Nevertheless, there are still opportunities in these markets offset by the strong downturn in European and some global economies in the early 1990s. Discretionary expenditure on leisure is the first to suffer.

Overall conclusions on country specialization

The threat comes not from the country but from companies located there. There is always danger from generalizing about the character of a country's people ('dour', 'fun-loving', etc.) and much of it can be completely useless in business strategy as well as plain wrong. The aim here is much more limited and concentrates on proven knowledge, skill and cost areas.

In a global context, the Asian 'Tiger economies' (Singapore, Malaysia, Hong Kong, Korea, etc) present a further dimension in country specialisation: low labour costs and developing skills. Some global companies, such as Philips Electronics, have taken advantage of this form of specialisation and transferred production to those countries.

COMPANY SPECIALIZATION

This is more familiar territory for most managers. We will look at three examples which show different aspects: BASF AG and Bayer AG (how two large companies in the same country can specialize in world markets in different ways over time); ICI plc (how a company has become more profitable by taking a more specialist route); and BMW AG (the results of specializing within a classic European market).

Case Study: BASF and Bayer, Germany

Data
The world's first and second largest chemical companies.
1992 turnover (DM million)

BASF AG		Bayer AG	
Oil and gas	6782	Polymers	7198
Chemicals	6699	Organics	5472
Agriculture	4671	Ind. products	7579
Plastics and fibres	9092	Healthcare	8928
Dyestuffs	7637	Agrochemicals	5154
Consumer	8824	Imaging Technologies	6864
Other	816		
Total	44522	Total	41195

Return on capital:	4.2% (versus 14.8% in 1988)	8.7% (versus 14.4% in 1988)	
% sales in Europe:	68	57	
% sales in home country:	na	na	
% sales in rest of world:	32	43	

European and global activity
The companies have similar sales but Bayer is noticeably more international because it is less vertically integrated with a wider, more specialist product range. From a specialization viewpoint, the two companies have grown totally differently.

BASF is the world's largest *basic* chemicals company. It suffered in the cyclical downturn in global markets in the early 1990s. It has been shutting down production capacity to recover profitability; a classic volume producer strategy. The company produces products in 35 countries. It is involved in world markets and the single Europe is not the main focus of its operations.

Bayer is a specialist company with a wide range of special products, e.g. inorganics includes pigments, ceramics, polyurethanes and coating raw materials. Each product area will be subject to the market demand changes of many varied customers: profitability will be more complex and stable. Healthcare has proved particularly profitable: differentiated product.

In August 1988 Bayer acquired a company in the US for $500 million, specializing in automated diagnostic testing: it is consolidating its position world-wide rather than in the new single Europe. It also has major activities in South America and Asia.

Keypoint on specialization
Specialization has produced a more stable but complex market for Bayer. Profitability has held up better in the world recession. Given the size of both companies, they can sustain good arguments for continued investment. But these considerations are related to world, not European markets.

Additionally, both companies are operating on a world scale (and recent activity reflects this).

Special keypoint for British readers
Although Bayer's return on capital may not look all that attractive at 8.7%, this must be set in context. Price inflation is only 2–3% and the cost of capital is lower in Germany: Bayer is probably as 'profitable' as many British companies with much higher returns on capital in terms of shareholder earnings. *This is crucial to assessing other European competitors.*

Case Study: Imperial Chemical Industries plc, UK

Data
The world's fourth largest chemical company.

Turnover (£ million)	1992
Bioscience	2978
Speciality chemicals and materials	5256
Industrial chemicals	3224
Regional businesses	1164
Intersegment	(561)
Total	12061

	1990	1992
Return on capital:	13.5%	9.5%
% sales in home country:	37	37
% sales in rest of Europe:	22	21
% sales in rest of world:	41	42

European and global activity
The profitability of ICI in the early 1980s was regarded by the company as insufficiently high. Strong measures were therefore taken to change the basic product mix of the company: this is reflected in the increase in profitability shown in the figures, helped by an upturn in world activity.

ICI has strengthened its activities in the following areas around the world:

Consumer & speciality products
Pharmaceuticals: co-operation with Merck (US) and Yamanouchi (Japan). It has now demerged this area to form a separate company; Zeneca.
Paints: a world leader with manufacturing in 29 countries. Has acquired Berger Australia and an Italian paint company, purchased a coatings business in Spain and entered a joint venture with Du Pont.
Speciality businesses: has strengthened individual areas and claims to be world leader in polyurethanes and advanced aircraft materials. Close partnerships with US and Japan.

Industrial products
General chemicals: a joint venture with Enichem (Italy) and took over production in Germany, Austria, Sweden, and the UK of a range of basic chemicals.
Petrochemicals: one of the world leaders, but suffered in world downturn.
Fibres: World leader in acrylics market.
Explosives: the largest free-world supplier.

Agriculture
Agrochemicals: one of the world's largest companies but in a volatile market.
Plant breeding: a new area with big potential world-wide.
Fertilizers: its strategy is to cut back capacity to meet future demand.

ICI has also moved four of the group's product head offices out of the UK to Belgium, Canada and the US. It operates on the world stage but is also making some moves to consolidate its European position in areas of weakness.

Keypoint on specialization
Around the mid-1980s, ICI concluded that its basic chemical profits were subject to severe competition and cyclical market changes. It therefore took the decision to specialize: the process involved technical development of new products as well as searching for market niches and areas of specialist chemical demand.

The company increased its profitability as a result of these actions. However, it still suffered in the global downturn in the early 1990s; some areas of specialisation became so weak that ICI considered total withdrawal.

Case Study: BMW AG, Germany

Data
One of Europe's two top luxury car makers.
1992 Turnover (DM million)

Cars	22918
Motorcycles	457
Leasing	2884
Other	4982
Total	31241

1992 return on capital: 6.6%
% sales in home country: 42
% sales in rest of Europe: 32
% sales of rest of world: 26

European and global activity
BMW has for many years established itself in a position behind the six volume car manufacturers in Europe but at the top end of the market: its main competitor has been Daimler-Benz. In 1992, it announced it was to start manufacturing cars in the USA – the first time outside Germany. The explanation for this was: 'It is no longer possible to absorb the effect of the exchange rate and the extremely high production costs in Germany.' In 1994, it acquired Rover (UK); this is discussed in chapter 17.

Keypoint on market specialization
BMW has been developing its up-market stance for years. In addition, all production has been concentrated in Germany. This is not expected to change with the single Europe because it is the way for a smaller manufacturer to obtain economies of scale. Thus, market specialization is coupled with concentration of production to achieve high profitability.

Overall conclusions on company specialization

Top European companies are using specialization in the following ways:

1. Building customer loyalty by satisfying specialist customer need;
2. Protecting against competition by building special relationships with customers;
3. Increasing profitability – customers will pay extra in some cases for products and services that are specially designed for their needs;
4. Using economies of scale that arise from specialist production to increase margins or reduce prices and remain competitive; and
5. Achieving market dominance in a specialist area: a strong strategic position.

Overall, there is no point in specializing in an area that is so obscure that market demand does not justify the extra effort required. Generally, specialization strategies have followed some well-worn paths: higher quality/higher price/ higher service levels; specialist product performance; and avoiding areas where a competitor already has an edge, unless there is real product or service innovation.

Before finishing our consideration of company specialization, let us briefly examine two more issues: the distinction between specialization and segmentation; and the problems of selling existing non-specialized products more widely in European and global markets.

Market specialization and segmentation

For clarity of thought, it is worth just briefly considering the 'market segmentation' beloved of marketing managers. Market segmentation starts and finishes with the business of splitting markets into parts in order to appeal particularly to a part of a market.

Market specialization is broader covering production, personnel, R&D, etc., though it has a similar end in that there is no point in specializing if the result achieves few sales. Specialization may lead to *market dominance*, whereas market segmentation does not in itself lead to this position but is rather a signpost for analysis.

Selling existing products more widely in European and global markets

The single Europe and GATT result will enable the diversity of speciality products in EC countries to be available to a wider population as barriers come down. For companies involved with this type of product, there is every reason to try selling the *same product* to a wider European market: Scottish haggis and Greek goat cheeses could potentially be consumed by a larger community within the EC and North America.

However, it needs also to be recognized that where a product or service is much the same as elsewhere in Europe and only protected at present by a national barrier, there is not the same reason to try selling it elsewhere: we will look at what can be done in Part II of this book.

For companies with products that do have some special national character, wider sales are worth exploring. The point here is that the company (in the context of the larger market) is *already specialized* in its products. It needs, initially at least, to concentrate on European or global marketing and distribution of its existing products, rather than developing new products.

CHAPTER 4

Building a 'Euro-brand' or 'Global-brand'

If you are one of Europe's 20,000 small manufacturers making shoes, then you can skip this chapter as it is irrelevant except out of academic interest. We are concerned here with building branded products across Europe and the world and the substantial costs and benefits that will arise.

Because the costs of doing the job adequately are so high, there is really no point in undertaking detailed work unless the resources are available and potential sales are achievable. In a sense, this is the reverse of the previous chapter where specialization was considered: this could potentially be on a small-scale, though we did look at some large companies.

Now, we are concerned with the *pan-European or global branded opportunity*. Certainly it could be specialist but will still involve substantial resources. For the right company with the right planning, there may be attractive profits. Let us look at the situation now.

Leaving aside the obvious difficulties in ranking the performance of Coca Cola above or below Christian Dior, there are some important areas to emerge from Table 4.1:

1. It is not necessary to have massive sales to have an important European brand: Adidas and Jaguar are impressively high on the list although neither company appears in the Top 400;
2. None of the companies have been in the market place for less than five years, many for lengthy periods;
3. While it may partly be a function of the way the list is constructed, all the companies have laid much emphasis on quality performance in their development, and not just those positioned up-market; and
4. All the names have benefited from substantial advertising, promotional and public relations support over the last few years: the newer ones in the table perhaps more than some of the older names.

One other salutary lesson is to examine the profitability of those companies appearing in Europe's Top 400 (see Table 4.2). While the list is dominated by car companies with all their special features, it nevertheless does not make impressive reading. Building a Euro-brand does not guarantee profits, whether in a buoyant year like 1987 or a more difficult year like 1992.

Probably Nestlé is closer to where many companies would expect to be:

Table 4.1   Europe's 20 most popular brands

			How well known	*Esteem*
1.	Mercedes Benz	Ger	4	2
2.	Philips	Neth	2	8
3.	Volkswagen	Ger	3	12
4.	Rolls Royce	UK	15	1
5.	Porsche	Ger	10	3
6.	Coca Cola	US	1	66
7.	Ferrari	Ita	18	5
8.	BMW	Ger	20	4
9.	Michelin	Fra	12	26
10.	Volvo	Swe	14	25
11.	Adidas	Ger	19	21
12.	Jaguar	UK	31	11
13.	Ford	US	8	103
14.	Nivea	UK	16	53
15.	Esso	US	11	83
16.	Sony	Jap	29	24
17.	Nescafé	Swi	6	193
18.	Colgate	US	9	141
19.	Christian Dior	Fra	38	14
20.	Nestlé	Swi	24	45

Source: Landor Associates.

Unilever with many famous European brands also has higher profitability. Even so, the conclusion stands: profitability is still elusive.

CRITERIA FOR EURO-BRAND BUILDING

So, what lessons can be drawn from this evidence? There are three main ones: resources across Europe or around the world; quality; and timing.

Resources across Europe or around the world

For any company considering this route, it will be necessary to have an advertising and promotions budget of at least US$60 million for three years. Therefore if the sales and profit margins do not generate these funds, there is no point in pursuing the matter. As an order of magnitude, this means sales of the order of *US$600 million per annum* to justify this type of resource allocation.

For Coca Cola, such a figure would be attainable with the right product. For some other smaller brands, this is not feasible and it would be better not to attempt the process. Alternatively, a phased launch with lower funding levels might be feasible; but this might not be pan-European or global.

Quality

All the brands in Table 4.2 (and many more not on the list) are impressive in the consistent quality they deliver to customers. Delivering this across Europe or the world all the time is not to be underestimated.

Top Euro-brands demand top quality and procedures to ensure that this is

Table 4.2   Profitability of some Euro-brand companies

	Return on capital (1987)	(1992)
Daimler Benz	13.9%	2.6
Volkswagen	4.6%	(0.1) loss
BMW	11.1%	6.6
Michelin	10.8%	10.4
Volvo	13.7%	(3.7) loss
Ford	10.3%	0.01
Nestlé	22.5%	23.0

Source: Company reports.

maintained are an essential element of the cost of a European or global launch. Without them it would be better to launch on a more modest scale.

Timing
All the listed brands have been working at the matter of Euro-branding or world branding for some years. Nothing has happened quickly and, unless work has already started, it will certainly not happen in the early 1990s. The necessity to have a long time horizon is vital to a successful development brand policy: it will be both expensive and difficult to build a brand in under five years. Do not expect short-term returns.

Case Study: Nestlé SA, Switzerland

Data
Europe's largest branded goods company.
Turnover 1992 (Sfr million)

Europe	26632	Beverages	13521
North and South America	19214	Dairy and dietetics	14890
Rest of World	8654	Prepared dishes and miscellaneous	15718
		Chocolate and confectionery	8598
		Pharmaceutical	1773
Total	54500	Total	54500

Return on capital: 23%
% sales in home country: not available but low
% sales in rest of Europe: 49
% sales in rest of world: 51

European and global activity
One of the world's great branded goods companies: it has grown both by internal investment and by acquisition. The recent purchases include:

1978	Chambourcy
1985	Carnation Dairy
1985	Hill Brothers Coffee (US)
1986	Herta

1988	Rowntree (UK) confectionery
1988	Buitoni (Italy): '3rd largest Italian food company'
1988	Perugina (Italy) confectionery
1992	Perrier mineral water

Nestlé has made strong moves to enhance its franchise in important branded food areas over the last few years: surely not unconnected with the single Europe. For example, as a result of its acquisitions, it has immeasurably strengthened its share of European chocolate confectionery (20% compared to Mars 16% and Philip Morris 18% in 1992).

This company will benefit from the economies of scale and presence operating in Europe. In the early 1990s it acquired companies in Hungary, Poland and the Czech Republic.

Keypoint on Euro-branding
Nescafé is the world's leading instant coffee brand. It has been carefully advertised and promoted since the earliest days and remains the biggest single area for the company. As well as branding, the product has also been enhanced by product improvements: it is not just a matter of advertising but also of quality products.

In looking at Nescafé, we need to distinguish two types of activity. First, basic global branding with production concentrated in a few key countries and some advertising/design. This is strategic, with benefits in economies of scale and economies of advertising message as the world becomes more mobile. Second, national advertising, promotional support and public relations activities. This is both strategic and tactical with scale benefits in central buying/printing and PR activity across the EC or individual countries.

The first area above probably makes more Euro-branding sense than the second which needs more tailoring to individual areas. There would be considerable loss of competitive response time and thrust if the second type of activity were to be centralized. Individual markets need to be able to maintain the initiative and tackle individual taste preferences and attitudes.

Euro-branding must not be taken too far in terms of central decision making. The balance with national markets must be worked through.

Case Study: Heineken NV, Holland

Data
One of Europe's top six brewers.
Turnover 1992 (Dfl million)

Beer	7266	Europe	
Soft drinks	1013	Netherlands	2164
Spirits & wine	412	Other	4405
Other	93	Western hemisphere	1127
Total sales	8784	Africa	509
Service proceeds	160	Australasia	579
		Services	160
Total	8944	Total	8944

Return on capital: 14.0%
% sales in home country: 25
% sales in rest of Europe: 50
% sales in rest of world: 25

Europe and global activity

Heineken is still family controlled and operated from Holland, where it dominates the market. It is heavily involved across Europe having acquired many brewers (outside Germany) before the single Europe was even a gleam in a politician's eye. Much has been spent on rationalizing brewing capacity, particularly in southern Europe, to produce modern efficient and profitable plant.

With the ending of the German purity law restrictions (the Reinheitsgebot), Heineken is still 'studying' Germany. Apart from this, much of European brewing on an international scale is now tied up, either by the company's own deals or by British and French brewers. Further single market activity will be difficult but Heineken is already well represented. However, it acquired its first company in Eastern Europe by buying Komaromi, Hungary, in 1992.

Keypoint on Euro-branding

In spite of its international brand recognition, the Heineken brand name is not operated as such throughout Europe. Probably partly because of the growth by acquisition, Heineken has started with local brands: Dreher (Italy); Aguila (Spain); Amstel (Canada); Murphy (Ireland); and Heineken (Netherlands, UK and USA).

More recently, it has identified a core range of international brands: Heineken, Amstel, Buckler (non-alcoholic) and Murphy's Irish Stout. It is now introducing these globally.

Case Study: Olivetti SpA, Italy

Data

Europe's second largest computer and office products company.

Turnover 1992 (Lire billion)

Products	2825
Systems	2985
Service	2215
Total	8025

Return on capital: 3.0% (loss)
% sales in home country: 39
% sales in rest of Europe: 44
% sales in rest of world: 17

European and global activity

Computers and office products are sold on a world-wide basis (see Chapter 7) and Olivetti has therefore adopted a global approach. Until mid-1989, 22.5% of its shares were owned by the US telecommunications giant AT&T: this stake was then exchanged for shares in an Italian holding company.

Like all the European, and some of the global computer hardware companies, Olivetti is loss-making with only limited prospects for improvement. It has shed 6000 jobs and is rationalising further. It claims a 6 per cent share of the European market, which it aims to build through alliances and joint ventures: DEC (US) computer technology; Canon (Japan) ink jet printers; AT&T (US); Matsushita (Japan) and Marubeni (Japan) in small computers.

During 1992, it also developed contacts with Bull (France) and Siemens Nixdorf (Germany). Whether this network of links and alliances addresses the global strategy issues of service, specialisation, downsizing, rapid technology change and new channel strategy remains unclear. Nevertheless, 'Olivetti is ready to play a part in the restructuring of the European industry'. Olivetti's global ambitions have yet to be realized.

Keypoint on Euro-branding
Olivetti has established its name throughout Europe without massive expenditure: it has a credible presence in most countries. However, this has been built over many years and has not yet led to consistent profitability. Euro-branding and profitability do not necessarily go together.

Case Study: European fast-moving consumer goods companies

Data
Not all Europe's top consumer goods companies operate under well-known Eurobrand names: private label, unbranded commodity foods and national brand names are a significant part of the total.

Other key brand names, principally associated with US companies, do not quite make it to Europe's Top 400 but have been included for the sake of completeness. It should be noted that these are generally companies with world brands, having substantial sales in the US and elsewhere which fall outside the scope of the data in the following table of selected European branded goods companies. Even so, a few US companies with important market stakes in Europe are excluded: for example, Mars. Unfortunately, they do not publish any useful company data for Europe.

In addition, some major European companies do not appear because their overall size excludes them from Europe's Top 400, eg BIC, France. Other famous brand names such as Guinness, Shell and Volkswagen appear in other categories, wines and spirits, oil and petrol, cars.

	Country	1992 sales (US$m)	Return on capital (%)	home country (%)	Destination of sales rest of Europe (%)	rest of world (%)
Food and consumer goods						
Nestlé	Swi	41313	23.0	na	49	51
Unilever	UK/Neth	40820	22.6	na	59	41
BSN	Fra	11356	13.3	45	48	7
Eridiana Beghin Say	Ita/Fra	9814	12.6	22	58	20
L'Oreal	Fra	7452	19.8	33	45	
Dalgety	UK	7387	27.2	38	4	58
ABF	UK	6534	15.4	90		10
Hillsdown	UK	6396	12.4	55	23	22
Cadbury Schweppes	UK	5573	20.8	44	22	34
Tate & Lyle	UK	5563	16.7	25	23	52
United Biscuits	UK	5153	15.1	50	14	36
Christian Dior	Fra	3950	not available: private			
SME	Ita	3700	group being broken up & sold			
SuedZucker	Ger	3534	9.7	54	46	
Campina MelkUnie	Net	3349	9.7	53	30	17
Northern Foods	UK	3348	40.1	100	0	0
Reckitt & Colman	UK	3147	21.0	19	27	54
Beiersdorf	Ger	3063	14.9	39	39	22

Barilla	Ita	2540		not available: private		
Unigate	UK	2236	16.6	79	0	31
Wessanen	Neth	2224	18.7	11	25	64
SMH	Swi	2094		not available		
Allied Lyons	UK	1983		not available		
Procordia	Swe	979*	13.9	61		39

* food turnover only

Some US companies are heavily involved in Europe and global markets: home sales are for the USA; European sales are the total for that area in the table that follows.

Philip Morris Food sales	US	29048	na	70		30
Procter & Gamble	US	29362	17.5	53	28	19
Eastern Kodak	US	20183	na	54		46
Pepsi Inc	US	19608	14.1	77	7	16
Johnson & Johnson	US	13753	26.9	50		50
Sara Lee	US	13243	15.6	66	27	7
Coca Cola	US	13074	48.0	33	30	37
Colgate Palmolive	US	7007	19.6	36	31	33
Heinz	US	6582	28.7	58	28	14
Kelloggs	US	6191	37.3	57	27	16
CPC International	US	6189	25.8	37	40	23
Quaker	US	5576	27.5	69	24	7
Gillette	US	5163	36.8	31	42	27

Care needs to be taken in examining the above data; the companies do not all compete against each other in the same markets. The aim is to indicate comparative size rather than full details.

European and global activity
Larger companies tend to have developed by dominating national markets; even the largest, Nestlé and Unilever, have strong national or regional strengths. Some now seek to extend their influence to other European countries. This has either required the financial muscle of large resources, eg PepsiCo's purchases in Spain cost US$ 320 million in 1992, or some form of collaborative deal or simply the extension of brands across Europe. The following reflect this approach:

Wessanen merged with Bols, the Dutch drinks group, early in 1993. The former is particularly strong in the USA and may be able to help the latter there.

ABF has some tea and coffee interests in France and Belgium but is mainly UK based. Its last major acquisition was British Sugar in 1990 for £880 million.

Unigate still has the same wide interests from dairy to transport; some strategists would say that it still has the same lack of focus in its business range.

Tate & Lyle: one of Europe's top three sugar companies, along with Sucre et Denree and Suedzucker. T&L moved into the US in 1988, when it bought Stanley Industries, and into Australia two years later. In the stable European sugar market, any acquisition in that area by T&L would either be too expensive or blocked by the European Commission on competition grounds. European joint ventures would also be ruled out.

Eridiana Beghin Say is part of the Italian Ferruzi empire. At the time of writing, the whole group was the subject of bankruptcy proceedings. Individual companies were still continuing to trade.

Reckitt & Colman has a range of products in niche markets around the world. It has not really considered its strategy as being specifically European.

Sara Lee bought the Dutch beverage company, Douwe Egberts, in 1987. It also owns the Kiwi polish and Radox bath products brands. In 1991, it extended its beverage business by acquisitions in Eastern Europe.

Colgate Palmolive, Heinz and Gillette have all been established as European branded companies for many years. Reference is made elsewhere in this book to the economies of scale they have obtained in production and logistics in pan-European operations.

Kelloggs, General Mills and Nestlé are engaged in a battle for the European and global breakfast cereal market. This is described in detail in my book *Cases in European Marketing*.

Global tobacco products

'Home sales' may take on a special meaning for companies in this category: BAT Tobacco has only a limited franchise in its home country but extensive European sales; Rothmans International does not really have a home country; American Brands is market leader in the UK through its subsidiary Gallaher, but has only a small franchise in the USA. The data therefore needs to be read with care.

	Country	1992 sales (US$m)	Home	Europe	Rest of world
Philip Morris					
Tobacco sales	US	25677	47		53
BAT	UK	19660		43	57
RJR Nabisco	US	9027	68	32	
American Brands	US	8157	22	78 mainly UK	
Hanson/Imperial	UK	7589	90 estimated	10	
Tabacalera	Spa	4567	90 estimated	10	
Rothmans Int'l	Swi	3984		51	49
Seita	Fra	2661	75 estimated	25	

European and global activity

Once market share is gained, it is not given up lightly: the French and Spanish former tobacco monopolies, Seita and Tabacalera respectively, still dominate their home markets by controlling distribution. Equally, Gallaher and Imperial Tobacco (part of Hanson) dominate the UK market. BAT is strong in Germany and elsewhere. Rothmans is actually part of Richemont International and owns the global brand Peter Stuyvesant. Philip Morris claims the world's largest tobacco brand in Marlboro.

With strong and fairly stable national franchises, international strategies have recently concentrated on extension beyond western Europe. For a description of BAT's move into Eastern Europe, see my book *Cases in European Marketing*.

BAT and Gallaher also exchanged some brands across Europe in 1993 to strengthen their respective market positions (Financial Times 30 June 1993, page 25 for details). BAT acquired the US tobacco interests of American Brands in 1994, but not its European sales (see under Gallaher in Chapter 17).

Keypoint on Euro-branding

The above data shows that some highly profitable European companies do not operate pan-European brands: they may have branded goods, but many are essentially national brands. Some are starting the Euro-branding process, eg BSN discussed later.

But it is the *US branded goods companies* that have really made the most of Euro-branding which may be easier in the single market. It would be ironic, but not wholly surprising, if the USA was to benefit more than Europe from the single European market. This is quite likely on present evidence.

CONCLUSIONS

Euro-branding and global-branding have not truly taken off yet in some areas because of organizational, economic and cultural differences. For example, the packaging colour green is seen as cheap in Spain, yet has the image of being environmentally sound in the UK.

Moreover, there is still a need for local labelling, local ingredients, and so on, so some aspects are not clearly cost effective. While this will supposedly change after 1992, it remains to be proven and will still not allow for cultural diversity.

Nevertheless, for the well-researched and well-supported product or service, there are real rewards and real competitive strengths to be gained by following the Euro-branding route. However, it will only work with some products and, in fact, some of Europe's most profitable companies do not follow this approach at all.

CHAPTER 5

Defining Critical Success Factors

In the last three chapters we have looked at three vital aspects of the European and global analysis: preparing background material; market specialization; and building a Euro-brand. Before proceeding further we need to analyze the critical success factors (CSFs) for the European and global markets in which we are involved. These are the aspects of the market and thus the parts of our own business which it is absolutely essential to understand in the new European and world environment. We might need to make some changes. CSFs are important because they crucially affect profits.

Now no two situations are the same so there is no single way of approaching this. Here are some key questions that you can ask that will help to clarify CSFs:

1. What really important *market trends* are now taking place? Growth? Cyclical trends? Essentially static? Massive cheap imports? Major new product innovation?
2. How important is our existing *home market* to our business? Is it essential to defend this?
3. Why have *competitors* grown to the position they now hold? What have they done and what skills do they have? What advantages can they offer our customers? Will they be persuasive? Why? Price? Service? Advertising? Salesforce? Distribution arrangements?
4. What are the largest *cost areas* of the business? Are they critical? Do our competitors share the same cost profile?
5. How important is *research and development* and market innovation, even if original research is not involved? What areas are we strong in?
6. Is our business *capital intensive*? Are there long lead times for customer orders? How do our resources and order book compare with the competition?
7. What *worker and management skills* are particularly crucial? How do these compare with our competitors?
8. How important are sudden movements in *currency* to our business?

CSF ILLUSTRATIONS

All these need to be combined together and honed down to the most important areas: every manager will have something to say under every heading but only some will be *critical*. These are the ones we are looking for and they usually amount to around only four or five. Let us take some examples.

CSFs in fast-food retailing. Examples include location: quality of food; speed of friendly service; and cleanliness and design of store. I was once told by a senior manager in such an organization that the really important factors were location and location and location.... I think he was exaggerating but I can see what he meant.

CSFs in electricity supply distribution: Continuity of service; price; speed and resolution of faults; safety costs; and energy supply costs and trends.

CSFs in branded coffee: Price; in-store distribution and display; plant capacity utilization; and advertising and promotion.

CSFs in pharmaceuticals: Product performance; research & development; cost structure; and salesforce skills and resources.

CSFs in iron and steel: Plant investment; distribution arrangements; product specializations; and continuous production.

Case Study: United Biscuits plc, UK

Data
Europe's second largest biscuit manufacturer.
1992 turnover (£ million)
Biscuits

UK and Europe	831
Keebler: US	1051
KP Snacks	530
Ross/Youngs prepared meals	520
Terry's confectionery	176
Other	10
Total	3118

Return on capital: 15.1%
% sales in home country: 50
% sales in rest of Europe: 14
% sales in rest of world: 36

European and global activity
United Biscuits (UB) is UK market leader in biscuits and second in Europe overall behind BSN. UB acquired Verkaede biscuits, Holland, in 1990. It has also long been involved in the USA: it acquired Keebler in the early 1980s. In 1992/93, its American biscuit operations came under severe price competition from the US market leader, Nabisco. This did not stop Keebler buying a US manufacturer of private label biscuits in 1993 for £47 million: even after this purchase, Nabisco will still be three times as large as Keebler.

UB is also heavily involved in snack markets: it beat its global rival, PepsiCo (US) to purchase the Australian company, Amatil, for £195 million in 1993. UB has major snack operations in the UK, where its subsidiary, KP Foods, is snack market leader, and in the rest of Europe where it made a series of small acquisitions in the late 1980s.

Beyond all this, UB has interests in UK frozen food through Ross/Youngs, which it bought in 1988 for reasons that make little sense against its global ambitions. UB sold its Terry's Chocolate business to Philip Morris (US) in 1992.

Keypoint: CSFs for UB in biscuits
■ Product innovation;
■ Price/value;

- Instore distribution and display;
- Plant capacity utilization and unit costs; and
- Advertising support for lead brands.

These are CSFs for biscuits. They suggest that UB's involvement in US biscuit manufacture could still prove difficult. In Europe, its second place to BSN will need radical thinking about CSF's if it is to overtake the market leader.

Case Study: Glaxo plc, UK

Data
1992 turnover (£ million)

Anti-ulcerants	1807
Respiratory	964
Systemic antibiotics	681
Antiemesis	259
Dermatological	145
Cardiovascular	63
Antimigraine	43
Other	134
Total	4096

Return on capital: 31.3%
% sales in home country: na
% sales in rest of Europe: 42
% sales in rest of world: 58 (of which 42% North America)

European and global activity
Glaxo has built its recent success on its world leader in anti-ulcerants, Zantac. It has a vigorous research programme and, as the above data shows, is by no means reliant on its ulcer drug (eg Ventolin is one of the world's leading anti-asthma drugs).

Glaxo has not been actively seeking major European initiatives, nor does it expect to: 'International marketing has been a key factor in our success..... Glaxo pursues a global strategy and we do not expect the promise of a single internal market in Europe from 1992 to require significant changes in the group's operations.' Company strategy has been to continue its strong research programme, despite global pressures on drug profitability.

Keypoint:CSFs for Glaxo in pharmaceuticals

- International marketing and distribution;
- Research & development;
- Cost and timing of drug approval process; and
- People management skills in development jobs.

Again, the CSFs for the company and market point up what is really important rather than an endless list of what might be useful to know. Unfortunately, it is usually necessary to go through the long analysis to arrive at the final shortlist.

Case Study: Cockerill Sambre SA, Belgium

Data
One of Europe's top five steel producers.
1992 turnover (Bfr million)

Integrated iron and steel activities	58504
Distribution	66777
Construction	17337
Mechanical engineering	9139
Motor vehicle components	13863
Services	2067
Other	7200
Total	174887

Return on capital: 0.25% (versus 15.2% in 1988)
% sales in home country: 26
% sales in rest of Europe: 70
% sales in rest of world: 4

European and global activity
Like the other leading European steel makers, the company has been reorganizing over the last few years: it is not a profitable business. Its activities are almost exclusively within Europe.

The company is the largest distributor in Belgium and Holland. With the new single market, it has established new agreements with other companies: for example, Usinor Sacilor (France); Stinness (Germany); and in the building industry, Bouygues (Spain). It sees global activity as 'difficult because of significant differences in production cost structures between different regions of the world.' In other words, European steel is expensive to produce.

Keypoints: CSFs for Cockerill Sambre in iron and steel

- Distribution agreements;
- Unit costs and capital investment; and
- Special products and product margins;
- Joint ventures with other groups, particularly large customers.

We will come back to the steel distribution issue later. This is a key factor in a number of major industries. The key strategies of Cockerill are elaborated further in its 1992 annual company report.

Case Study: Renault SA, France

Data
One of Europe's top 6 car producers: government owned

Turnover (Ffr million)	1987	1991
Automobiles	114375	133949
Commercial vehicles	28383	26760
Other	4752	5265
Total	147510	165974

Return on capital:	7.3%	10.3%
% sales in home country:	51	48
% sales in rest of Europe:	37	41
% sales in rest of world:	12	11

European and global activity

Renault has been investing heavily over the last few years to bring its plant up to modern standards. It is still heavily reliant on its national market which remained subject to protection into the 1990s.

Essentially, it is one of the leading European manufacturers of cars but it does not have the specialist market positioning of some that would assist in the new single market. Potentially, it is one of the losers, particularly in the event of a renewed Japanese inflow. To build economies of scale in research and component supply, it negotiated a minority share exchange with Volvo (Sweden) in 1990. An attempt at outright takeover was rejected by its Swedish target in 1993. At the time of writing, it still needs a strategy for global survival.

Keypoint: CSFs for Renault in cars

- Strong marketing and market positioning;
- Distributorships and servicing;
- Plant investment and unit costs;
- Design and development skills; and
- Government and EC links (to maintain protection).

CONCLUSIONS

The construction of the best concentrated list of factors for a specific company coupled with all the material that has already been developed, is the basis of the European and global strategy. We will come to this in Part II, but in the next three chapters we highlight some pitfalls in our analysis where real profits can be lost.

Before leaving the issue of CSFs, we would do well to consider two overall areas that have proved crucial to international business prosperity in the early 1990s:

- economic downturn;
- currency movements.

Economic downturn will have an impact on all companies. However, for some businesses recession is not merely something to be endured, but hits at the company's ability to survive. For example, companies needing to operate a plant at 95 per cent capacity – float glass making (Pilkington); polyethylene (BASF) and car manufacturing (Volkswagen) – will identify international economic trends as critical.

Currency movements affect all companies operating internationally; most companies develop instruments and insurance to hedge against the risks. However, for some countries this is insufficient; currency movements are critical to survival, because profit margins are low and dependent on predictable currency fluctuations. For example, the very survival of Metallgesellschaft (Germany) was called into question in early 1994 primarily as a result of injudicious currency management. This can also be critical to success.

CHAPTER 6

Recognizing Hidden Barriers

As the 1990s progress, world trade barriers are likely to come down. There are two principal reasons: the single European market and the implementation of the General Agreement on Trade and Tariffs (GATT). Many companies will have considered the market opportunities that this will bring; the difficulty is that some barriers will remain hidden yet could have the biggest impact on profits.

Because the situation is so complex and varied, governments will find it almost impossible to legislate for all eventualities: many barriers rely on unwritten understandings rather than formal laws. It is these *hidden barriers* that will be the real problem. These are the ones that can cost money because:

- they negate the sales effort at an advanced stage;
- they make a nonsense of planned economies of scale that cannot be realized on any reasonable timescale;
- they cost money to negotiate around; and they are the competitive advantage of other companies and will not be given up lightly.

THE NATURE OF THE PROBLEM

What are the hidden barriers? Where are they likely to emerge? What will they cost in lost profit opportunities? One answer to the question is, of course, that no one can know because they are difficult to pin down. However, that is clearly not a satisfactory basis on which to plan. While accepting that detailed assessment has to be carried out by industry and is therefore beyond the scope of this book, let us make some attempt to estimate where problems might arise.

The starting point has to be the three basic areas where barriers may still exist: physical barriers (cross-border checks, customs and all the documentation that accompanies this); technical barriers (national industry standards, technical controls and laws, plus national procurement policies); and fiscal barriers (principally VAT and excise duties). Now we can cast a critical eye over some examples.

Case Study: Bouygues, SA, France

Data
Europe's largest construction company.
1992 turnover (Ffr million)
Construction

Public	23801
Roads	21303
Real estate	5508
Offshore services	3558
Electricity	1508
Waterproofing	2778
Ground and frozen products	2987
Engineering design	1034
Film production	180
Other	63
Intersegment	(660)
Stock change	1132
Total	63192

Return on capital: 8.1%
% sales in home country: 71
% sales in rest of Europe: 10
% sales in rest of world: 19

European and global activity
Bouygues is one of Europe's leading construction companies (eg it is a member of the Eurotunnel consortium). As a family-controlled business, it has used construction profits to acquire interests in other unrelated areas. There appears to have been no clear pattern to this activity.

Keypoint on hidden barriers
During the Summer of 1989, Bouygues bid for a public works bridge building contract in Denmark. After submitting its bid, the company complained that it was unable to make a full and fair bid because of bias by the authorities in Denmark: this hidden barrier clearly caused expense to the company. After intervention by the European Commission, the company was allowed to resubmit a bid, but it was still unsuccessful.

Because Bouygues had relatively limited experience of construction working inside the single Europe, it effectively went through a learning experience. No doubt it will be wiser next time and arguably the bid was worthwhile for this alone.

The company is itself protected by high barriers in France (along with other French construction companies): France and Germany have been identified in an EC survey as the most difficult countries for technical building certification. The problem is that such certificates are mandatory in these countries and all levels of construction management rigidly follow the national technical regulations. Perhaps Bouygues should not have complained too strongly to the Danes.

Generally in European construction, some of the more essential areas (eg stability, fire safety and health), may be harmonized. But there will still be plenty of argument over many other practical areas starting with electricity voltage, water pressures and plug sizes. The hidden barriers will continue in construction for many years. The same will apply in global markets.

Here are some lessons that seem to come out of the Danish bid described above: gain information from experience; if you can afford it, take part in bidding for contracts to gain experience; accepting that hidden barriers will continue in some industries, see if you can put a cost on the extra time involved so it can be costed into the bid.

Case Study: Selected EC construction companies

Data

Let us look at this area across Europe: there is a vast range of companies within Europe's Top 400, ranging from road and housing construction through to cement and tile manufacture. Many of the companies have international involvement but this means world construction contracts and USA subsidiaries rather than single Europe activity. There are few non-European companies engaged in European construction.

The cement companies have made the most progress towards European integration and are covered separately in this book. They are therefore excluded from the table.

	Country	1992 sales (US$m)	Return on capital (%)	Home (%)	Source of sales Rest of Europe (%)	Rest of world (%)
Bouygues	Fra	12536	8.3	71	10	19
Dumez*****	Fra	9107**	loss	na	but mainly France	
Soc Generale d'Entreprise****	Fra	8808**	na	58	32	10
Holzmann	Ger	7000	8.9	57	15	28
Skanska	Swe	5690	(5.4)	85	15	
Hochtief	Ger	5073	3.4	72	2	26
Tarmac	UK	4850	(1.4)*	78	7	15
Poliet***	Fra	3930	12.5	90 est	10	
Redland	UK	3454	9.8	24	52	24
Wolseley***	UK	3229	23.2	49		51 (all USA)
BICC/Balfour Beatty	UK	3054**	loss	na	but mainly UK	
Fomento de Construcciones	Spa	2928	na	na	but mainly Spain	
Wimpey	UK	2687	(11.3)	78	4	18
P&O/Bovis	UK	2512**	loss	na		
Hanson	UK	2416**	3.0	na		
Trafalgar House	UK	2148	loss	na		
Taylor Woodrow	UK	2026	4.1	80	4	16
Euroc	Swe	1680	6.7	42	43	15

* before major restructuring costs
** only part of total turnover
*** mainly wholesaling and builders merchants
**** wholly owned by Compagnie Generale des Eaux (Fra)
***** merged with Lyonnaise des Eaux (Fra) in 1992

The above data excludes cement, property deals, engineering construction and services; all these have rather different strategies.

European and global activity
Construction was hit hard by recession in European economies in the early 1990s. The business strategies were therefore those of survival rather than the search for growth opportunities; cost cutting and asset sales to stave off bankruptcy.

Construction across Europe is fragmented with many small and medium size companies; the large firms listed above tend to tackle the big government contracts, eg road construction. They then subcontract part of this work to the many smaller enterprises. The large companies thus have two roles: contract procurement and then contract management. Strategies will reflect this structure.

Bouygues, Dumez, BICC and Trafalgar House are all part of the Channel Tunnel construction consortium; this is the most obvious area of cross-European activity.

Dumez has small companies in Spain, Germany and the Czech Republic. It has a large electrical distributor in North America, United Westburne.

Redland has weathered the storm of depressed European construction markets better than some. It manufactures in some 30 countries, including six roof tile plants set up in the former Eastern Germany and a plant in the USA and South East Asia.

Holzmann is the largest German construction company and has taken advantage of the massive investment in infrastructure in Eastern Germany. It also has significant US subsidiaries and is involved in energy and environmental technology.

Tarmac is typical of Europe's construction companies attempting to cope with severe recession. It is particularly dependent on the UK and USA.

Skanska is Sweden's largest construction company. It has also been badly affected by Europe's difficult economic recession.

Keypoint on hidden barriers
Companies like Holzmann, Dumez and Tarmac have moved from the national to world markets rather than the single Europe. One reason for this is that the hidden barriers (public procurement policies and national building regulations) are high.

Other reasons include the growth in world markets for large-scale construction projects and the cost of transporting construction materials across Europe, which distorts economies of scale and needs special local sources. It would therefore be wrong to conclude that hidden barriers are the only reason for the lack of growth in the single market in this area.

Let us look at another example of a national organization that has declared itself as welcoming EC contracts.

Case Study: Deutsche Bundespost Postdienst

Data
Europe's largest postal carrier.
1992 turnover (DM million)

Letter mail	14040
Info post	2727
Freight	3976
Newspaper post	1046
Other	3845
Total	25634

Return on capital: 2.7% loss
% sales in home country: over 90
% sales in rest of Europe: low

European and global activity
Following reorganisation in 1989, the company has been operating as an autonomous enterprise. It will be privatised in the mid-1990s.

Postdienst has been active in rebuilding the infrastructure of the former East German postal system. Nevertheless, there has also been a focus on international mail; the company became a member of a new European data processing initiative called CAPE (Computer Aided Post in Europe) and sponsored by the EC. It has also joined a new worldwide venture called GD Express along with the postal services of France, Canada, the Netherlands, Sweden and the transport company TNT Australia.

Keypoint on hidden barriers
As part of its large investment in East Germany, EC laws insisted that Postdienst contracts were open to companies from other EC countries. This was recognised in the 1987 Annual Report of its predecessor company, Deutsche Bundespost Telekom; 'We are trying to open up procurement beyond national frontiers and create the single internal market within Europe by 1992.' No data is available on how successful the company has been. Its changing role and legal status will make it more difficult for outsiders to obtain contracts.

This suggests:

- research customers carefully or time and resource will be wasted;
- national government institutions are more visible and thus more vulnerable to opening up their tendering procedures in the new Europe, so they may be worth trying.

Case Study: Fiat SpA, Italy

Data
One of Europe's six large car producers.
1992 turnover (lire billion)

Automobiles	27446
Commercial vehicles	8044
Tractors & construction machines	4585
Metallurgical products	1162
Vehicle components	2881
Batteries	1079
Industrial components	2642
Production systems	1326
Civil engineering	2641
Rolling stock & railways	282
Aviation	1231
Publishing & communication	475
Snia BPD	2038
Financial services	2970
Insurance	1995
Retailing	4499
Inter-company	(6190)
Total	59106

Return on capital: 3.2%
% sales in home country: 49
% sales in rest of Europe: 35
% sales in rest of world: 16

European and global activity
In spite of the tremendous range of products, most of Fiat's production essentially revolves around cars and trucks: 72% of the company's employees in 1992 were located in Italy which indicates how concentrated on Italy the whole operation is.

Keypoint on hidden barriers
Importantly, the company's sales are sustained by its home market. While this is perhaps slightly more protected than some, all Europe's car operations work behind considerable barriers including: documentation and inspection; type approval; VAT differences on company purchases; varied sales taxes; tax incentives on environmental emissions; and national vehicle requirements.

In view of this list, some may ask whether hidden barriers are needed. But these are just the type of barriers which may disappear because they are well documented and they are the sort of thing that the EC can legislate for. But these barriers offer real competitive advantage to Fiat and the other car makers in their own countries. Does any company really think it will all be sweetness and light? There will be a strong need to look for further competitive reaction: hidden barriers will be set up.

Here are some pointers on barriers based on the above:

■ Expect a competitive reaction from major home companies as barriers to entry come down;
■ Anticipate new barriers to emerge that are at present hidden; and
■ Estimate in advance what hidden barriers are likely to go up by studying the market and take appropriate action in advance.

Case Study: Total Oil, France

Europe's fifth largest oil and petrol company.

Data
1992 turnover (FF million)

Exploration and production	6787
Trading and Middle East	39159
Refining and marketing	70345
Chemicals	18744
Mining	1133
Corporate	440
Intersegment	(30409)
Total	136608

Return on capital: 8.5%
% sales in home country: 43
% sales in rest of Europe: 28
% sales in rest of world: 29

European and global activity
Total has refining and marketing operations across much of western Europe with the exceptions of Scandinavia and Italy. It is concentrated in its home country where it is second only to Elf – it has built this position over many years with the cooperation of the French government who hold a majority of Total's shares.

Both its exploration and production activities and its trading and shipping interests are truly global, rather than European. Over the last few years it has been faced with difficult market conditions in trading. Its strategic development process involved careful examination of objectives, and then a refocussing on specific projects based on two criteria:

- specific operations requiring special expertise: the aim is to differentiate its product and generate high value added.
- carefully selected geographical areas: the purpose here is to minimise business risk.

In chemicals its strategy has also reflected this approach, it has sought 'high value added speciality' chemicals. Hence it acquired Bostik adhesives and developed Coates printing inks and Hutchison rubber products into European market leaders in specialist areas.

Keypoint on hidden barriers
Because petrol and oil are traded globally there are ostensibly fewer hidden barriers than might apply with some other products. In practice for a company like Total, there can still be significant barriers – much of the company's activities rely on compliance with national regulations on imports, taxes and technical specifications. Learning all this from scratch would take too long for most companies; the alternatives are to buy in expertise, eg from a good local distributor, or recruit local nationals.

As part of its business strategy, Total has sought to develop speciality products. It might be thought that their special nature would overcome hidden barriers. The degree of protection provided here will depend on how specialist the products are against competition.

Here are some pointers to barriers to entry based on Total:

- specify in detail the barriers to be overcome; and
- consider setting up national companies or selecting a good local distributor to overcome them.

Case Study: Wellcome plc, UK

Data
World's 19th largest pharmaceutical company.
1992 turnover (£ million)

Prescription drugs		Non-prescription drugs	
Anti-virals	826	Cough & colds	132
NMB's	106	Tropical anti-infectives	54
Anti-inflammatory	105	Analgesics	19
Cardio vascular	90	Other	32
Immuno-suppressants	70		
Systemic bacterials	49		
Central nervous system	47		
Topical anti-infectives	43		
Cough & cold	22		
Other	103		
Subtotal	1462	Subtotal	237
Total sales	1699		

Return on capital employed: 33%
% sales in home country: 8
% sales in rest of Europe: 26
% sales in rest of world: 65

European and global activity

Wellcome is, by world pharmaceutical standards, a small company with strong involvement in the USA. Over the last five years, it has begun to build a European presence. It has used strategic alliances with nationally-strong drug companies to achieve this in Italy and Germany (with Hoechst). Such a strategy is not confined to Europe; it has also built alliances in the Far East, for example Japan (with Sumitomo). The key here is to have something special to offer. Wellcome has its unique drug Retrovir.

Keypoint on hidden barriers

In Europe, along with all other companies in this market, it is faced with a series of barriers particularly over the registration of new drugs. Whilst the EC has made some strides in gaining common technical standards for new products, there are still considerable differences over the practicalities of registering new drugs, which can take up to three years and involve different methods in each EC country.

While this was not the reason Wellcome developed its new anti-AIDS drug 'Retrovir', it does illustrate one way of getting around some of the barriers. The drug has been shown in the USA to be a break-through in treating the symptoms. Although it will certainly have to meet various national approvals, its revolutionary nature has helped its acceptance across Europe. It will break some of the rules and therefore overcome some of the hidden barriers. Here are some pointers on barriers arising from the above:

■ if you want to avoid hidden barriers, investigate breaking the rules completely;
■ totally new products and services are much more likely to do this than ones that mirror what is already available.

CONCLUSIONS

In the nature of the changes, there is bound to be some attempt to maintain barriers. Nevertheless, they will undoubtedly come down from the mid-1990s onwards and companies who have tried the market prior to this time will be best placed to move.

CHAPTER 7

Dealing with Excess Production Capacity

There is no doubt that some companies may go out of business in the new European and global markets because of the excess production capacity that will arise as barriers come down. Companies must identify if this will happen to them: if it is likely, then damage limitation now will save even more grief later. It is a sure way to lose large sums of money in the new situation if not tackled vigorously at an early stage.

HOW WILL EXCESS CAPACITY ARISE?

Essentially, it will come from more efficient companies trading across market barriers and thus generating spare production capacity. There are certain types of industry that are more likely to give rise to it than others. For example:

- Industries that have traditionally been *protected by national governments* (eg railway rolling stock and defence);
- Industries that have operated on a national basis behind tariff and other trade barriers but which have *spare national or European capacity* (eg cars and public telephone switching equipment);
- Industries where a *highly efficient possible competitor* with the potential to add to capacity has developed in one country (eg parts of the food industry); and
- Industries that are *highly fragmented* in one country but more concentrated in other countries (eg boiler-making and boiler-servicing).

Coupling these considerations with estimates of European and global market size and existing production capacity will show if there is a significant problem. However, many national industries know that the dire predictions made about them by the European Commission in 1988 had not happened by 1992. Either the EC got it wrong or new markets for the capacity were found. Let us examine the evidence.

COMMISSION EXAMPLES

In 1986–88, the European Commission sponsored research into the matter of excess capacity in the new single market. It produced examples from six industries (see Table 7.1).

For a variety of reasons, this overcapacity had not necessarily resulted in closure by 1992. But the threat has not yet passed. Let us look at the main

Table 7.1   Overcapacity in selected European industries

	Market size (ECU) 1986	Estimated capacity utilization	Significance of intra-EC trade
Boilers	2000	20%	negligible
Turbine generators	2000	60%	negligible
Locomotives	100	50–80%	negligible
Mainframe computers	10000	80%	med. to great
Public switching	7000	approx. 70%	medium
Telephones	5000	90%	negligible

Source: Cecchini, *Benefits of a Single Market.*

industries in Table 7.1 and the strategies they have adopted to overcome the difficulties. We will look at public switching and telecommunications equipment later in the book.

Boiler-making and turbine generators

According to the EC, there was massive overcapacity in this industry. Traditional customers have been in the thermal and nuclear power industries and in the oil and gas industry. As these have declined, plastics, electronics and food and drink have become more important. There is considerable exporting beyond the EC but little intra-EC trade.

In the five countries surveyed on boiler-making, the EC predicted the number of firms to decline from 16 to around 4. In practice, production and numbers employed in the industry were largely static between 1987 and 1992. [*Source: Panorama of EC Industry 1993*, pages 7–24.] Demand for turbines and generators is derived from the industries they serve. The main related industries are shown in Table 7.2.

Table 7.2   Related national industries for turbines and boiler-makers

Germany	Chemicals
	Automobiles
	Mechanical engineering
	Energy
	Anti-pollution
France	Nuclear power (overcapacity)
	Automobiles
	Oil
	Food & drink
UK	Oil
	Energy
	Harbour & shipping
	Iron & steel

Source: European Commission, Panorama of EC Industry 1989.

As demand has declined in one area, capacity has been switched to another. In addition, companies have moved towards rapid and flexible servicing. Where high levels of skill are required to maintain boilers, eg nuclear industry, strategies have included the provision of other related services. All these new strategies may assist as European markets are opened to competitors with lower labour costs from the Far East and Eastern Europe.

Let us look at one of the world's largest turbine manufacturers, the European company ABB.

Case Study: Asea Brown Boveri, Switzerland and Sweden

Data
One of the world's major engineering companies: world leader in several categories.
1992 turnover (US$ million)

Power plants	6497	EC	5971
Power transmission	5606	EFTA	5862
Power distribution	3345	North America	2115
Industry	4430	Asia/Australasia	2111
Transportation	2662	Others	1773
Financial services	805	Western Europe	17467
Various activities	10027	Eastern Europe	351
Intergroup	4207	North America	4931
		South America	896
		Africa	1980
		Asia/Pacific	3990
Total	29615	Total	29615

Return on capital employed: 14.2%
% sales in home country: irrelevant because two home countries
% sales in rest of Europe: 60
% sales in rest of world: 40

European and global activity
ABB was formed in January 1988 by the merger of the electrotechnical operations of ASEA (Sweden) and Brown Boveri (Switzerland). Both companies felt the need for size, growth and rationalization to operate their businesses more successfully in world markets. They also recognized the economies of scale and spare capacity issues that would arise increasingly in the *world* markets in which they operate.

While the combined company has its HQ and major manufacturing in Sweden and Switzerland, it is also a substantial employer in the EC. The company has 42,000 employees in Sweden and Switzerland, 76,000 in the European Community and another 95,000 elsewhere in the world.

After the agreed merger, ABB set about sorting out its world-wide interests in several markets. Thus, for example, it negotiated takeovers or joint ventures with much of the Italian power engineering industry, including Finnmeccanica. It is also reported to have taken over companies in Spain and has a nuclear power technology agreement with Siemens, Germany and a turbine agreement with Rolls Royce, UK.

Pursuing its world-wide ambitions, ABB purchased major companies in the US and Canada in 1989. Subsequently it consolidated its European acquisitions, divesting some parts that were 'non-core'. It also made investments in Eastern Europe 'to safeguard the group's long-term market share in these countries.'

Both in terms of sales and employees, ABB is a truly international company. Let us look specifically at the two market areas under discussion.

Keypoints on boilers and turbines

ABB power plant orders received 1992 (US$ million)

Gas turbine power plants	1570
Utility steam power plants	2024
Power generation industry	791
Hydro power plants	737
Nuclear power plants	612
Power plant control	479
Other	708
Total	8322

The company is well represented with a range of products in this market: 'power plant control' shows how it is able to mount more than a bolt-on operation to other suppliers. It can offer a broad range of services to customers.

In 1988 ABB reported substantial overcapacity in the industry. Nevertheless, it continued to invest to maintain its position as a low cost producer. By 1992, it was reporting steady growth worldwide as it integrated Eastern Europe capacity into its operations; Asia was likely to show the greatest growth.

Locomotive and railway rolling stock

The EC study predicted that the 50 per cent capacity utilization will lead to a reduction in the number of companies from 16 to 3 or 4. Importantly, it expected this to take place over 'decades' which would allow time for adjustment. By 1992, production in current prices was the same as in 1988 and the same numbers were employed in the industry. [*Source: Panorama of EC Industry 1993*, pages 11–38.]

Nevertheless, many companies in the industry have seen restructuring over the last few years. Belgium now has 2 manufacturers compared to 27 some 25 years ago. In France, one company has bought out another six. The merger to produce ABB brought about another of the many rationalizations in the industry.

Let us now turn to another area, mainframe computers, and examine the EC viewpoint on overcapacity which is rather less clear than for boilers and locomotives. It is important to interpret the data accurately, otherwise prediction is difficult.

Mainframe computers

While the EC acknowledges that this is already highly competitive, with significant trade within the EC, it has still identified it as an area where overcapacity will lead to 'some continued rationalization of the industry'.

Certainly rationalization is likely but it may not occur as a result of over-capacity. It is more likely to happen because of straightforward competitive pressures and some fairly dumb marketing. The overcapacity conditions outlined at the beginning of this section simply do not apply here:

- there is no large national protected industry;
- there is strong intra-EC trade and a large net import into the EC;

- the market still has reasonable growth to soak up capacity; and
- the largest competitor (IBM) already has access to all the major European markets.

Case Study: Leading European computer and information technology manufacturers

Data

	1992 Sales (US$ m)	Return on capital (%)	Home (%)	Europe (%)	Rest of world (%)
			Home	Europe	Rest of world
US Companies					
IBM	64523	(16.4)	38	35 est	27 est
Hewlett Packard	16410	16.3	44	37	19
DEC	13931	(10.2)	37	48	15
Unisys	8422	16.1	49	29	22
Apple	7086	29.0	55	27	18
European companies					
Siemens Nixdorf	8755	loss	62**	32**	6*
Olivetti	6126	(3.0)	39	44	17
Groupe Bull	5330	loss	not available		
Rank Xerox	5031	na	100		
ICL*	4775	na	100		
Japanese companies					
Fujitsu	29844	na	67	17	16
Hitachi	24664	na	na but mainly Japan		
NEC	15559	na	na but mainly Japan		

* ICL is a wholly-owned subsidiary of Fujitsu
** 1991 data
Note: in the above table, 'Europe' means total European sales for US and Japanese companies. For European companies, it means '% sales in rest of Europe'.

European and global activity
Business strategies have had to cope with rapid technological change, low-cost Far Eastern competition, innovative distribution channels and increased emphasis on total customer service.

Considerable rationalisation has therefore taken place in the computer industry around the world. Within this, European industry over the last few years has seen:

- Siemens bought the troubled German computing company, Nixdorf in 1990. Despite substantial re-organisation costs, there is still no sign of profitability;
- Groupe Bull acquired Honeywell (US) and Zenith (US) in the late 1980s, but is still making major losses: see next case;
- Fujitsu bought ICL (UK) in 1991. The UK company then acquired Nokia Data (Finland) in 1992 for £230 million; Nokia itself had previously bought Ericsson Computer Division (Swe) in 1988;
- Olivetti's myriad links across the computer industry are described in chapter 4.

Keypoint on overcapacity
Quite why the European Commission's researchers described European computer manufacturing as having excess production capacity remains a mystery – against the global whales of the US and Japanese computer companies, European

competitors are comparative minnows. Small market share is not usually associated with high profitability. In the context of small market shares and rapid technological change, excess production capacity would seem to be largely irrelevant.

Apple Computer (US) and Amstrad plc (UK) have shown the way to survive and grow by innovation and specialist products directed towards market niches. It was noticeable that when Amstrad went on to compete directly with other companies in mainline minicomputers it became unstuck. Again this has nothing to do with overcapacity.

Let us look in more detail at one European computer company that has found one method of survival; handouts from the French government.

Case Study: Groupe Bull, France
(French government-owned computer company)

Data
1992 turnover: 30187 (FF million)
Return on capital: 25.6% loss
% sales in home country: 38
% sales in rest of Europe: 36
% sales in rest of world: 26

European and global activity
In October 1989, Bull acquired the microcomputer business of Zenith (US) for US$ 500 million. The aim was to push Bull towards being in the top five computer manufacturers in the world. The company then reported a net loss for every year after this to 1993; a total of US$ 3 billion over this period.

Subsequently, it has built some other international links:

■ technical agreement with IBM in 1992, from which IBM gained 5.7% of Bull's shares;
■ cooperation agreement with NEC in 1993; the latter holds 5% of Bull's shares.

But the company never really came to grips with its mid-size position in the world computer market. It was still organized by geographical region until late 1993, rather than by product or service. Its major acquisition of Zenith was an irrelevance – it needed to move manufacturing to low-cost production facilities in the Far East, rather than acquire extra production facilities in the high-cost USA to add to its high-cost French factory.

Groupe Bull also needed to develop low-cost marketing and distribution possibly with another computer manufacturer. It also had to differentiate its products so that it could consider higher prices. Essentially it has become a high-cost producer with undifferentiated products, in an industry with substantial low-cost global production capacity.

Keypoint on overcapacity
In late 1993, Bull was reported to be asking the French government for US$ 1.5 billion of additional help. The company's strategy for dealing with overcapacity was designed to deal with its structural mistakes of the past – it needed the funds to close its minicomputer production plants in the USA and France.

Even if this was agreed, the company still appeared to be without any longer term strategy – compare this approach with Hewlett Packard (US) who were announcing around the same time; 'Computers that gave the same performance at a fraction of the cost'. Such a trend only underlines the need to look beyond overcapacity in an industry if this strategy is to be anything more than a short-term solution.

GENERAL STRATEGY TO TACKLE OVERCAPACITY

One way out of overcapacity problems is to redefine the market. A large homogeneous market may have excess capacity in some areas. However, a company that can provide a special service in a specific market area to a limited number of customers stands some chance of survival. Thus, in locomotives, companies might specialize in small transit systems suitable for commuter travel. In boilers, providing a high level of service for an industry that has need of this type of operation might provide a route forward. In both cases, the key to success is to check out exactly what the *customer* wants.

We will return to strategies to analyze and tackle this important problem at the end of Part II.

CHAPTER 8

Protecting the Home Market

For the majority of companies seeking international expansion, their principal sales will come at present from the home country. Home sales must be defended for two reasons: because without them there is no future; and because it is often easier strategically to defend than attack (and therefore more profitable). This reasoning must form a part of the European and global initiative. Failure to do this will hit the profit line hard.

Thus, although some companies may be tempted to make their focus Europe or world markets instead of the home country, this needs to be undertaken with some caution. A company's first responsibilities are not to pioneering for its own sake but to its owners, managers and workforce.

ASSESSING THE NEED FOR ACTION

The key to the exercise is to strike a *balance* between defending the existing situation while taking advantage of the new larger international markets. This chapter is about one aspect of that balance and, specifically, about measuring its importance and the actions that follow. In assessing the situation, there are several important principles to be adopted.

If there are major uncertainties, then the balance favours defending the home market. If sales are heavily reliant on the home territory at present, then the situation is very different from those companies who already have substantial knowledge of Europe or beyond. This must be reflected in the decision-making process.

Another key consideration here is concerned with what can be offered to the new markets. If it is what other companies are already selling in their home markets then it is right to pose another question: why should customers in that country change? (If the only answer is 'lower price' then this really is a slippery slope to profit problems.)

If the decision looks at all dubious, then the balance shifts to defending the home market at present. After further advances, it may then make sense to tackle Europe or the world.

Where customers are loyal and markets are not growing fast, the balance favours protecting the home market as a first priority. There is nothing more valuable to a company than a group of loyal and satisfied customers. They are worth defending and might expect to be defended. This is usually more difficult where markets are growing fast, quite possibly because of technical change. In this case, fast growth is more likely to be accompanied by new customers entering.

Such customers are less likely to be loyal unless you are offering a unique product. Hence, the balance may favour European or global development.

However, even in fast growing markets, there are plenty of circumstances where it is better to be well established in one area than poorly established everywhere.

If barriers to entry are reasonably difficult to overcome and European or global competitors are not standing on the doorstop already, then the balance moves to first defending the home territory. Here we are talking about the hidden barriers as well as the more obvious areas. If it is quite difficult to make a move, then competitors may take their time.

Similarly, if potential competitors are preoccupied with their own home markets for whatever reason, then again the threat is lower. The first priority must be to protect the home market.

However, if some have a strong reputation for international expansion (and you can often get a 'feel' for this at international exhibitions or trade fairs), then to expect them to stay out of your home territory is courting disaster. Here too, the first priority must be home protection, though in this case the best way to do it might be a European or international launch: we will come back to this at the end of Part II.

Can your potential competitors 'rewrite' the way the market does buiness? If so, then you must resolve this threat on home territory first. We will look at an example of this shortly, but by 'rewriting' is meant a radical new product or service that changes the way customers will view your product. If there is a threat here then it is better to resolve it in home territory rather than be stretched by an international strategy.

We have now examined some of the guidelines governing the defence of home territory. Let us look at some examples.

Case Study: Rank Xerox plc, UK

Data
European leader in photocopying and important player in complete office systems market.
1992 turnover (US$ million)
Total 5031 including Fuji Xerox (Japan)
No details published by either Rank Organization plc (UK) or Xerox Corporation (USA).

Return on capital: 14.8%
% sales in Europe: 100
% sales in home country: n.a.

European and global activity
It was many years ago that the American company, Xerox, entered into a 50/50 partnership with the UK company, Rank, to manufacture and sell copiers throughout Europe. With high technical quality and good marketing, Rank Xerox quickly gained market leadership in Europe which it has held until recently. In the mid-1970s, Canon and other Japanese copier companies started to attack Xerox worldwide with new marketing ideas and technical innovation.

Since the early 1980s, Japanese copier companies have marketed their products in Europe at lower prices than the main European/US companies; Rank Xerox, Oce (Netherlands) and Olivetti. In 1987, the European Commission judged the Japanese products were being dumped in the EC, ie sold at lower prices than in Japan, and it therefore imposed a 20% import duty.

If the objective of the duty was to protect the European home industry, including Rank Xerox, it was unsuccessful. Prices of Japanese models were not raised after the duty was imposed. European copier companies were therefore unable to raise their profitability, production utilisation and market share. All that happened was that Japanese *imports* were reduced with companies such as Canon setting up European production.

Keypoint on home protection
For Rank Xerox, Europe is home territory. Entry strategy for Japanese manufacturers was not just a question of lower prices; the copier market rules needed to be 'rewritten' for them to be successful.

Rank Xerox had a strong sales force calling regularly on customers to maintain their photocopying machines. Canon rewrote the rules by introducing a machine range that had replaceable parts that needed little maintenance. It also chose a target group that was inefficient for Xerox to call: smaller businesses. The Japanese company now has market leadership by volume of the European photocopying market.

Case Study: Lufthansa, West Germany

Data
One of Europe's top three airlines.
1992 turnover (DM million)

Passenger traffic	12464
Freight traffic	2480
Mail traffic	306
Maintenance	913
Catering	390
Travel and commissions	204
Insurance sales	125
Hotels	124
Other	234
Total	17240

Return on capital: 1.8%
% sales in home country: 19
% sales in rest of Europe: 34
% sales in rest of world: 47

European and global activity
The company is one of Europe's major air carriers. It is helped by its alliance with American Airlines (US) and its dominance of Germany, Europe's largest airline market.

As a result of the pressures on airlines described in Chapter 2, Lufthansa has been struggling to remain profitable. It has been particularly hampered by its high German wage structure which has become 'increasingly problematical'. It has also had more limited protection on its trans-Atlantic routes than some rivals, as a historical result of more limited bilateral agreements between Germany and the

USA. It has also been caught by the strength of the Deutsche mark in international price comparisons. This is a powerful package of difficulties for the airline to overcome.

Keypoint on home protection
Along with other national airlines, Lufthansa needs to seek out ways to protect its home market. The analysis above suggests part of the problem, and therefore the solution, rests at government level. The company needs to lobby its government and the EC hard. It also needs to find a lower-cost solution, either by locating some activities in a lower-wage economy or by finding some means of reducing costs in the home country. Global market exposure really does emphasise the need for careful home defence.

Case Study: Repsol SA, Spain

Data
Spain's largest oil company and ninth in Europe.
1992 turnover (Ptas billion)

Exploration and production	139
Refining and marketing	1547
Petrochemicals	106
Distribution of gas	186
Intercompany	(71)
Total	1907

Return on capital: 15.2%
% sales in home country: estimated around 85
% sales in rest of Europe: over 10
% sales in rest of work: under 10

European and global activity
Although Repsol operates within global markets for oil and petrol, its primary sphere of operation is Spain. In the late 1980s, the company was faced with three major strategy issues:

■ privatisation in 1990 by the Spanish government;
■ liberalisation of the Spanish oil market;
■ search for growth in its relatively static markets.

In the course of resolving these issues over the period to 1993, the company concentrated its strengths in Spain – its main activity outside the country was to strengthen its oil supply links with Pemex, the Mexican national oil company, and to purchase 250 petrol stations in the UK – beyond this, it concentrated on Spain. Growth was achieved by acquiring companies in gas distribution, Gas Madrid and Gas Barcelona.

Keypoint on home protection
As part of Spain's entry into the European Union, the European Commission insisted that the Spanish government relinquish its control of Spanish petrol supplies and retail sites. This posed a direct threat to Repsol, the largest Spanish oil company and government-owned. Through a series of deals, Repsol was able to gain dominance of the Spanish retail market. Crucially, government/Repsol cooperation was vital to this strategy of home protection. More detail is given in my book, *Cases in European Marketing*, Kogan Page 1994.

Case Study: IRI, Italy

Data
Italy's largest company but now being privatized.
1991 turnover (Lire billion): 79901
Return on capital: largely meaningless with such a varied range of products and
services, but it made a loss after tax and interest.
% sales in home country: 80
% sales in rest of Europe: 5
% sales in rest of world: 10

European and global activity
Up to 1992, IRI (Istituto per la Ricostruzione Industriale) was essential to Italian
business strategy. It was set up to reform the banking system after the great
depression of the 1930s. It quickly moved into industrial areas such as telephone
services and steel manufacture. By 1990, IRI's three major banks controlled 14% of
Italian loans and 11% of deposits: Banca Commerciale Italiana, Credito Italiano and
Banco di Roma.

In 1991, IRI's share of production was:

	% home market	% EC market
cast iron	87	11
steel	45	8
power plants	70	10
shipbuilding	70	10
cement	9	2
ice cream and frozen food	26	na
milk	11	na
mass distribution	9	na
highway mileage operated	49	10
electrical railway transportation	60	12

Source: IRI Yearbook 1991/92 English edition.

IRI also had controlling interests in Alitalia (airline), STET (telephone service), RAI
(state radio and television service).

To know IRI was to know Italian industry. Now all this will change as the group is
broken up and privatized over the mid-1990s.

Keypoint on home protection
Up to 1992, IRI owned 62% of SME, the Italian food products, retailing and catering
group. During 1992/93, SME was split up into three main areas:

■ frozen food and ice creams: IRI stake was sold to Nestlé for US$ 410 million in
1993;
■ canned foods and olive oil division, CBD; this was sold to an Italian agro-
industrial holding company in 1993. The company then sold the olive oil part to
Unilever. The Anglo–Dutch company had originally made a bid for all of CBD but
only wanted this part;
■ motorway restaurants and chain stores.

From a home protection stance, the rapid change of ownership and control of key
Italian markets could have a significant effect on existing companies. Nestlé and
Unilever are powerful competitors who were strengthening their position in Italy.

'Home protection' therefore takes on a new meaning. Business strategy is like a game of chess, with each player needing to see the full implications of the moves made by others.

CHECKLIST ON PROTECTING THE HOME MARKET

Table 8.1 sets out some key questions that therefore need to be asked, relating principally to defending the home territory:

Answering the questions covered in the table should provide plenty of ideas on where your own company stands with regard to protecting the home market. We will come back to this at the end of Part II when developing the theme of a European or global strategy.

Table 8.1   Home market protection checklist

Topic	*Recommendation*
Your company	
1. How reliant are you at present on sales from the home country? And how profitable are those sales?	Highly reliant? Move with caution. Highly profitable? Prepare for global or European competition!
2. How well are you organized to operating outside the home country now, even if the sales have yet to materialize?	Well organized? Proceed with caution. Need to organize? Undertake full evaluation before moving.
3. What are you able to offer to other countries now: more of the home product or something different if required? And will the product you offer be something better than is currently available there?	Home product only? Move only with caution. Something different? Better but not a strong basis for moving in itself. Something better? A basis for moving.
Your home markets	
4. Are they growing fast with much activity? Or are they only growing slowly?	Fast? Tackle these first. Slow? Possible to look elsewhere.
5. Does your company have a high market share in its home market? And is it market leader? Or is it only one of several products or services?	High share? Defend. Leadership? Defend. Fragmented? Not so important to defend.
6. How important is marketplace technical innovation? And does this involve high capital expenditure or research and development?	Important? Maybe Europe or the world would offer a wider area, but competitors may also see this. Same true for R&D.
7. How likely are your home customers to want to change? Are they loyal to you or would they move at the first opportunity? Are they tied to you so that they cannot move anyway?	Loyal? Defend without doubt. Move easily? Maybe still defend by building loyalty and beware competition!

Your home competitors

8. Are they mainly in the home country? Or are there substantial imports?

Home? Defend. Imports from Europe or elsewhere? Attacking their territory may be best defence. Imports from elsewhere? Depends on how successful and why.

9. What do you know about potential European or global competition in your home country? Not very much or a great deal?

Not much? Defend until clarified. A great deal? Act accordingly.

10. Are other international companies waiting to attack your home market or is there a likelihood of a move in the next two years?

Foreigners waiting to attack? First priority is to defend but there are various ways to achieve this (see Part II).

11. On what basis might an attack at home be mounted? Full frontal assault on you, or would competitors pick off a part of your market? With what weapons?

Full frontal assault? Probably need to defend. Specialist attack? Can be very dangerous, especially if innovative. Analyze and defend.

Your home costs

12. Is transport a significant part of total costs? Or is it relatively cheap to offer the goods or services in other countries?

Significant? Expect potential competitors to think hard. Cheap? Expect competition.

13. Can you set up internationally without incurring major capital costs (eg factories)? Or is it necessary to have local facilities?

Major capital involved? Competitor moves will be much more predictable: watch the markets.

14. Will it be expensive to meet the different requirements of other national markets? Or will it involve a few simple label changes, for example?

Expensive? Some protection. Cheap and simple? Trouble much more likely.

Finally, in the long term for some companies, Europe as a whole will be the home territory. But because of the history of the way some European markets have developed, it is highly likely that there will be strong regional markets in some products and services well into the next century. Don't hold your breath waiting for an instant European market!

CHAPTER 9

Analyzing the Current European and Global Situation: Summary and Conclusions

We have now come through the background work and can answer some important questions:

- Is there a European or global opportunity?
- What is the size of the opportunity?
- What will our company bring to the market to tackle it?
- What about the environment, ie world, European Union and national government factors? Cyclical and global trends?

The key point here is not analysis for its own sake but a *prediction* about the future environment of the company. Inevitably, there will be uncertainties in this and these need to be identified. Whether the implied risks are acceptable is then a value-judgement the company can make; each will be different depending on its resources, ownership, values and culture.

In assessing the various environmental factors, the essential criteria will be:

- their ability to deliver the company's objectives;
- the extent to which achievement is hindered by the environment and structure in which the company operates.

This clearly implies clarity on the objectives of the company – this is an area that we explore shortly in part 2 of the book. It is likely that amongst these criteria there will be some measure of company profitability. As a first step in this process, we have been monitoring 'return on capital' throughout this part of the book for the top European companies.

Back in 1990 for the book's first edition, I constructed Table 9.1 which summarizes profitability in the sample companies. The table is only a rough guide; some years are special in some industries. Some companies, especially those providing public services, do not regard profitability as their prime objective. Some organisations will look on profitability as only part of the way shareholders derive company benefit, eg the hotels, brewing and leisure sector was influenced by the large proportion of UK companies in the sample. The companies may have substantial property portfolios which were not reflected in the data, but may earn significant wealth for the shareholders.

Beyond this, most companies do not have the strategic option of switching

Table 9.1   1987 average return on capital of Europe's top 250 companies

Retailing	19.2%	Private service	11.2%
Food & consumer goods	19.1%	Cars, trucks, spares	11.2%
Pharmaceuticals	18.0%	Telephone & postal	11.1%
Construction	18.0%	Rubber	10.5%
Publishing	17.0%	Aerospace & defence	9.3%
Oil & petrol	16.1%	Computers & office	8.2%
Chemicals	16.0%	Metals & mining	8.2%
Paper, packaging & glass	14.9%	Electricity	7.8%
Gas	14.6%	Heavy eng. & ships	7.1%
Trading	14.5%	Insurance*	4.3%
Electronics & elec. eng.	14.1%	Banks*	3.9%
Telecommunications equip.	13.7%	Steel	2.4%
Hotels, leisure, brewing	12.9%	Coal	1.0%
Transport	12.3%		

* Insurance and banks declare their financial data in such a fashion as to make these figures of limited value.

from one sector, such as coal, into another more profitable sector, such as pharmaceuticals. Hence for strategy purposes, Table 9.1 has limited value. Moreover, the situation changed during the early 1990s. Because of European and global recession, most companies were less profitable. Some even sustained major losses such as coal and steel.

However, as a reminder of the fallibility of strategy, the difficulty of forecasting and the problem of dealing with major structural weaknesses in some parts of European industry, it serves a purpose. It is surely ironic that the two least profitable sectors were steel and coal. These were formed into the European Coal and Steel Community in July 1952 and were the precursors of the European Community of April 1957: hardly one of Europe's successes.

Overall, there is no guarantee of profitability from European and world markets. What is needed is a successful strategy, which is what we will deal with in Part II.

Developing a Successful European and Global Strategy

We have now moved beyond the stage of analyzing the situation. We have made the decision to go international. Our opportunity and task now is to find the best way to do this.

For most companies, there will be an obvious but important constraint on this basic decision: we will work from the skills, products and resources that the company has already developed. Daimler Benz is unlikely to want to start selling decaffeinated coffee and Ford Motors is equally unlikely to launch a range of colour TVs. Few companies have the realistic option to start afresh. Hence, our objective is not just to move beyond national boundaries but also to do this with the existing broad range of products or services.

There are some important qualifications to this:

1. We may choose to adapt our products or services to meet different customer tastes.
2. We may decide to communicate to customers in a different way from our existing markets.
3. We may decide that we should do this in partnership or by acquiring another company.

There will be other considerations based on our resources, the sheer size of European and global markets and what our competitors have already done. We need to start by mapping out the task of international strategy development.

Let us begin with three working definitions:

1. The purpose of a strategy is to meet a set of *objectives*.
2. The *strategy* is a set of principles by which those objectives will be met.
3. Detailed *plans* then follow from this.

This is not a basic book about business theory or strategy so we will not debate these matters at length, but use the definitions as our way of working: others may use different terminology.

In developing our international strategy, we need to analyze the first two elements and follow up the implications. In Part II therefore, after examining the establishment of realistic objectives, we look at the development of strategies to meet them. In the latter analysis we will cover the four main elements of strategy useful for global and European markets:

1. Company strengths strategy.
2. European and global customer strategy.
3. European and global competitor strategy.
4. European and global channel strategy.

These four areas have been especially developed to bring out the main issues of international development but make no claim to represent a unique solution to business strategy: the objectives are clarity, pragmatism and successful strategy development.

Finally we will cover such questions as defensive and offensive strategies and the best ways to tackle the particular opportunities and problems of single European and global markers.

CHAPTER 10

Developing and Setting Realistic European and Global Objectives

'THE EUROPEAN AND GLOBAL CHALLENGE'

There has been much publicity about the 320 million European Union population and the tremendous sales scope this offers for any company. For the vast majority of companies this is misleading tosh: there is no realistic prospect on any reasonable time horizon of successfully targeting all European countries from scratch, let alone global markets.

Out of the top 400 European companies, only some 150 actively market across all 12 EU member states. This does not mean the products of the remaining 250 companies are not sold elsewhere, just that some use distributors and agents to import products and others currently have largely national interests. Nor does it mean that this figure will not increase over the next 10 years: clearly it will.

But if some of Europe's largest companies do not actively sell right across Europe or the world, what chance do smaller companies have? Some may say that there is an opportunity here and, in some limited cases, they will be right: for example, with a really unique new product. But how many of these are there likely to be? For the vast majority of companies, realistic objective setting on a reasonable time scale will dictate limiting the countries covered. As we discussed in Part I, this will probably mean, in practice, a *selected advance* internationally in terms of countries.

Now you can see why the heading to this section is in quotation marks: it is not very meaningful for most companies. However, it needs to be recognized that over time a larger number of countries may be covered. The question is what is the correct timescale?

TIMESCALES FOR OBJECTIVES

Any move internationally is an *investment* in time, people and of funds. It needs to be judged as such and not fudged by a grand feeling that it is worthwhile in itself, or something else equally woolly. The company's investment criteria for new business therefore apply. It is partly for this reason that some of Europe's top companies have largely ignored Europe in the period 1987-94 and invested elsewhere, particularly in the USA and the Far East. Europe does not necessarily offer the best prospects.

Depending on the company's objectives and resources, company new business criteria need careful evaluation for international expansion. It may be appropriate to allow some leeway for the experimental nature of such development given that the size of the eventual return in some cases could be very high.

In practice, timescales will vary with the product or service as well as with the criteria that the company normally uses to evaluate its investments. For example, what is realistic for a grocery product – a payback of five years with a positive profit contribution after two years – may be totally unrealistic for a telecommunications project that will take 18 months to design and install and may take 8 years to pay back.

There is no point in denying that European and global development will carry its own risks and therefore does deserve to be limited and reassessed after a finite period. It is important therefore to set up some criteria that do not drift out too far. Some suggested rules for investment might therefore be:

■ Time horizons of 3–5 years are realistic for at least some initial return;
■ Time horizons of 8–10 years are too uncertain to be realistic in most cases; and
■ Time horizons under 2 years may well apply but only where the profit margins on individual products are very high.

For many companies, European and global expansion does represent a real challenge which has been accepted with enthusiasm: Electrolux and Ericsson are examples of this. Amidst the folklore of strategy is the adage that 'it is best to be first into a market'. Should a company therefore accept this enthusiastic approach and keep its timescale very short? In most western European and North American markets, this perfectly good guideline needs to be treated with some caution. All such countries have relatively highly-developed economies with many of the obvious consumer and industrial products: thus it is not really a question of being first into a market, because there may well be another company already there with something similar.

However, if there is the prospect of *acquisition* in an advanced economy, then there is a strong case for moving fast because the best companies go quickest. The difficulty is that, for Europe's top companies, this is nothing new: this book demonstrates that the takeover trail has been a major priority for some time. But there are still some good candidates, so, here, there is a clear case for acting quickly.

RELATIONSHIP TO COMPANY OBJECTIVES

As has been indicated, company development internationally has to stand up to the investment and development criteria that are used elsewhere. To this extent, there is magic about a particular area such as the single Europe. It is beyond the scope of this book to look in detail at the fundamentals of setting company objectives or mission statements. We are concerned with opportunities and threats in Europe and global markets and the best ways to tackle these: nevertheless, the starting point has to be the company objectives set by the main Board. They may need to be expanded to include the new international horizons.

For many companies the European and global markets do represent a real challenge. This will only be met if it is done enthusiastically, professionally and with some aggression. The main Board has a responsibility to set *challenging objectives* for international expansion which will stimulate this attack. Only ambitious objectives will provide sufficient stimulus for good executives to strive harder to make a success of European and global markets.

We will take as our starting point that a decision has been made to explore international markets with some aggressive objectives. The question that follows is how to tackle this. This is the matter of strategy which we will deal with next.

DEVELOPING STRATEGIES TO MEET THE OBJECTIVES

At the kernel of the strategy analysis is the problem of how to identify the market correctly: the difficulty is that most markets can be divided in an infinite variety of ways. We looked at the relevance of 'Europe' and 'global markets' as opportunities for the company in Chapter 1.

If a business has not resolved what market it operates in from the broadest perspective, then its chances of assessing European or global markets are low. You really do need to sort out the basics.

What we will do here is to plot a middle course and set out fundamental issues that companies need to tackle, whether it is for the new Europe or for a broader base. Our strategy development and market definition is therefore primarily concerned with European and global market analysis.

European and global strategy development

To develop the best strategy, we must develop policies in 'the four Cs': company strengths; customers; competitors; and channels of distribution.

Company strengths strategy
It is essential to establish what the company is really good at and where its strengths really lie, because that is the route forward.

European and global customer strategy
At the heart of a good strategy is the customer because the objective is to make a sale. The world has rather a lot of them and the challenge is to sell to what can be a diverse group. Companies also need to understand who really is the customer and what is the nature of customer demand.

European and global competitive strategy
To put this after customers in strategy development may come as something of a surprise to those obsessed with competitive advantage and theories of marketing warfare. These are fine and form an important part of our armoury, but they are no more important than the customer.

European and global channel strategy
Finally, one of the most difficult tasks for most companies tackling international markets will be that of obtaining distribution for their products or services: the channel to reaching the customer. We will look at the best ways to do this.

Naturally, all four topics are only aspects of the same issue so we then need to combine them together. We will look at ways to undertake this in Chapter 25, at the end of Part II.

From all four routes above, what we want to end up with is a series of short statements, probably only half a page each, listing the strategies in each area for tackling European and global issues: these may well be backed up by a thick file of analysis but the basic strategy statements must be short and succinct.

CHAPTER 11

Company Strengths Strategy

As a result of our analysis of the current European and global situation in Part I, the company will have extensive data on opportunities and threats from these markets. To make sense of these, we need first to look at what the company is good at and where it is weak. This is always a difficult process because it is so easy to be over-optimistic about strengths: every company seems to have the perfect salesforce and excellent senior managers with no weaknesses in sight. We will look at three areas: conglomerates in Europe; company strengths defined; and how to evaluate possible strengths.

CONGLOMERATES IN EUROPE

There was a fashion in the 1960s for acquiring companies in totally unrelated industries to 'provide another leg' that would balance the existing businesses. There seemed to be no thought of being strong in related areas and building on areas of strength. The rise of the conglomerate has been followed by the breakup of many over the last 10 years.

Thus there are few in Europe's Top 400 and those that are there are subject to special scrutiny. For example:

- *Ferruzzi:* Italian holding company involved in corruption scandals in the early 1990s (see *Financial Times* 24 June 1993, p. 19);
- *Hanson plc:* whose skills at selling unwanted businesses outside its core basic industries were considerable; more recently, growth has slowed;
- *IRI:* which is the Italian state holding company and thus a special case; it was examined in Chapter 8;
- *Suez:* the French financial holdings company being restructured;
- *Paribas:* the French industrial holdings company;
- *Lonrho:* the UK hotels to agriculture holding company being restructured;
- *Société Générale de Belgique:* which was the subject of a major takeover battle in the late 1980s; Suez (above) has 61 per cent shareholding.

Out of the top European companies, the conglomerates have seen more than their share of comment, some of it aimed at breaking them up. Arguably, the best of them are also so large that different parts have sufficient skills to be capable of capitalizing on their strengths in each area.

However, Sir James Goldsmith did not agree with this. He made a contested bid for BAT, arguing that the company needed to turn back to its core strengths in tobacco (and he was right). In fairness, this is the policy that the company subsequently adopted during the early 1990s, albeit in insurance as well as tobacco.

The vast majority of European companies have a consistency of businesses, even if the spread is sometimes wide: even Philips NV, which had a very broad spread, sold its defence business and its domestic appliance interests because they were too small to operate successfully and not vital to its core business.

When it comes to European and global development, there is a clear case for concentrating on core areas already familiar to a company, rather than moving into totally unknown markets. *Concentration of force* rather than defending a weak position is another way of expressing the same principle. The important point for the vast majority of companies is that they need to develop from existing strengths. So what is a company strength?

COMPANY STRENGTHS DEFINED

There can be no one definition of company strengths because it all depends on a series of factors covering markets, competition, general business prospects, shareholding structure and company objectives. However, in practice, it is possible to analyze a company under a number of common headings which will provide clear pointers to areas of strength:

1. *Markets* in which the company operates and competes: growth and factors influencing this.
2. *Products/services* of the company in its markets: not only market share but also competitive advantages versus competitors (which may in turn involve other areas below).
3. *Product/service quality* for its ability to meet customer requirements at an acceptable price.
4. *Management and worker* performance and skills.
5. *Financial* strengths and weaknesses.
6. *Production and distribution* strengths and weaknesses, including relative unit costs of production.
7. *Research and development* resources and abilities.
8. *Investment practice* and future plans for the company.
9. *Profit performance* and ability.
10. *Clarity of purpose* and objectives.

No one area in the list is more important than another. However, in analyzing a specific company, certain areas will quickly turn out to be crucial, with others of lesser significance. Critical success factors identified in Chapter 5 may provide some guidance.

Correct assessment of the factors is a most important preliminary step to the development of a European or global strategy. The difficulty for many companies will not only be to make the analysis in the context of home markets but to *ensure that it has the necessary European or global dimension.* Let us examine some major European companies and look for their particular strengths.

Case Study: Alcatel Alsthom SA, France

Data
World's largest telecommunications equipment manufacturer with important energy equipment interests.

1992 turnover (Ffr million)

Telecommunications equipment	76081
Telecommunications and energy cables	33082
Energy and transport	27514
Electrical engineering	15382
Batteries	3400
Services	6218
Total	161677

Return on capital: 7.1%
% sales in home country: 29
% sales in rest of Europe: 42
% sales in rest of world: 29

European and global activity
The group's main subsidiary is Alcatel NV in which it has a 100% shareholding. Alcatel was transformed in 1986 when it bought the telecommunications and electronics interests of the US company ITT. This major European and world initiative has resulted in the world's largest telecommunications company in a market where size is important. Subsequently, Alcatel sold ITT's television division to Nokia, Finland.

The company also has a subsidiary in gas turbines, Alsthom, which has linked with GEC (UK). Both have 50% of the combined company which has been better able to compete in world markets.

The group has really grasped the issues of world size and tackled them vigorously. It has managed to weld together companies of different product ranges and cultural backgrounds such as Alcatel and ITT. GEC Alsthom, the gas turbines company, has also prospered after a difficult start.

Keypoint on strengths
In terms of company strengths, the company has clearly built a powerful position in world telecommunications. Additionally, it has resolved its position in turbines.

Arguably, its return on capital is not high enough, even if the cost of capital and inflation are low. But this is a consequence of its major development and world economic depression. More importantly, the group also believes it is important to spend behind its strengths: 47% of its capital expenditure in 1992 went into telecommunications, following 54% in the previous year.

The real difficulty at the company will be to decide when it is appropriate to look for profits from Alcatel and slow down the rate of spending. These areas, particularly with their long lead times, have a habit of moving backwards.

Case Study: BSN Groupe SA, France

Data
Europe's third largest branded food company.
Turnover (Ffr million)

	1988	1992
Dairy	11065	26102
Grocery and pasta	9177	13081
Biscuits	8275	13457
Beer	6260	6552
Mineral water	3476	5979
Containers	4997	7046
Intergroup	(1073)	(1377)
Total	42177	70840

1992
Return on capital: 13.3%
% sales in home country: 45
% sales in rest of Europe: 48
% sales in rest of world: 7

European and global activity
Over the last few years, BSN has shown the way to a European, but not global, strategy in branded food as much as any other company. It has undertaken two major acquisitions which have added significantly to its products and brands: the outright purchase of Nabisco Europe's biscuits and snack operations for US$2.5 billion; and the acquisition of 60% of Galbani, the Italian cheese company, with the option to purchase the remainder. As a first step, this has taken BSN to number one in the European biscuit market: spending behind strengths again.

Second, it has also immeasurably strengthened the company's position in dairy products in Italy: the company has not only bought two good brands (Dolcelatte and Bel Paese) but, in many ways more importantly, it has secured distribution for its dairy products in the notoriously difficult Italian grocery distribution chain. We will come back to this strategy later.

BSN has left other European food companies standing by these two bold moves, particularly strengthening its position in the fast growing markets of southern Europe. It has also acquired dairy companies in Eastern Europe to consolidate its position as the largest in the world. In the early 1990s it also bought mineral water companies to become the world's largest producer in this area as well. Fundamentally, it has been opportunistic but kept to the product areas it knows.

Keypoint on strengths
One fundamental aspect of strength is the share it holds of various markets. In the case of BSN, the following is the approximate position:

	Brand(s)	Countries	Market share strength
Dairy	Gervais Danone	Fra, Ita, Ger, Bel, UK, US	Strong
Grocery	Panzani, Amora, Stoeffler, HP Sauce	Fra, Bel, Neth, UK	Collection of small products: together viable

Biscuits	De Beukelaar, Nabisco, Lu	Fra, Bel, Neth, Ger, Ita, UK	Was viable, now strong
Beer	Kronenbourg, Wuhrer, Perroni, San Miguel (minority)	Fra, Bel, Spa, Ita	Strong: some countries
Mineral water	Evian, Badoit, Volvic	Fra, Ita, US, UK	Viable with some strong countries
Containers, glass jars, etc.		Fra, Neth, Spa	Larger producer in some national markets: viable in those areas.

It has taken BSN some time to assimilate its purchases into the group. We will come back to implementation in Chapter 25. In the meantime, the BSN strength in market share will be accompanied, as long as the implementation is successful, by consequent strengthening in other areas, for example: lower unit production costs; lower unit sales force costs; and lower distribution costs. This will provide further benefits over the competition. Quite correctly, BSN has not acquired companies in other food areas. A major strategic weakness is its heavy reliance on European sales. In 1994, BSN Groupe changed its name to Danone in order to reflect its claimed global leadership in dairy products.

Case Study: Marks & Spencer plc, UK

Data
Europe's fourth largest retailer (clothing, food and household goods).
Turnover (£ million)

	1988	1992
UK and Eire	4220	5015
Europe	132	245
Canada/US	180	534
Total	4532	5794

Return on capital:	41.3%	21.6%
% sales in home country:	90	87
% sales in rest of Europe:	3	4
% sales in rest of world:	7	9

European and global activity
Marks & Spencer has been nothing like as successful in its overseas ventures as it is in the UK. It has moved very gingerly into Europe with the cautious opening of stores in Paris and Lyons followed, more recently, by others: they have never been really significant to the company.

Over several years, Marks & Spencer had moved into Canada and the US but had not been successful up to 1992, with much retrenchment taking place. In 1988, it bought the up-market men's clothing operation, Brooks Brothers: its prime task over the succeeding years has been to ensure that this is successful. In 1992, it earned a small profit from its US operations, but was still losing money in Canada.

Keypoint on strengths
Despite its undoubted strengths in UK retailing, the company has never been as successful in its overseas operations. One of the reasons is that its North American expansion never relied on its strengths in the UK, eg its shops in Canada and its Kings Supermarkets in the USA were not built on the UK retail 'formula', high price, high quality. Its European expansion has chosen to adopt the UK approach. But shop openings have proceeded at a modest pace so far.

An area of strength in the UK for Marks & Spencer is its stringent quality standards, agreed with its suppliers and rigidly enforced. Because of the retailer's importance in terms of profits to some suppliers, it has become so powerful that it has been able to demand more from that supplier than other retailers. Customers in the UK are actually willing to pay more at Marks & Spencer stores than other retailers for the quality of goods that are on sale. A real strength.

Case Study: Continental AG, Germany

Data
Europe's second largest tyre and rubber products company
1992 turnover (DM million)

	1988	1992
Continental	1567	1842
Uniroyal	985	1085
Semperit	842	890
Merchandise & services	406	920
General Tire (US)	2498	2105
Industrial products	1521	–
Other	87	260
Conti Tech		2285
Gislaved		302
Total	7906	9690

Return on capital:	12.1%	8.7%
% sales in home country:	30 approx.	36
% sales in rest of Europe:	40 approx.	35
% sales in rest of world:	30	29

European and global activity
Continental made a major switch in business strategy in the early 1990s. It followed a successful attempt to avoid being taken over by Pirelli in 1991/92, and a largely unsuccessful bid in the period 1987–90 to become a global tyre company. It now trades under a number of brand names and has plant spread across Europe:

- 4 Uniroyal plants   Belgium
  France
  UK
- 4 Continental plants   Germany (2)
  France
  Spain
- 2 Semperit plants   Austria
  Ireland
- Gislaved/Viking   operation in Norway

In 1987, Continental acquired General Tire in the USA. It was following a global strategy that also involved a joint venture with two Japanese partners, Yokohama and Toyo.

According to Continental, the world tyre industry became more concentrated over the ten years up to 1988. The following shows global shares.

		1978	*1988*	*Acquisitions*
Goodyear	US	19%	20%	
MIchelin	Fra	17%	16%	*See below.
Bridgestone	US	7%	15%	Firestone 1988
Continental	Ger	3%	7%	Uniroyal Europe 1979, Semperit 1985, General Tire 1987
Sumitomo	Jap	2%	6%	Dunlop 1985
Goodrich	US	6%	5%	Uniroyal and B.F. Goodrich 1987
Pirelli	Ita	5%	6%	Armstrong 1988
Yokohama	Jap	3%	4%	
Toyo	Jap	3%	3%	
Others		37%	15%	

Source: Continental AG.
* Note: The data here does not take account of Michelin's acquisition of Goodrich in early 1990.

Continental was still a small player by global standards. It saw profits disappear as it assimilated its acquisitions against a depressed world tyre industry. Pirelli chose this period to attempt to acquire Continental, but was stopped mainly by a collapse in Pirelli's own profits: it could not afford the takeover. Continental was then able to rethink its unsuccessful global strategy.

Keypoint on strengths
Continental decided to concentrate on its strengths which were in quality rather than volume tyres. Hence it chose 'to concentrate on selling products with higher added value and niches in the market.' Its speciality tyres include truck tyres and snow tyres. It went even further: 'The future belongs to suppliers of complete systems. As a manufacturer of tyres, airsprings, anti-vibration and sealing systems, hose assemblies and vehicle ventilators, we are in an excellent position to benefit from this trend.' It may have been building on strengths, but its new strategy coincided with the 1990s global downturn in the car industry; timing also matters in strategy.

Let us turn for our final case study on strengths to another industry where global markets are in operation.

Case Study: The European Cement Industry and Holderbank SA, Switzerland

Europe's top cement, concrete and aggregate companies are:

	Country	1992 sales (US$m)	Return on capital (%)	Destination of sales		
				Home (%)	Rest of Europe (%)	Rest of world (%)
Holderbank	Swi	5940	10.5	10	43	47
RMC	UK	4500*	na	27	66	7
LaFarge Coppee	Fra	4273*	na	but see chapter 30		

Heidelberger Zement**	Ger	1431*	9.9	81	19
Cimentries CBR	Bel	1350	na		
Italcementi	Ita	1105	na		
Blue Circle	UK	1010*	na		

* only part of company turnover
** European and global activity

Cement strategy relies on economies of scale, good supplies of quality raw materials and low transport costs (because of the weight of the product). Hence, global companies need to locate close to sources of raw materials and, ideally, near to their customers. Central manufacture in one country and export to others is therefore not usually a viable strategy in major industrialized countries, though it can be where the export target has no national cement industry. To be European or global in cement therefore means setting up or acquiring national or regional companies, in addition to the skills involved in managing high volume, low cost operations. European and global activity therefore relies on local representation and manufacture.

Holderbank SA, Switzerland
Europe's largest cement company.
1992 turnover (SF million)

Cement, clinker and lime	4412
Ready mixed concrete, aggregates	1835
Concrete, chemicals, other	2323
Intergroup	(734)
Total	7836

Return on capital: 14.5%
% sales in home country: 10
% sales in rest of Europe: 43
% sales in rest of world: 47

European and global activity
Holderbank operates on a world scale with extensive operations in North and Latin America and elsewhere. It lays great emphasis on its strategies of vertical integration, ie aggregates as well as cement, geographical spread and investment in capital equipment.

Keypoint on strengths
The company has achieved its position by a single-minded pursuit of top quality cement production wherever it has set up. In comparison with both the second and third largest companies above, Holderbank has no gypsum and biochemicals (like LaFarge) and no DIY retailing and builders merchants (like RMC).

Holderbank has grown by doing what it does best: building on its strengths. However, both LaFarge Coppee and RMC might argue that they are in the construction business and can economically sell a wide range of products to the same customers: 'strengths' needs careful definition.

HOW TO EVALUATE POSSIBLE STRENGTHS

One of the difficulties with evaluating strengths is that it is possible to end up with pages of analysis, all essentially unformed. Making sense of it is not easy. A British chief executive of a food company is said to have humorously described the process in his company as griping, groping and grasping for a solution.

One way of evaluating possible strengths is to *test them against issues that the company faces:* in the Introduction to this book four issues were raised about Europe and the world that might serve as the agenda for some more detailed issue questions. Purely as examples of issues only, we might take the following: Will our planned brand investment programme and cost reductions be enough to defend our home market share? ... Have we jointly agreed enough target companies with competitors for planned reduction in production capacity? ...

Table 11.1   Checklist for company strengths

Main area	*Questions*
Market share	How do we measure up to the competition?
	Any areas we dominate or at least have a strong share?
	How do our marketing strengths and investment compare with the competition?
Market growth	Are we involved in some growth areas? Are they swallowing cash or merely providing the growth all companies need for survival?
	Are we mainly involved in declining markets with a struggle to survive?
Product quality	Are our products or services good value for money? Do we have a good quality record in relation to the price we ask or do we have a record of customer complaint?
Management & workers	Do we have a good industrial relations record?
	How does our management resource compare with the competition?
Financial strengths	Are we financially sound or are we stretched?
	What has been our profit and earnings per share record over the last few years?
	Do we have any difficult shareholders?
Production costs	Are we a least-cost producer?
	What is our record on plant investment?
	How do we compare to the competition?
Distribution	Do we have adequate distribution to our identified target group?
	Are our competitors under any particular pressure in this area? How do costs compare?
Research & development	Is this important in our industry?
	Have we had major successes? How does our record compare to the competition?
	Are we cost-effective?
Investment practice	What is our record on company investment and how does it compare to the competition?
Profit performance	What is our profit record? How does it compare to the competition?
	What is particularly good about it?
Clarity of purpose and objectives	Does the company state these clearly? Are they known to those involved?
	Are they measurable?

Will our investment in the new IT system achieve the economies of scale projected? ... Is direct selling the best route to extra sales in our two lead countries?

The objective is to test the assessment of our company strengths and focus company judgement in this difficult area. Overall, for the vast majority of companies tackling European and global strategies, it will be essential to capitalize on core strengths. In most cases, this is far more important than worrying about company weaknesses as long as they are not terminal: and, if they are, what on earth is the company doing expanding internationally anyway?

In conclusion, Table 11.1 provides a checklist of company strengths. These clearly are unique to particular companies but the Table sets out some questions that you may care to ask about your company as the starting point for your own analysis.

Not all questions are important to all companies. Some areas need expanding for some companies and markets. The key to responses is to concentrate on strengths rather than analyze every weakness.

CHAPTER 12

Customer Strategy: Establishing Customer Requirements

In part I, we examined sources of material on our customers and the background influences to the market. In particular, we looked at European and global opportunities. Our starting point now must be to return to these and set out what we know about our customers in order to identify the target group. In practice, there are likely to be gaps in our information that they may be possible to fill at reasonable cost. We also need to examine this through customer research but we will start with targetting.

CUSTOMER TARGET GROUPS

As we have seen, most companies will have existing products or services for international markets. The target customers identified for the home country must surely be a starting point for such markets. But the worst strategy error would be to assume all other countries are like home territory. We need to re-examine customer target groups.

Based on the material now assembled, we should be able to specify potential customers for our product or service. For example, we may know: who is buying the product in the home country; who is buying rival products elsewhere in our target countries; and why they are making their respective purchases. We will also have background on the countries that make up the geographical area and the special market characteristics that make them either different or similar to those we are already serving. We are also likely to have formed some view on whether we will cover a whole region or select one country.

From this material, it should be possible to develop the first cut at a *target group profile* of customers for our product. It may be that it is still drawn fairly broadly and may contain more than one sub-group of potential customers.

From the viewpoint of customer strategy, what we are seeking is to identify a customer target group that our products or services are particularly likely to appeal to. The two main areas we will be researching are:

- Broad target groups which have the merit of high sales but the problem of being difficult to hold exclusively for our own company (eg all housewives in the single Europe aged 25–35 or sheet steel users).
- Narrow target groups which may have lower sales but often remain loyal to our company because of the niche product or service we offer (eg

housewives in the single Europe aged 25–35 with a full-time secretarial job or sheet steel users in shipbuilding).

Clearly, this oversimplifies the business of customer targetting: the examples are used to illustrate what, in principle, we are seeking, rather than a precise formula. We will return to this subject when we consider developing competitive advantage later in Part II.

A common error in drawing up such profiles is to assume that the same reasons for making the purchase and method of buying apply across similar target groups in different countries. For example, instant coffee target groups are not radically different in the UK and Germany, but the product is used more frequently and is stronger tasting in Germany. It is therefore important to develop information not only on the target but also on other aspects of the customer. It is often here that background data is no longer enough and customer research is needed.

CUSTOMER RESEARCH IN EUROPEAN AND GLOBAL MARKETS

There are three main ways of finding out about customers in international markets: by market research; by test marketing; and by acquisition, joint venture or marketing agreement. We will look at each of them.

Market research

This has the great merit of being reasonably cost-effective. We spent much of Part I setting out areas that need to be covered: it encompasses the *whole range of information* available to a company, not just some specially commissioned work undertaken in a named country: this is back to the multidisciplinary team discussed in Part I.

Case Study: SKF AB, Sweden

Data
The world's leading producer of bearings and related products.
1992 turnover (SKr million)

Bearings and seals	22385
Tools	1865
Special steels	2399
Total	26649

Return on capital: 5.7% loss (compared to 9.4% profit in 1988)
% sales in home country: 5
% sales in rest of Europe: 56
% sales in rest of world: 39

European and global activity
By the single-minded pursuit of its goal, SKF has become the leading global company in roller bearings. It claims 20% of the world market, excluding China and the former Eastern bloc countries. It is twice as large as its nearest competitor, which is either FAG (Germany) or one of several Japanese companies, depending on the precise market definition.

Compared to its peak in 1989/90, the company's European business declined 20% during 1992. This was a result of economic recession throughout the region. It has nevertheless benefited from European integration by:

- cutting its inventory locations from 24 to 5;
- siting the 4 international warehouses around Europe plus another at its headquarters located 100 km east of Brussels.

Back in 1988, SKF identified the single Europe as leading to real cost savings: it has succeeded in achieving these.

Keypoint on customer requirements and research
SKF's strategy has been to provide a full-range service. Rather than merely sell bearings, it has chosen to offer the best solution to a customer's problems regardless of the type of bearing required. The specific strategies to achieve this are to:

- offer a premium service that handles unusual bearing problems;
- maintain a world geographical presence at some significant cost through its own salesforce or distributors;
- concentrate on this core *service*, so enhancing its leading position.

As a strategy for obtaining and retaining loyal customers, it is difficult to beat. But it only works as a result of carefully establishing customer requirements by working closely with them over time.

SKF does this using its extensive salesforce, eg there are 44 sales companies in SKF Bearings Services. Importantly, it uses all parts of the company, not just the salesforce, to gain customer data. However, the company also recognizes that some customers have standardized requirements that do not require special design. For this reason, it is organized into three main areas:

- SKF Bearing Industries: responsible for sales to the auto and electrical industries where bearings are relatively standard;
- SKF Bearing Services: after-market and distributor responsibility;
- SKF Speciality Bearings: customized design products with higher prices for the services charged.

This example has been deliberately chosen because it is the industrial area that is supposed to be more difficult to investigate. SKF shows that it can be done and done profitably.

Test marketing

This tends to be expensive and resource-consuming, yet it can be useful for some products and services. The main pros and cons are set out in Table 12.1. There is no single answer to the question of whether it is the best method or not, though it is difficult to envisage circumstances that would justify test marketing in all 12 EC countries.

As some marketing managers might admit, it is extremely difficult to read results in one country, let alone in all 12. Yet test marketing has helped companies to obtain the best product and marketing mix and thus contributed to profits, mainly in branded consumer products and largely in tests in one country. Test marketing is explored more fully in chapter 5 of my book; *European Marketing*, Kogan Page 1992.

Table 12.1 Advantages and disadvantages of test marketing in Europe

Advantages	Disadvantages
■ Real live customers ■ Market place response ■ Test full marketing mix ■ Probe quality and service aspects more effectively ■ Test repeat purchase	■ Expensive ■ Can be messed up by competitors ■ Not suited for products with high custom design ■ Not suited where large one-off products made ■ Not suited where large capital plant required

---

Case Study: Cadbury Schweppes plc, UK

Data
One of Europe's top 4 confectionery and soft drinks companies.
1992 turnover (£ million)

Confectionery	1464
Beverages	1903
Total	3372

	Confectionery	Beverages
Return on capital: 21.6%		
% sales in home country:	53	40
% sales in rest of Europe:	18	23
% sales in rest of world:	29	37 (especially USA)

European and global activity
The company has two main product areas: confectionery and beverages. In terms of business strategy, they are quite different: Cadburys chocolate is particularly strong in the UK but is not a Pan-European brand. Unlike its rivals, Nestlé and Mars, Cadbury has made no attempt to develop European brands. However, it has acquired some European confectionery companies.

   In 1989, Cadbury bought Chocolat Poulenc SA, France for £94m to 'distribute Cadbury products in that country and a small range of Poulenc products elsewhere'. Subsequently, Cadbury bought the Spanish company Chocolat Hueso in August 1989 for an undisclosed amount, acquiring at the same time 14% of that market. In 1992, it acquired the German and Dutch confectionery companies, Piasten and De Faam, respectively. Cadbury sold most of its US confectionery interests to the US market leader, Hershey, in August 1988 for £186 million.

   By contrast, in soft drinks, Cadbury Schweppes has followed a global strategy in the US and in Europe. It bought Procter & Gamble's soft drinks brands for $220 million giving the company a 4% share of the large US market. It holds 26% of the North American drinks company Dr. Pepper/Seven-Up. It purchased the North American company, A&W Brands, for US$ 334 in late 1993. Schweppes' total strategy for the US market remained unclear at the time of writing, but it was certainly building global brands and alliances under the Schweppes and Canada Dry brand names.

Keypoint on test marketing
When Cadbury launched its highly successful chocolate countline, Wispa, in the UK in the early 1980s, it did so after two UK test markets. The estimates of sales from

the tests were important in making the large financial commitment required to build the national-scale production plant and in the marketing expense and techniques for the national launch. The result showed that skill and imagination could be turned into profit.

When it came to launching in other parts of Europe, Cadbury naturally needed to follow local requirements on labelling and ingredients changes. But no further major test marketing was mounted, nor justified.

The reality is that, if selling internationally is to mean anything at all in terms of economies of scale, then a major revamp of products from the home country for each of the international opportunities is an expensive luxury: what is wanted is to take an existing product or design and modify it to suit individual countries' legal requirements, labelling laws, etc. with the minimum of other changes. Otherwise, where is the saving?

Thus, test marketing is only appropriate for many companies in the sense of taking a product and trying it in other countries, suitably modified where required, before final harmonization of national laws. Anything more detailed is the way to lose profits.

Acquisition, joint venture or marketing agreement

As a way of gauging customer demand, this will surprise some readers. But over the last few years, it has been used as extensively as any other method by Europe's Top 400 companies. Two points need to be made clear: we are not talking about mega-moves in this context – only small ventures compared to the present size of the company; and we will explore the merits of mergers and acquisitions for business purposes in Europe and the world later in Part II of this book. Our consideration now is concerned only with their merits for market research.

Table 12.2 **Advantages and disadvantages of using acquisitions, joint ventures or marketing agreements for international customer research**

Advantages	Disadvantages
Provides much broader range of data than sole company test market launch	More in-depth commitment than some companies would prefer
Accepts that major problem is often not the product so much as the establishment in new country	Takes longer to organize because of greater complexity of negotiation
Starts the process of cutting across country boundaries which has to be faced as part of the decision-making process	More expensive in immediate cash outlay
Quicker to become established once agreement reached	

Note: This table concerns *market research* only: full discussion of the merits of acquisitions and joint ventures comes later in the book.

For clarity, 'marketing agreement' here means some contractual deal, short of joint venture, involving close company co-operation across international borders. Acquisitions and joint ventures are as normally understood. The advantages and disadvantages are shown in Table 12.2.

The balance of the decision will vary with the company and its products or services. But, in principle, this route forward is possible for small as well as large companies, as long as the other company concerned is no larger in size and with complementary interests.

Case Study: St. Gobain SA, France

Data
One of the world's largest producers of glass products.
Turnover (Ffr million)

	1988	1992
Flat glass	11727	13099
Glass & other insulation	8265	9404
Fibre reinforcements	3574	3108
Containers	7627	12352
Building materials	6694	6294
Pipes & machinery	9383	8347
Industrial ceramics	2123	10724
Paper & wood	8467	8733
Other	1579	2424
Inter-company	(564)	(478)
Total	58875	74007

	1988	1992
Return on capital:	18.1%	9.5%
% sales in home country:	45	37
% sales in rest of Europe:	35	40
% sales in rest of world:	20	23

European and global activity
St. Gobain is the world's leading producer of many glass products (eg car windows and perfume bottles). The glass activities are highly profitable and form the major part of St. Gobain's international expansion:

1988: buyout of a US glass fibre minority shareholding
    : a glass container joint venture with a German company
    : acquired a vinyl fittings manufacturer in US
1989: buying an optical glass manufacturer in France
    : acquiring a French company making suspended ceilings
    : buying 73% of Vetri, the second largest Italian manufacturer of glass jars and bottles
    : negotiations with Italian packaging company and three Italian companies in building materials
1990: acquired company in Argentina
    : UK distributor of glass products, Solaglas
    : Norton, US, for US$ 2 Bn
    : Italian and Portuguese companies
1991: Oberland Glas (Germany), second largest glass packaging company
    : Austrian company
1993: Italian company

St. Gobain is obviously determined to maintain its position in glass throughout Europe and also to take a position in building materials: this latter area is closely connected with its strengths in glass fibre, plastic pipe manufacture and other building products distributed to similar outlets. This is a clear example of channel strategy in operation.

Importantly, the company has also seen the need to develop in the USA: in reality this is the key to a strong world position in the 1990s. It has therefore acquired companies in North America, especially Norton in 1990 which accounted for the major increase in industrial ceramics turnover.

Keypoint on acquisitions

Whilst St. Gobain did not make its international acquisitions for the purposes of customer research, its customer knowledge will have increased substantially as a result. In a difficult area for market research such as building materials distribution, this represents a valuable way to obtain important information on the market. In relation to the total investments of St. Gobain, the cost is relatively small.

Chapter 24 contains a further comment on the company's clever acquisition of a UK glass distributor in 1990.

As a result of the market research and earlier background data, we should now have a clear idea of our potential target group of customers, probably on a country-by-country basis. But we have a fundamental area to explore at this point: are we absolutely clear that we have identified the right customers? We will tackle this next.

CHAPTER 13

Customer Strategy: Identifying the Customer

Before moving on to other aspects of customer strategy, we need to be sure that we have correctly identified the right customer in the marketplace.

As many business people will immediately recognize, it is not only the final consumer who makes the decision whether to buy or not: the well-known example is food retailing where it is not enough to have an excellent product but vital to persuade at least a handful of top grocery buyers to display it or no sales will be made. This applies across Europe and in some global markets, even in lesser developed economies like Greece and Portugal.

Intermediate purchasers have a profound effect on customer strategy. In this case, we need to split customer strategy into two parts: strategy for the final customer; and strategy for the intermediate purchaser. Fortunately, the broad areas that need to be established for them are the same, even if the answers are different. They are also inter-connected: the intermediate buyer wants to know the final consumer's actions to make sure products do not sit on the shelves or in the warehouse.

Naturally, if a final purchaser is large enough (eg a government buying organization), then the seller deals direct even though the industry has intermediate purchasers.

Table 13.1 does not pretend to be conclusive, rather an indicator of where intermediate customers need to be considered. No doubt there will be some industries that could come under both headings: for example, iron and steel sells both directly to some consumers for further manufacture but also to intermediate stockholders to be sold on subsequently.

Let us pick out two areas to illustrate strategy development: European retailing and European trading companies. By trading companies, we mean those companies with a primary business of buying and selling products as intermediaries, rather than manufacturers. Because both groups of companies act as intermediaries to the ultimate customer, they raise the questions of what special opportunities they might offer across the single market and what strategies are required to sell to them.

Table 13.1   Some European industries where (a) the intermediate purchaser matters and (b) where companies deal mainly with the final customer

Intermediate purchaser	*Final customer*
Grocery products	Chemicals
Cars & trucks	Packaging
Iron & steel (some)	Hotels & leisure
Pharmaceuticals (some)	Telephone & postal services
Coal (some)	Electricity & gas
Metals & mining (some)	Insurance
Construction	Banking
Consumer electronics	Defence
Office equipment & computers	Heavy engineering
Travel & transport (some)	Media
Textiles & clothing	Retailing
Oil & petrol	Trading companies
Publishing	
Rubber & tyres	

Case Study: European retailing

Data

		1992 sales (US$ m)	Return on capital (%)	Home (%)	Rest of Europe (%)	Rest of world (%)
Primarily grocery retailers and wholesalers						
Aldi	Ger	20204			na	
Leclerc	Fra	20100			na	
Intermarche	Fra	20089			na	
Carrefour	Fra	16081	11.0	69	19	12
J. Sainsbury	UK	15207	20.6	89	0	11
Auchan	Fra	15007			na	
Ahold	Net	12910	15.4	47	0	53 [USA]
Tesco	UK	12528	16.6	100	0**	0
Casino	Fra	12218	9.4	80	0	20
Delhaize	Bel	10675	19.7	28	1	72 [USA]
Argyll	UK	8587	22.3	100	0	0
ICA	Swe	7961	8.9	100	0	0
Coop	Swi	7901	1.2	100	0	0
GIB	Bel	7449	8.1	85		15
ASDA	UK	6800	estimated: not available			
Docks de France		6360	10.8	84	9	7
CWS	UK	5010	na but high home %			
Kwiksave	UK	3550	na but high home %			

Other retailers with some wholesaling

Note that some have extensive grocery business such as Tengelemann and Migros.

Company	Country					
Tengelemann	Ger	30200			na	
REWE	Ger	25640			na	
Promodes	Fra	16704	15.6	59	37	4
Karstadt*****	Ger	12448	6.5	96	4	0
Pinault Printemps	Fra	12400			na	
***Metro	Ger	12009			na	
***Kaufhof	Ger	11672	14.8	100	0	0
Migros	Swi	11465	2.4	95	5*	0
Schickedanz	Ger	10950			na	
KF Group	Swe	10506	4.9	100	0	0
***Asko	Ger	9715	2.9	100	0	0
Marks & Spencer	UK	9574	21.6	87	4	9
Edeka	Ger	8613	7.3	100	0	0
Boots****	UK	6548	22.2	70	20	10
Kingfisher	UK	5863	16.2	100	0**	0
Vendex	Net	5660			na	
Kesko	Fin	5652	1.7	100	0	0
C&A Mode	Ger	5500			na	
Hertie*****	Ger	4700			na	
Comptoirs Moderne	Fra	4024			na	
WH Smith	UK	3515	20.7	94		6
Sears	UK	3368	5.3	95est	5	0
Dixons	UK	3282	9.5	67	0	33 [USA]
Rinascente	Ita	2900			na	
Benetton	Ita	1462	24.4	34	39	27

*but note move into Austria in 1993
**but note moves into France in 1993
***shareholding strong link through Metro Switzerland
****includes manufacturing turnover
*****see text

European and global activity

Unravelling business strategy in European retailing presents problems only matched by those amongst the European banking companies. Some companies have developed cross-shareholdings and excessive secrecy that make normal commercial judgement exceptionally difficult. However, retailing is a much greater threat to European competition policy than banking because of the dominance of a few retailers in specific countries.

Probably the worst example is Germany where the antiquated company disclosure laws have allowed three groups, Tengelemann, REWE and Metro, to control around 50% of German retailing, yet reveal little of themselves (*Financial Times*, 8 December 1992, p 21). The influence of such companies extends well beyond their national boundaries, eg Metro has retail outlets in at least 8 European countries. Tengelemann has a major store chain in the USA (Atlantic & Pacific). It is surprising that such a combination of secrecy and large market share is legal under Article 85 of the Treaty of Rome. But European Commission bureaucrats no doubt hold a different view.

European supermarket retailing is a relatively mature industry in the sense that major large-scale market growth has now been completed, particularly in northern EU countries. In their existing countries, it is now quite difficult for large retailers to find sufficient new locations and new product areas for expansion. Some have therefore sought openings in North America. Until recently, southern Europe was under-supplied with large stores and certainly eastern Europe is still undergoing retail reform.

Thus, the developments of the last few years include: Delhaize (into the USA and more recently Hungary); Carrefour (south America and Spain); Marks & Spencer (USA and, much less successfully, Canada, plus a slow expansion into Europe and through franchise shops into the Far East); J. Sainsbury (USA); Ahold (USA); Docks de France (Spain and USA); GIB (USA); Promodes (Spain and USA).

Retailers need to tackle the lack of growth and, at the same time, to obtain scale economies, buying power and cost-cutting. Beyond expanding geographically, their main strategies have been either to join pan-European retail alliances or to acquire fellow competitors.

Retail alliances can take a number of forms. Purchasing groups are an alliance to improve buying power, eg Eurogroup has GIB, Coop Schwiez, REWE, Paridoc (France) and Vendex as members. The European Retail Alliance goes beyond buying into broader cooperation: it includes Casino, Argyll and Ahold along with Migros, Dansk Supermarket (Denmark), La Rinascente (still controlled by Fiat) and ICA.

Acquisition has included Tesco's purchase of Catteau in northern France; Kingfisher's takeover of Darty (France) to create a major new force in electrical retailing; Migros' acquisition of Familia supermarkets in Austria. One practical difficulty is the real variation that exists in national tastes, service and local laws, thus making economies of scale through company purchase more difficult to achieve. Another problem is justifying the price premium over asset value usually needed for acquisitions.

Amidst all the activity, one retail sector has shown significant growth against a depressed European economy: the *discounted price, no-frills grocery store*. Aldi has been particularly successful with this retail formula: it expanded from Germany into the Netherlands, Belgium and France and is now moving into the UK. The threat has been so great that UK and French supermarket chains, such as Carrefour and CWS, have opened their own discount stores. The UK is particularly attractive for discounters because the higher profit margins taken by some UK retailers allow the discounters a low-price entry strategy.

Keypoint for intermediate customer strategy
For companies familiar with dealing in one country with major retail buyers, the experience will be no different in other parts of Europe. Similarly, for other markets involving intermediate purchases, the basic procedures will be much the same.

What will be different in the new Europe will be the pressure on manufacturers from the new buying organization described above. It is likely that it will eventually involve trans-Europe sales negotiations, sales monitoring and deliveries. This is a very powerful combination, both as a source of sales and as retailing threat to manufacturing profit margins, unless handled carefully. Suppliers need to come to terms with this quickly and sort out their customer strategy for the new situation.

Case Study: European trading companies

Within Europe's Top 400 companies, there is a group engaged in trading activities. Every one of them is part of a larger group but each has a quite distinct operational area concerned with buying and selling a product range. We can group their activities into two areas within this overall category: industrial trading and general trading. Up to 1991, there was a third group trading in food commodities, but the three companies involved, Berisford (UK), Dalgety (UK) and Tate & Lyle (UK) have now largely withdrawn. It was not sufficiently profitable and the risk exposure is significant (see Metallgesellschaft below): the strategy involves taking a small profit on buying and selling near-commodities, value-added is low. There are, of course, other companies continuing to trade in food commodities in Europe that are not listed in this book. Companies seeking to sell their products internationally may well meet these companies as intermediate purchasers of products.

What also seems to have happened is that some European manufacturers have become traders. Some now handle much greater sales volumes as intermediaries than they manufacture. In any event, they may therefore be in competition with a company seeking distribution through an intermediary.

All of the companies operate on a world-wide basis. Because they are part of larger groups, there is usually little detail on profitability. The following table covers selected European trading companies.

Industrial trading		1992 sales* (US$m)	Products traded
VEBA	Ger	13291	Oil, chemicals, coal
Thyssen	Ger	9698	Steel, oil, coal, construction
Metallgesellschaft	Ger	8836	Metals, ores
Preussag	Ger	8058	Non-ferrous metals & alloys, steel, chemicals, building
Viag	Ger	4958	Chemicals, general
Krupp	Ger	4400	Steel, plant, food, agriculture
Pechiney	Fra	3124	Metal trading
Ruhrkohle	Ger	2645	Coal trading
MAN	Ger	2395	Steel trading
Cockerill Sambre	Bel	2182	Steel

*Company turnover in *trading* area only in all cases.

There is no company in the above table engaged solely in trading. Many have become involved in order to sell their products or secure distribution (we will come back to iron and steel in Chapter 25). Most of the companies already have the expertise to operate across Europe, where appropriate, so the single market will make little difference.

Metallgesellschaft traded heavily on international markets without proper controls in 1993. The company became exposed to heavy losses and had to be rescued by the German banks in early 1994.

General traders		1992 sales* (US$m)	Products traded
Mitsui*	Jap	21079	General trading
Sumitomo*	Jap	12465	General trading
Haniel	Ger	8950	Solid and liquid fuels, freight, metals, food, pharmaceuticals
Mitsubishi*	Jap	8550	General trading
Lonrho	UK	1600	Cotton merchants, plumbing, freight
Inchcape	UK	1557	Sourcing services, electronics, wines & spirits, timber
Volvo	Swe	979	Food, other consumer products

*Turnover for Japanese companies is European turnover only.

The two UK companies in the list of general trading companies have extensive trading contacts based on Britain's past historical contacts with Africa and the Far East. All operate internationally.

Turning to the future of trading companies in the single Europe, the main differences will clearly arise as barriers come down and pan-Europe trading becomes easier. However, all these companies are experienced in this area so that the main effect will be an increase in profit margins from higher efficiencies rather than some more fundamental shift in business focus.

For those companies engaged in global trading, the single Europe is unlikely to have a major impact.

Keypoint for intermediate customer strategy
All the above companies may represent a means of gaining distribution within Europe, but not all have their main strength in the EC. Indeed, some have no substantive EC activity.

Yet picking the right company can be instrumental for distribution. Some years ago, the Japanese car maker Toyota sold some overseas distribution rights in its cars to Inchcape: the company now distributes Toyotas in 10 countries and sold 130,000 vehicles in 1989. In early 1990, Toyota agreed with Inchcape that it would take an increasing shareholding in the company, rising to 51% over 8 years, for which it would pay around US$100 million. The Japanese company wanted both to cement its relations with Inchcape and to take a higher share of its own rapidly increasing European car sales over the period.

By early 1990 the Japanese car company, Nissan UK, had not been able to reach a similar contract with its UK importer. Nissan therefore set up its own distribution company. The implication for dealing with intermediate customers is clear: the medium term as well as the short term needs to be considered. Intermediate customers can be important.

In many respects, what we have been examining with trading companies is the company that has existed for centuries: the importing company. But it is no less useful for that and does represent a route into Europe and global markets for some businesses to examine.

There are many smaller companies acting as importers that are not represented in Europe's Top 400 companies. The trading company case study only picks out those owned by Europe's largest companies. In some circumstances, the smaller companies may represent a much better opportunity for international business deals because they are not tied to the major existing nationals. However, because of their size, they may not have the distribution clout.

In any event, intermediate customers need to be considered as part of the overall development of customer strategy. Their needs must be specified as part of the overall analysis.

CHAPTER 14

Customer Strategy: Differentiating the Product or Service

Having analyzed what customers want, the next step is to explore product or service differentiation. (To avoid unnecessary repetition, 'product' is used in this chapter, but the comments apply equally to services.) We need to look at this in relation to competitive products and customer expectations.

We therefore enter the bridging area that covers both customers and competitors. Some readers may feel it would be better to consider this as part of competitor analysis: this is possible but the *result* will still need to be tested against customers so we will explore it here.

Differentiation of the product or service may involve real or perceived differences in performance as seen by the customer. For convenience, we can separate out three principal sources of differentiation: (1) In the real performance of the product; (2) In the product's presentation (perceived differentiation); and (3) In the product's value for money (perceived differentiation). All these need to be judged against the reactions of the target group of customers. Usually at this stage it is better to consider differentiation options rather than fix on one route: market segmentation focusing on a market niche may be involved.

Occasionally, when defending against competitors, a strategy without product differentiation is needed: we will discuss this later. Let us concentrate on the main issues and examine the three routes to differentiation.

REAL DIFFERENTIATION FROM PRODUCT PERFORMANCE

Moving internationally into other advanced economies with a product or service that is very similar to existing offerings could be a recipe for trouble. Why should a customer change? Why should a distributor stock the product? Because it is cheaper? That is not a route to long-term profitability unless your factory has spare capacity and unit costs, compared to the competition, are already low.

This is not to deny that the Japanese have been very successful at establishing themselves in a market by persistently pricing below existing products. But, even here, there has almost always been some attempt to investigate product differentiation before fixing on price.

Another difficulty is that many such markets are well-developed. Even specialized national products, from French goat cheeses to Scottish single malt whisky, are now readily available. Finding a totally new product is therefore quite difficult. Moreover, most companies will best gain economies of scale by working with their existing product areas.

However, it is very doubtful whether a significant thrust should be launched without some product differentiation, even within an existing product area. For example, Procter & Gamble (US) or Unilever (UK/Netherlands) are unlikely to launch a major new household detergent product without some form of performance differentiation. Equally, Henkel, which is strong in detergents in Germany, will always look to produce superior performance as a means of holding off Unilever and P&G in that country. (However, if the brand share of an existing product was under threat, then a similar product might be launched as a short-term tactical measure.)

What is needed may well be a balance between total innovation, which might require major change, and some lesser differentiation from products already on sale in a particular part of the single European market.

Case Study: Rhône Poulenc SA, France

Data
Broadly-based, global chemical and pharmaceutical company.
1992 turnover (FF million)

Agriculture	10262
Health	30479
Organic and inorganic intermediates	15812
Speciality chemicals	14274
Fibres and polymers	12486
Inter-group	(3095)
Total	81709

Return on capital: 8.6%
% sales in home country: 22
% sales in rest of Europe: 35
% sales in rest of world: 43

European and global activity
Rhône Poulenc has been transformed over the ten years 1984–93 from a sleepy French national chemical company, into a global and broad-based chemical and pharmaceuticals concern. It now claims world leadership in several speciality chemicals and to be amongst the top five in each area of its global businesses.

It has achieved the turnaround over the last few years with a series of acquisitions and disposals of subsidiaries; specifically it spent over US$ 7 billion on acquisitions, and raised US$ 1.7 billion on disposals between 1986 and 1992. It will be evident that this imbalanced switch in assets has increased company debt – gearing stood at 86% in late 1992. Such high levels of indebtedness were made easier because the company was government-owned and would only be privatized in 1993/94.

Over recent years, the new company has purchased the following: Rorer, the US pharmaceuticals business for US$ 1.7 billion; Connaught, a Canadian vaccine company; RTZ Chemicals from the UK; GAF from the USA. It has reduced its dependence on basic chemicals and fibres, which have been subject to fierce global price competition, and raised its presence in drugs where product differentiation has allowed higher prices.

During 1992/93, it made smaller acquisitions in Poland and Slovakia to enhance its eastern European presence. It also joined forces with Italy's SNIA (a Fiat subsidiary) to create a new fibres company that will be 'number 1 in polyamide yarn'. This is not necessarily quite as grand as it reads – world chemical fibre markets have excess production capacity and depressed prices. The main effect may be to deconsolidate this area from the two parent company balance sheets and make the two owners look more profitable.

Keypoint on product differentiation
Rhône Poulenc has sought product differentiation in its development in a systematic and detailed way. It has reorganised its research and development and doubled expenditure over the last few years. It has also focussed efforts on specific developments, especially in the pharmaceuticals and speciality chemicals sectors. As a result for example, it claims world leadership in chemical surfactants and in dairy fermentation processes for food ingredients.

The difficulty with R&D-based product differentiation is that there is always a risk that the development will not produce sufficiently attractive results. For example, the chemical companies BASF and ICI both stopped development in 1992 of especially toughened plastics for the defence industry, after investing substantial R&D funds – breakeven was still too far into the future.

Case Study: Siemens/Nixdorf, Germany

Data
European leader: seventh in the world.
Turnover (DM million)

	1988	1991
Germany	2802	7544
Other Europe	2167	3939
Other	378	642
Total	5347	12125
Return on capital:	3.4%	2.8%
% sales in home country:	52	62
% sales in rest of Europe:	41	32
% sales in rest of world:	7	6

European and global activity
Here is a national company, which expanded with vigour and determination on the back of fast growing markets, but has failed to develop a special niche outside its home country: the computer hardware market has become increasingly commodity-like and global. Additionally, with its rapid growth, the company suffered from very slack management controls. Nixdorf's strength has been in Germany but the market is so international that this is no real protection. By 1989, it had moved into losses.

In January 1990, it was acquired by Siemens and combined with that company's computer business to become the largest in Europe with a turnover of US$ 9 billion in 1992 but still losing money and no clear strategy for recovery.

Keypoint on product differentiation
There is no doubt that spreading research and development costs over one combined company, rather than two separate firms, has assisted the economics of the merger. Additionally, since both Siemens and Nixdorf are strong in Germany, this has provided a strong share in that market. But what has really changed?

Neither company had a strongly differentiated product internationally. Neither had international strength in niche markets. Nor is it at all clear how economies of scale can make the difference.

Siemens/Nixdorf nevertheless bought time for redevelopment of its products, so that it could produce real differentiation from others and real economies of scale from combined production. In seeking differentiation, it will need to reappraise its target group on an international scale: currently, it may be too broad with too many needs for the company to satisfy through specialist products. The problem is to find a large enough, narrower target (or targets) to justify the development costs. And one that cannot be easily imitated by larger rivals at lower cost.

At the same time, it must protect its existing business. Siemens/Nixdorf may still need an international partner or joint venture to provide global scale and some real product differentiation in the medium term.

The slippery slope still beckons, and the angle is just as steep.

Case Study: European chemical industry

Data

Here is an industry in which the largest companies operate on a world scale. Some have attempted to benefit from specialization. Because of differences in markets, costs and business strategies, we will separate general chemical companies from those engaged primarily in petro-chemicals.

General chemical companies

		1992 sales (US$ m)	Return on capital (%)	Home (%)	Rest of Europe (%)	Rest of world (%)
Hoechst	Ger	30868	7.4	58		42
BASF	Ger	29961	4.9	68		32
Bayer	Ger	27722	8.7	57		33
ICI	UK	19932	2.8	18	27	55
Rhône Poulenc	Fra	16209	8.6	22	35	43
*MontEdison	Ita	12739	loss	na		
**Ciba	Swi	10267	6.6***	na		
AKZO	Net	10073	14.3	9	53	38
Henkel	Ger	9489	9.8	29	51	20
Solvay	Bel	8317	8.0	7	66	27
DSM	Net	5325	3.5	16	60	24
Norsk Hydro	Nor	4200	na			
**Unilever	UK	3637	na			
**Degussa	Ger	3128	na			
**Sandoz	Swi	2789	na	45		55
Courtaulds	UK	1562	23.9	41	20	39****
Alusuisse Lonza	Swi	1150	na			
Viag	Ger	1076	na			

* part of Ferruzzi: see beginning of chapter 11
** only part of total turnover shown above
*** after tax profits
**** sales by source, not destination

In the above table, Elf Sanofi and Roussel Uclaf are not shown separately because they are majority-owned by other companies already listed, Elf Aquitaine and Rhône Poulenc respectively.

Petrochemical companies

Royal Dutch Shell	UK/Net	9855
Elf Aquitaine	Fra	9772
Enichem	Ita	9533
Veba	Ger	6850
BP	UK	4895
Total	Fra	3718
Petrofina	Bel	2634
Neste	Fin	2138
Repsol	Spa	1001
Statoil	Nor	902

Note: for all the above petrochemical companies, chemical products are only part of total sales. No further detail is published on profitability or sales destination.

Some major US chemical companies active in Europe

Du Pont	USA	37799	8.6%	56	34	10
Dow	USA	18971	8.7%	50	29	21
WR Grace	USA	5518	8.5%	59	29	12

There are many other North American chemical companies operating globally and in Europe. The above represents a selection. Home sales are for the USA with European sales covering the whole of Europe.

All the above data needs to be treated with some caution, since it mixes companies in speciality chemicals with those in basic large-scale production. However, the aim is to provide an indicator of comparative size rather than full details.

European and global activities
Against a background of depressed world chemical markets and low-priced imports from the Far East and Eastern Europe (particularly in petrochemicals and artificial fibres), there has been considerable retrenchment in the industry in the early 1990s.

Unlike some other sectors in this book, such as retailing, the chemical industry already acts on a pan-European and even global scale – the data on destination of sales above makes this reasonably clear. The difficulty is that global trading also gives entry to global chemical competitors from outside Europe, some of whom can sell at lower prices. The European chemical industry has devised two principal strategies to counter this threat over the early 1990s:

- seek lower costs through economies of scale and other means;
- move into speciality chemicals.

To produce lower costs from further economies of scale, leading companies have been swapping assets. For example, Du Pont and ICI exchanged ICI's nylon turnover (US$ 1.2 billion) for Du Pont's acrylic plants in North America (sales US$ 500 million) plus US$ 400 million cash. In giving permission for these moves, the EU Commission also attached some stringent conditions since Du Pont ended up with 43% of the European market.

Around the same time, Royal Dutch Shell was planning to merge part of its plastics business with a subsidiary of MontEdison. Neste and Statoil were also considering whether to combine their petrochemical interests in a company called Borealis. ICI was also negotiating to sell part of its plastics interests (sales US$ 3 billion) to BASF. At the time of writing in early 1994, all these deals were awaiting regulatory approval by the European Commission.

The above exchanges and mergers are made more complex by the reality of large-scale chemical processing – some plastics are made as by-products during the manufacture of other goods. Many companies are vertically integrated or have common overhead costs. All these issues mean that a simple strategy to exit a part of the industry could impact elsewhere on the business and therefore be more difficult.

An additional complication is that some chemical companies are state-owned, eg Enichem, and receive state subsidies to keep them in operation. This has meant that the private sector has been unable to enforce the reduction in total European production capacity required – the state industry is not subject to commercial pressures and can just keep going, even though it might be the state companies that are the least efficient! The same problem has arisen in the European iron and steel industry (see chapter 23).

For some companies, the strategy has therefore been to seek out speciality chemicals, ie a form of product differentiation. We examine this below.

Keypoint on product differentiation
In theory, speciality chemicals will have higher profit margins but, by their specialist nature, rather lower sales than the bulk chemicals above. AKZO, ICI, Ciba, Sandoz and Rhône Poulenc have all followed this strategic route during the early 1990s. However, it is not without its problems.

Demand is still derived from customers in other industries and, in times of economic depression, all will suffer. Moreover, it has been difficult in some cases to produce specialities that can be patented – if they are not and demand is proven, then other chemical companies have entered the same specialist market.

Nevertheless, product differentiation has been partially successful in chemicals. The key strategies are a precise understanding of the needs of the selected target group, coupled with strong links to research and development. The objective is to develop products to match such specialist demand.

Case Study: BOC Group, UK and Air Liquide, SA, France

Data
Two of the world's largest specialist manufacturers of industrial and commercial gases.
1992 turnover (US$ million)

BOC Group		Air Liquide	
Gases	3270	Gases	4275
Healthcare	876	Welding materials	754
Special products	464	Engineering & construction	321
Discontinued	117	Chemicals & other	588
Total	4727	Total	5938

Return on capital:	17.4%		13.6%
% sales in home country:	24		} 57
% sales in rest of Europe:	5		
% sales in rest of world:	71		43

European and global market activity
Both companies have grown up from different backgrounds and therefore have different associated products. BOC is more associated with health and hospitals, thus it has health products including anaesthetics, US home healthcare, etc. Air Liquide has a background in construction, so it has pipelines and chemical plant interests.

Both companies have strong national sales and both have important US connections. The consequence of this is that neither had major pan-European interests in the early 1990s. Arguably, this will change and probably by the same route as in the USA where both companies have made growth by acquisition. In 1993, BOC purchased a German gas supplier to extend its European interests.

BOC itself said that it is one of two companies competing on a truly global basis. Both it and Air Liquide have made major moves in the Far East. BOC has plant in Taiwan and Japan and Air Liquide has plant in Japan and a joint venture with the Japanese company Showa Denko. The demand for specialist gases for electronics in these countries lies behind this expansion.

Keypoint on product differentiation
The world market for specialized gases is reportedly large enough to sustain two manufacturers. They have differentiated their products sufficiently to form a new specialist sector of the market for industrial gases. Here, differentiation has been prompted as much by product developments as by the target groups, though clearly such customers need to be satisfied to pay the higher prices charged.

The advantage of specialization for these two companies is that the investment required in plant and service for any further entrants is high, thus deterring newcomers. This is a profitable strategic position for the two companies concerned.

Within product differentiation, Air Liquide in particular claims to have shifted the emphasis of its product development towards closer customer linkages. It has been working with long-term industrial customers to build specialized products and services unique to that customer. Matching product differentiation with the needs of individual large customers can be a powerful strategy.

PERCEIVED DIFFERENTIATION THROUGH PRODUCT PRESENTATION

For some target customers, the way the product is presented is just as important as its function. This applies particularly in consumer markets and, more recently, in some industrial markets. Customers buy products because they satisfy a broad range of needs beyond the functional: for example, fashion, taste, status and professional style. Europe and global markets are remarkably homogeneous across a number of product and service areas, from Benetton and Gucci in fashion to Coca Cola and McDonalds in food products.

Make no mistake: product performance has to be there. Fashion clothing has to be made with top quality materials, and hamburgers with at least 90 per cent beef. But the essence of the differentiation between products lies just as much in the way the product is presented as in its intrinsic performance.

More recently, these trends have been extended into professional areas: what new car or computer would be launched in Europe or North America in the 1990s without a major presentation to dealers? A brief handout might impart the technical data but the key to sales achievement lies partly in the way the distributors present the product or service. Good dealer presentation has always been a characteristic of the best of the marketing-led companies. It is now becoming an intrinsic part of product presentation and differentiation across international markets.

Five major guidelines

There are five major guidelines when developing product presentation.

Define the target group carefully

Accurate definition of the target group lies at the essence of this part of a product's development: the emotional needs that shape perceptions develop out of an understanding of the target as much as the product itself. The identified group may well involve a segment of the market.

In the UK, Lever Brother's (Unilever) differentiation of Persil washing powder from Ariel (Procter & Gamble) derived partly from careful research on what housewives wanted emotionally from a washing powder. I know because I did some of the early work.

Concentrate on pan-European or global presentation

Differentiation that can be applied internationally may be more relevant than concentrating on an individual country. Because of high promotional costs, it is usually advisable to consider pan-Europe or global applicability, even if the major launch is confined to one or two countries. Gillette's launch of Naturel in seven European countries was reported to be the result of economic as well as positioning requirements: centralized production and basic pack design is more cost effective.

Similarly, when Kraft General Foods (US) bought the Café Hag decaffeinated coffee company and production facilities in Germany, they did not only use them in that country. The product was launched across the main European markets with a similar packaging style and branding. The same designs were not undertaken out of indolence but because it made economic sense.

Clearly, this applies particularly to areas associated with the factory (eg the design of jar and can labels). It applies less to advertising which might be different between countries. Café Hag advertising in the UK, which includes some ridicule of German tourists, might not be especially convincing to German housewives.

Mars' (US) change of name for one of their Pedigree Petfoods dog food varieties in the UK from 'Mr Dog' to 'Cesar' was occasioned by the need for pan-European branding. Whilst there was a short-term change cost in the UK estimated at US$2–5 million, this will have a rapid financial payback from the annual cost savings in other areas.

Use price as part of the presentation difference

Pricing with its quality implications is an important indicator to customers about product differentiation: there are no cheap Daimler Benz cars anywhere in Europe. We will return to pricing shortly.

Consider visual designs which cross language boundaries more easily

All the best European and global brands use strong visual design elements that do not rely on language to present a unified visual identity: Coca Cola and Pepsi Cola are classic examples of what is needed.

Case Study: Coats Viyella plc, UK

Data
One of the world's leading textile companies.
1992 turnover (£ million)
Thread

Crafts	378
Industrial	439
Zips	89
Clothing	419
Homewares	273
Fashion retail	130
Precision engineering	119
Yarns and fabrics	249
Discontinued	14
Total	2110

Return on capital: 11.9%
% sales in home country: 48*
% sales in rest of Europe: 22*
% sales in rest of world: 30*

* By source, not destination

European and global activity
Coats Viyella is the largest pure textile company in Europe's Top 400. Its two main competitors are Courtaulds (UK) and Chargeurs (France). This is reflected in its world-wide sales: it is world leader in home sewing thread with strong sales in many parts of the world and it also has a strong world share in industrial threads. In 1990, it acquired the UK company Tootal for £400m.

Its range of retail shops and fashionwear is also international with shops in the UK, USA and Germany. Brand names include Jaeger, Country Casuals and Viyella plus Jean Muir in haute couture fashion. It also has a strong range of brand names in garments and knitwear with these having a more 'English export' approach rather than a strong local base. During 1991/92 it acquired various fashion and clothing businesses to extend its global fashion interests.

Yarns and fabrics include spinning and filaments: Coats Viyella has been under intense Japanese competition on a world basis for some time. Thus the company has invested in modern equipment to remain a low-cost producer and hold quality, whilst at the same time developing its branding in an area where customer loyalty can be very fickle. It has also been developing joint ventures, including one with a Korean company, to counter the threat of low-cost Far Eastern competition.

Keypoint on product presentation
Textiles are a classic area for differentiation through presenting the product well. Coats Viyella has a strong range of brand names in this area including the Jaeger mark. In household textiles and home furnishings, brand names include Dorma and Vantona. Products are also made under licence from Dior and Mary Quant.

Much effort has been undertaken to present these in up-market, modern, quality designs using both retail shops and advertising. This has given the company real differentiation in a product area where the danger of cheaper imports from outside the EC has become a reality. In reporting its financial results in the mid 1990s, Coats Viyella commented that its branded businesses stood up better than its commodity businesses, such as yarns and filaments, to the difficult global economic conditions.

Case Study: L'Oreal SA, France

Data
World's largest cosmetics company: Nestlé owns 49%
Turnover (FFr million)

	1989	1992
Salon and consumer	13263	18410
Perfume and beauty	10145	8464
Active cosmetics	–	3661
Other cosmetics	184	306
Pharmaceuticals	2909	6319
Other	668	406
Total	27170	37567

Return on capital:	19.4%
% sales in home country:	36*
% sales in rest of world:	64

* seems high: possibly by source, not destination

European and global activity
With its North American agents, L'Oreal effectively controlled over FFr 45 billion sales in 1992. For many years it was easily world market leader with such well-known brands as Lancôme skin products, Giorgio Armani fragrances and Helena Rubenstein makeup. To keep ahead, the company regularly outspent its competitors on R&D: around 3 per cent of sales in 1992.

In 1990, global competition was transformed. Procter & Gamble (US) acquired Richardson-Vicks, Shulton, Cover Girl and Max Factor. Unilever then replied with Chesebrough-Ponds, Fabergé, Elizabeth Arden and Calvin Klein Cosmetics. The Japanese groups Shiseido and Kao also made acquisitions in Europe and the US.

L'Oreal has increased R&D and marketing expenditure to counter this competition.

Keypoint on product presentation
Some may judge L'Oreal to be a special case because it is involved in a product area that lends itself to presentation. Any business able to make sales of well over US$9 billion cannot be that specialist and the company has built a strong strategic position.

Its products are carefully targeted at customer groups. It employs a vigorous product development programme and strong presentation. Importantly for global control, it places much emphasis on good local in-store presentation: differentiation must be followed through at local level in this type of market.

Case Study: Schweizerische Gesellschaft fur Mikroelektronic und Uhrenindustrie AG (SMH), Switzerland

Data
One of the world's leading watchmaking and electronics holding companies.
Turnover (Sfr million)

	1987	1992
Switzerland	374	
Rest of Europe	542	
Far East	264	na
Americas	438	
Other	101	
Total	1719	2762

Return on capital:	10.9%	18.1%
% sales in home country:	22	na
% sales in rest of Europe:	31	na
% sales in rest of world:	47	na

European and global market activity
SMH is the holding company for part of the Swiss watchmaking industry with brand names such as Omega and Tissot. The world-wide competition from the Japanese companies is well documented, particularly Citizen and Seiko. The Swiss industry clearly had difficulty competing against the whole trend towards cheaper, digital watches on a world-wide basis. Europe offered no protection at all, nor does it now. Between 1974 and 1983, Swiss watch exports halved.

SMH was restructured in 1983. The strong brand names and technical knowledge became the foundation for a new global strategy. Swatch (below) accounts for only half its production of watches. In addition, the company makes components for other world watch manufacturers.

Keypoint on product presentation
Product presentation is important but needs real product differentiation to survive against a major product innovation like cheap watches. SMH produced its own innovation in the late 1980s with the Swatch which had strong, modern design, new cheaper production technology and heavy promotion. It was a major success throughout the world and showed what presentation, coupled with product differentiation derived from innovation, can achieve. By 1993, SMH claimed it would become the world's biggest watch maker.

The combination of a product development programme and strong presentation targeted to a specific group is worth considering for European and global markets.

Most importantly when it comes to presentation, there is a clear case for involving an outside consultancy or advertising agency: specialist skills are often involved in such areas, as the Swatch project clearly demonstrates. Bringing in outside professional assistance at an early stage is usually worthwhile.

PERCEIVED DIFFERENTIATION THROUGH VALUE FOR MONEY

Price is the other aspect of differentiating products in international markets. But this cannot be separated from the way the product performs and is presented: they are three sides of the same triangle. Price is the major feature but is better seen as part of the *value for money* benefit offered to the target group. If a product is clearly differentiated, then a price premium over competition may be possible.

For international markets, pricing and value for money will be governed by a number of basic factors:

- Prices already operating in the home country, where relevant;
- Currency exchange rates with other countries, both actual and potential;
- Cost of tariff and other barriers;
- Any variation in the rate of value added tax and any other local taxes;
- Prices of similar products already available in the new country;
- Trade discounts and other special deals already operating in the new country

- ie regular discounts off the list manufacturer's price for display, reaching volume targets, etc.
- ■ Distributor markup already operating in the new country – ie the difference between the distributor's price and the customer's price.
- ■ For multinationals, the prices at which goods are transferred between subsidiaries.

We will come back to those matters relating to distributors when we look at distribution strategy later. They are listed here because they may have some effect on the ultimate customer (though many distributors keep all their discounts).

To arrive at a possible price range, the above factors will need to be researched in detail. The resulting information has then to be reviewed against the target group expectations and the sales objectives. Normal company pricing criteria will then be applied: all the usual knotty problems then feature in international markets as in the home country. They are not detailed here since this is not a basic textbook. If there is one area to highlight, it has to be currency: most companies have greater exposure in this area than any other.

Case Study: VEBA AG, Germany

Data
One of Europe's largest producers and distributors of energy, oil and chemicals.
1992 turnover (DM million)

Electricity	11924
Chemicals	10180
Oil	13400
Trading	19750
Transport	7648
Services	2511
Total	65419

Return on capital: 5.3%
% sales in home country: 73
% sales in rest of Europe: 16
% sales in rest of world: 21

European and global activity
As one of Europe's largest companies, VEBA has come to dominate sectors of German industry – it is a major electricity supplier to the German economy. It is also a major national oil company with refineries and petrol stations across Germany under the ARAL brand name. Its oil activities also have a more global dimension with production interests in Libya and Venezuela.

In chemicals, it produces a range of basic products largely in Germany under the Huels name. In trading and transport services, it operates under two company names: Stinnes and Raab Karcher. Both these companies operate across European and international markets. In Germany itself, the Stinnes name also covers a range of tyre service outlets. Raab Karcher includes products and services as diverse distribution fleets and fresh flower selling.

Overall, VEBA is the fourth largest company in Germany with strong international connections.

> **Keypoint on product differentiation**
> Much of VEBA's activities are located in basic industries and trading. With such large-scale involvement, product differentiation becomes more problematical; for example, it is difficult to differentiate electricity supply except on price. In such cases, it may be easier to develop strategies that do not rely on differentiation. One such route would be to become a low-cost producer. This strategy is explored in chapter 18.

Innovation deserves separate and careful study and is examined in the next chapter.

WHAT IF PRODUCT DIFFERENTIATION CANNOT BE PRODUCED?

After all the analysis, some companies may conclude that any differences they can come up with are small and largely irrelevant to customers. In these circumstances, the realistic options may be to seek a joint venture or takeover of a local company in the country concerned or to seek a lower cost base or both. We will come back to the action required for this in the last chapter of Part II.

While these may be the options, it is worth recording that some of the companies most skilled at moving into new markets, including Japanese companies, use joint ventures or takeovers only for distribution. Differentiation is still sought in basic market areas: this is achieved by targeting products to *specific market segments*. If meaningful differentiation has not been produced then it probably means that the target group has been drawn too broadly.

CHAPTER 15

Customer Strategy: Identifying Technical Development Issues

In part I, the large UK chemical company, ICI plc, was cited as devoting considerable resources over the last few years to the development of its speciality chemical businesses. The need arose from the cyclical nature of basic chemicals on which the company had been dependent up to that time, coupled with the attraction of the higher profit margins on more specialized products. This is an example of the vital step of applied technical development, in its broadest sense, to take advantage of international demand.

Technical issues need to be looked at in two ways: outwards to the market using the target customer group as a guide; and inwards to the company to make sure that the technical viewpoints and ideas of senior managers have been fully explored.

In examining outside activity, the best data on competitive developments may come from the technical manager or packaging buyer who has just been to a conference at which rival executives were presenting new developments or suppliers were somewhat indiscreet as to who had already taken delivery. Even job recruitment advertisements can be a useful indicator as to where new action is taking place.

Looking inwards, there is no management formula that can be stated to ensure that technical development issues are adequately covered: circumstances differ. But it is useful for our purposes to identify three analytical stages:

1. Establishment of the basic strategic need for a development process and the issues involved.
2. Exploratory discussions within a company to explore the matters raised and the means to their resolution.
3. Development of a specific plan to resolve these with objectives, resources and a timetable.

Let us take each of these stages and examine some of the points they contain.

ESTABLISH THE NEED FOR DEVELOPMENT

This will involve examining what customers want and also what is potentially available from competitors. It may therefore mean spending some time pulling to pieces competitive products, obtaining price lists, interviewing customers, etc.

The process of analyzing customers' requirements and existing products will throw up various pointers as to possible product and service developments. If the existing range is unique then it is unlikely that these need to be followed up. But for the majority of companies, their international market position will substantially improve if development can be undertaken.

Development may be needed both to produce a distinctive offering to customers and to provide *competitive advantage* against other existing products. We will consider competition in more detail shortly, but should recognize now that a major reason for development is its contribution here. However, development merely to gain competitive advantage, regardless of real consumer need, is less likely to succeed so it is right to consider it as part of customer strategy.

It is more difficult to co-ordinate development across European and world markets because of their greater size and diversity. Part I suggested some ways to simplify this but there is no substitute for working through the issues.

Case Study: Fried. Krupp GmbH, Germany

Data
One of Europe's leading mechanical engineering companies.
1992 turnover (DM million)

Mechanical engineering	3773
Plant making	1853
Automotive	2846
Fabricating	3465
Steel	7799
Trading	6539
Other	1591
Inter-group	(4709)
Total	23157

Return on capital: 3.1%
% sales in home country: 55
% sales in rest of Europe: 26
% sales in rest of world: 19

Note: the above data covers the period before the Hoesch merger.

European and global market activity
Germany's second and third largest steel producers, Krupp and Hoesch, merged their companies in mid-1992. They also merged their engineering interests. The steel interests of Krupp/Hoesch are discussed in chapter 22. Krupp/Hoesch mechanical engineering sector includes:

- Rail vehicle engineering where it is the leading state supplier;
- Shipbuilding where it has the same difficulties as others world-wide;
- Plastic and chemical processing plant which has weak demand world-wide;
- Machine tools and;
- Defence engineering – German battle tanks.

This sector is heavily dependent on Germany's international strength in engineering. Its products are widely spread and will not rely on the single Europe as such for growth. Although the majority of the group's sales are to the home market, some will be used in products that are then exported.

The company's plant-making activities also cover a wide spectrum of markets:

- Metallurgical plant: world-wide;
- Horizontal continuous casters where it is the world's leading supplier;
- Piping and construction: focussed on Europe;
- Cement plant design: world-wide.

Again all these areas have a strong international dimension.

The automotive area covers a range of parts for the car and truck industry: leaf springs, car jacks, etc. Demand will be dependent on German car production.

Overall, Krupp is experienced in many international markets and can therefore take advantage of the international opportunities from its major home base.

Keypoint on technical development
Krupp does not publish a list of the areas of technical development that it is pursuing (nor is it suggested that it shoud publish such confidential material). Nevertheless, based on other published sources, Krupp Hoesch will have considered technical development in, for example:

- Defence engineering (further development of the Leopard Battle Tank);
- Rail vehicle engineering (new designs/technology);
- Use of plant design expertise in other industries; and
- Optimisation of steel usage in automobiles.

It will be evaluating these both for customer sales potential and their contribution to competitive advantage.

EXPLORATORY DISCUSSIONS WITHIN THE COMPANY

Discussions need to be undertaken between those responsible for strategy and technical development within the company on the need for change, its resource requirements and timings. The scope and structure of this depend on the nature of the problems identified from the strategic analysis and also on the technical opportunities identified by company staff.

There are three dangers in this area that are worth highlighting:

1. Occasionally, the whole sales development is structured to hinge on a new technical advance. This can be high risk and may need a cold douche of reality if it is not to distort planning and resources.
2. Market research can only take the analysis so far forward because customer comments are based on what is available now: genuine advances cannot always be conceived by customers until they happen, so customer research can be misleading here.
3. There is too much talk and not enough action.

The multi-disciplinary team approach is needed but with a specific brief and a timetable to report back.

Case Study: Benetton Group, Italy

Data
A leading supplier of high quality clothing world-wide.
Turnover 1992 (Lire billion)

Italy	862
Other Europe	988
Americas	221
Other	442
Total	2513

Note: associated companies in which Benetton holds a minority shareholding are not consolidated in the above.

Return on capital: 24.4%
% sales in home country: 34
% sales in rest of Europe: 39
% sales in rest of world: 27

European and global activity
Benetton says that it has over 6,700 stores selling its products in around 110 countries but its accounts still show one third of its sales deriving from its home country. The company operates some of its activities on a franchise basis and some through minority interests. It has also negotiated a range of joint ventures, alliances and other participative agreements depending on national country requirements around the world. For example, it has minority interest companies in Egypt, Mexico, Japan, China and India. All these would alter the destination of sales data if they were to be consolidated in the company accounts.

Essentially, the company works on the basis of local franchising of the company name and products to individual shops or groups of shops. They stock only Benetton goods and the company only sells through them. The main product has been knitwear, typically in bright colours: 'The United Colours of Benetton'.

Benetton's expansion across Europe went well, but its venture into North America was dogged by some legal and marketing problems. In addition to franchising, its strategy has had three elements:

- to rely on craft suppliers from the fragmented Italian clothing industry;
- to operate with relatively high advertising expenditure in comparison to other clothing industry companies [around 5% sales];
- to develop close and extremely flexible links with suppliers so that it can respond to changes in fashion demand.

It has attempted to diversify into other related activities, eg footwear, but with more limited success.

Keypoint on technical development
For a company like Benetton, technical development means more than engineering and technical research. It involves the study of fashion, design, fabrics and fibres and a whole range of devices that link its suppliers, headquarters and franchises, ie the chain that 'adds value' to its purchases. Technical development needs to be seen in the broadest possible context of its contribution to *every aspect* of business strategy.

SPECIFIC PLAN

Once a development area has been identified, a precise action plan is required with measurable objectives, resources and timescales. Depending on the product area, these might cover 12 months or take several years to complete.

Some smaller companies might argue that they do not have a special development department, nor do they have the resources to mount a special effort. This would be to miss the point: even if the company is so small that the managing director is the sole person responsible for development, the same process applies. The stages must be analyzed honestly even if the M&D has to talk to himself!

Case Study: Solvay et Cie., Belgium

Data

One of the world leaders in alkali and peroxygen chemicals and a leading European manufacturer of thermoplastics.

Turnover (Bfr billion)

	1988	1992
Alkalis	77.8	80.9
Peroxygen	18.8	18.3
Plastics	80.6	65.6
Processing	45.9	50.4
Health	30.4	39.3
Total	253.5	254.5

Return on capital: 23.1%	8.0%
% sales in home country: 10	7
% sales in rest of Europe: 65	66
% sales in rest of world: 25	27 (mainly USA)

European and global activity

Solvay built its strength on alkalis and, until 1988, they formed the largest part of its turnover: it is the world's biggest producer of soda ash. The difficulty with this area is that it is essentially commodity-based and static. This did not discourage Solvay from acquiring Tenneco's (US) plant in the USA for US$500 million. It is also building a new plant in East Germany. Both these plants are low-cost producers to maintain its world lead.

Since the 1950s, thermoplastics have become important with the company, now amongst the world's top producers of PVCs and polyethylene. Solvay is already European leader in several areas here with emphasis on higher added value where possible, but it is still largely a bulk chemical concern and highly cyclical.

Solvay earns 44% of its turnover from three European regions alone (Benelux, France and Germany), so is already well placed to take advantage of single market activity.

Keypoint on development plans

Two parts of Solvay are the result of development opportunities identified in the 1980s: peroxygen and health. The world's biggest maker of peroxygen products, Interox, was 50% owned by Solvay with the UK company Laporte Industries having the other 50%. In 1992, Solvay acquired the remaining 50%.

This product area forms the basis for a bleaching agent which is reported to be more environmentally satisfactory than other agents such as chlorine: it therefore has good growth prospects. Solvay identified this several years ago and has developed it with a specific plan. This is now producing a healthy return. Its problem is that other chemical manufacturers have seen the high margins earned on this product and have entered the market, competing on price.

Similarly, Solvay bought the Duphar pharmaceutical company in 1980: it is involved in human and animal drugs. The company reports that it has grown at 20% per year since that time. However, it is small compared to world suppliers. Development here, again, has been characterized by a clearly identified market sector and then specific growth plans to tackle the opportunities over a number of years. But its lack of experience and resources in pharmaceuticals has meant that its major new drug, Fluvoxamine, has taken much longer to gain approval and reach the market than larger companies. In 1992, it negotiated a marketing alliance with Upjohn (US) to assist the North American drug acceptance process and then market it. Development plans need also to be seen in the context of competitive response (Peroxygen) and regulatory approval/marketing (drugs).

CHAPTER 16

Customer Strategy: Customer Service and Quality Issues

For many international industries such as the car industry, telephone services and some branded goods, the issue of product and service quality has increased in importance during the 1980s. The Belgian company Solvay, which we have just examined, launched a major quality initiative in 1992. Consideration needs to go beyond the immediate product or service performance into environmental issues: awareness is much higher than previously with countries such as Holland and Germany leading the way.

For all these, customer service and quality have become parts of fundamental company strategy. Make no mistake, they are real concerns in the 1990s.

In practice, companies such as the UK retailer Marks & Spencer and the German car manufacturer Volkswagen have had this as a key area for years. Japanese companies like Nissan and Sony have made such issues an important part of their global development.

Tackling European and global markets makes this task more difficult because of the wider geographic spread and the greater diversity of tastes and requirements. In the early years at least, it may impact on profits but still needs to be established, undertaken and regarded as an investment in the future.

STRATEGY AREAS

The specific issues will be established by analyzing the identified target group of customers. These may well include not only the ultimate consumer but also the distributor who may be the immediate customer as in Chapter 13. Four main strategy areas need to be considered:

1. Product or service quality standards: the criteria by which the customer will judge that value for money has been received. Will this be the same as in the home country?
2. Procedures for customer service: there is a service element for many products associated with their sale. It might be advice on operation or simply initial installation. How will this be tackled outside the home country?
3. Handling customer complaints: even the best run companies occasionally have problems. How will these be handled?
4. Environmental issues: country standards differ and expectations are also not always the same.

In answering these questions, it is important to *establish the policy without becoming bogged down in detail.* We are considering customer strategy here, not detailed plans.

Clearly, we are raising fundamental issues and will not be able to go into depth here. Also the strategies will vary with the company and its markets. Let us examine the issues by looking at how three companies are facing very different quality questions.

Case Study: Karstadt AG, Germany

Data
Germany's largest department store chain.
Turnover (DM million)

	1988	1992
Karstadt department stores		
Textiles	3412	4726
Household and furniture	2125	2718
Food	1646	1539
Catering	276	347
Services	19	20
Other	2663	3847
Neckermann	1848	4469
NVR travel agents	1573	2570
Other	191	351
Less VAT	(1378)	(2089)
Total group	12375	18498
Return on capital:	7.2%	10.8%
% sales in home country:	100 approx.	93
% sales in rest of Europe:	0	7
% sales in rest of world:	0	0

European and global market activity
Karstadt is a very important retailer in Germany with 164 stores primarily in Northern Germany, Westphalia and the Rhineland. Selling space was 1,502,000 square metres at the end of 1992 (+ 15% versus 1987).

The company competes directly against two other big publicly quoted retailers: Kaufhof and Hertie (which used to be part of BAT Industries, UK). Whilst some German retailers have clear international ambitions (eg Aldi and Tengelmann), Karstadt has announced no plans to move beyond its national boundaries. However, along with its two rivals, it has moved into Eastern Germany. The department store retail format has been under pressure from specialist stores and discounters, along with German economic recession. At the time of writing, it was reported to be seeking to join forces with its rival, Hertie.

Keypoint on quality
In common with all retailers across Europe, the company has carefully defined quality standards for the supply of goods. It also has procedures on customer service and complaints. Any manufacturer supplying Karstadt will need to establish the company's detailed delivery requirements, stock control on perishable items, returns of damaged goods, etc.

For most suppliers, there will be nothing totally new in any of this: for international goods, this simply means greater geographical distances and language difficulties, for which handling procedures have to be set up.

Case Study: STET, Italy

Data
Italy's state-owned telephone holding company, but being privatised.
Turnover (Lire billion)

	1988	1992
Telephone services	15235	22539
Manufacturing, installation and equipment	2067	4995
Publishing and marketing services		2037
Information processing activities		1461
Other		798
Intergroup		(4663)
Total	17302	27167
Return on capital:	6.7%	16.5%
% sales in home country:	80 + (est)	80 + (est)
% sales in rest of Europe:	95 + (est)	90 + (est)
% sales in rest of world:	5	10

European and global market activity
STET is a subsidiary of the Italian state holding company IRI. In turn, the company has majority shareholdings in the various urban and regional telephone companies that exist throughout Italy. This Byzantine structure is being simplified by merging STET with its subsidiaries over the next few years.

STET is primarily involved with resolving its complicated structure and preparing for privatisation. In addition, 'STET group continued to pursue its own expansion plan targetted towards foreign markets with particular emphasis on the EC and the Mediterranean basin, Latin America and especially the so-called "Southern Triangle" [Argentina, Peru, Uruguay and Paraguay] as well as the former centralised economy countries of central and eastern Europe'. Annual Report 1992. For example, in 1992, it won the contract to operate a mobile telephone system in Greece. Nevertheless, the organization's main task is to complete the modernization of Italy's telephone system which needs to be undertaken regardless of international expansion and prepare for privatization.

Keypoint on quality
Like some other national public telephone systems, STET publishes data on its quality of performance. The Italian system has had some notable difficulties. For example, Cesare Romiti, Managing Director of Fiat SpA, speaking on 1992 to *Fiat News* (April 1988) said: 'The nature of the competition will be different because the opening up of the continental market will change the meaning and strength of the competitive positions of the companies involved. Italian companies are production efficient but are unable to develop this competivity due to problems in the energy field, the inadequacy of our transport system and the inefficiency of our telecommunications system'.

With this comment from a leading Italian industrialist, the quality problems were all too clear. The STET 1992 Annual Report comments: 'A great deal has been done to improve quality: private numbers now take on average 15 days to connect and more than 94% of faults reported by residential numbers were repaired the following day.' The publication of official statistics on performance is the start of the improvement process.

The key to quality here is that it is being quantified. This has three advantages: it takes it out of the realm of opinion so it is less open to dispute; the improvement can be measured and monitored; and objectives can be set for improvements. All these are valuable lessons for quality standard setting.

One additional key to quality is that it has a *price* and there are certain customers who will be willing to pay extra: for example, Fiat may be prepared to pay extra for more reliable telecommunications circuits.

For STET, its monopoly position may be threatened by new competitors during the early 1990s. We will look at this later in Part II when we examine Europe's top telephone companies.

Case Study: Compagnie Générale des Eaux, SA, France

Data
Europe's top water supply and heating services company: a major supplier of public works and local services.

1992 turnover (Ffr million)

Building and construction	42480
Water	36323
Energy	32477
Urban and property services	13583
Waste management	8826
Healthcare	3769
Communal services	3427
Communications	2499
Total	143385

Return on capital: 7.1%
% sales in home country: 73
% sales in rest of Europe: 16 estimated
% sales in rest of world: 12 estimated

European and global activity
CGE is not only involved with water but a whole range of *local service* companies sharing complementary technical knowledge. Its strategy around this core was stated as being in 1988:

1. To strengthen existing services in water, energy, urban maintenance, construction and real estate;
2. To enhance new businesses in related areas (cable TV, healthcare); and
3. To broaden into Europe and the US.

This clear vision was then followed up by action over the years to 1992. With regard to water, three companies supplied 70% of France's drinking water: the largest was CGE. Because there were few remaining opportunities in France and UK water was being privatized, the company moved into the UK with bids or acquisitions of some water companies. The company also acquired US, Italian and Spanish water interests.

In energy management, under its subsidiary Groupe Générale de Chauffe, the company is heavily involved in heating and ventilation services. It acquired the UK market leader, Associated Heating Services, some years ago. The company also has fuel trading interests mainly in France. It has unconsolidated shareholdings in two major Belgian energy companies, Electrabel and Petrofina [see chapters 2 and 24].

Urban maintenance activities are mainly confined to France and the UK but there is a transport company in Spain.

In construction and public works, the company's main subsidiary, SGE, operates mainly in France but with other contracts for housing, airports, etc around the world.

German and UK companies have also been acquired. It is the third largest in Europe [see chapter 6].

Finally as regards media, CGE is France's leading cable TV operator.

The Group also has interests in Africa and Asia. It has had difficulty developing in Eastern Europe because of the lack of local funds.

Keypoint on quality

With over 800 companies, CGE has a real task to maintain quality. It does this by its emphasis on locally based services (ie devolving management responsibility down to *local level* rather than attempting to service from the centre). With the type of services it offers and around 200,000 employees, it is essential to operate in ths way.

Three fundamental quality issues derive from these principles:

1. A company must organize itself to achieve agreed quality standards: it cannot be left to chance.
2. Employees need to be educated to be quality-aware as well as about other company objectives.
3. Every employee has a personal responsibility for quality.

CONCLUSIONS

Importantly, quality is not a service operation imposed from the centre on a large group. It has to be part of every employee's daily responsibility if it is to be successful. It is much cheaper in the long run to provide the right service quality at the beginning rather than to be picking up the mistakes later.

Japanese and German car companies have shown that customers will pay a premium for greater reliability: this is achieved on the factory floor, not in a separate quality control office afterwards. Total quality management starts from this fundamental principle and needs to be built into international business strategies on this basis.

CHAPTER 17

Competitor Strategy: Market Data

After the analysis undertaken in Part I, market data should be available in two areas: market growth and market share. We need to look at both.

MARKET GROWTH

Growing markets usually have more opportunities for companies both to enter and to increase sales. The strategic opportunity from real growth needs careful management for its exploitation but first it needs to be classified.

Markets have been structured into a number of categories useful for strategic analysis. For example:

- Embryonic (the very early growth stages);
- Growing (still growing fast, eg +10 per cent pa);
- Mature (small steady growth, eg +2–3 per cent pa);
- Ageing (declining, eg –2–4 per cent pa); and
- Cyclical (growth, decline, regrowth, etc).

The advantage of these over mere numbers is that the definitions give a better indicator of strategic importance and hence the management action required. The disadvantage is that they can be somewhat arbitrary and, in the writer's experience, can lead to some contention inside companies. For example, when a market is classified as 'ageing' rather than 'mature': ageing is emotive and might mean the area was to be run down, much to the consternation of the immediate managers and against good strategy if it is still a good cash earner. The answer is to classify with care.

Let us examine the European car and commercial vehicle industry using these broad categories with the aim of strategic relevance rather than statistical accuracy.

Case Study: European car and commercial vehicle industry

Data
In spite of the different country regulations on type approvals, tax, emission control and vehicle safety, this industry has for some years been operating across European boundaries: for example, the Ford Granada made in Germany is exported to the UK. Yet the industry is less profitable than others because of strong competition, the need to invest heavily in plant to obtain economies of scale, the economic downturn of the early 1990s and excess production capacity worldwide.

Car and truck manufacturers and assemblers

1992 sales US$ million

		Cars	Trucks	Total	Return on capital (%)	Destination of sales		
						home (%)	rest Europe (%)	rest world (%)
Volkswagen	Ger	na	na	57471	1.2%	46	37	17
*Daimler Benz	Ger	26649	18088	44737	na			
*Renault	Fra	29760	4868	34628	11.2%	48	41	11
Peugeot Citroen	Fra	na	na	29376	8.0%	42	48	8
**Fiat	Ita	20935	6136	27071	na	49	36	15
General Motors	USA	na	na	26319	14.0%	76	22**	12
Ford	USA	na	na	25927	loss	57	24**	19
BMW	Ger	na	na	21023	6.6%	42	32	26
Volvo	Swe	7958	5433	13391	na			
Rover	UK	6088	—	6088	loss	na		
***Saab Scania	Swe	4817	—	4817	4.3%	31	42	27
MAN	Ger	—	5317	5317	na			
Toyota	Jap	na	na	95428	na	55	9**	36
Nissan	Jap	na	na	65126	na	46	20**	34
Honda	Jap	na	na	38613	na	33	10**	57

*only part of total turnover of company included
**all Europe
***see text below

The six volume car makers in Europe are Volkswagen, Fiat, Renault, Peugeot Citroen (PSA), Ford and General Motors (Opel in Germany and Vauxhall in the UK). All Japanese companies in total accounted for only 12% of the European car market in 1993.

European and global activity

Cars
Cars account for 90% of all vehicles produced by number in Europe. Strategic effort across the world has been focused on reducing costs through:

- Designing-in cost reductions before cars ever reach the production stage
- Selecting and developing car component supplier relationships
- Reorganising production to take out costs, eg just-in-time delivery of supplies.

Europe's largest car manufacturer, Volkswagen, is located primarily in Germany, which has the highest total labour costs and a strong currency: two major contributors to VW's search for lower-cost production over the last few years. Partly for these reasons, the company has over the last ten years acquired companies in low-cost countries: SEAT, Spain, and Skoda, Czech Republic. Another strategy in 1993 was to recruit some senior executives from General Motors who had made their reputations driving down supplier prices whilst holding quality.

Other manufacturers have sought cross-shareholdings, joint ventures and outright acquisitions as a part of their strategy. For example:

- Fiat bought Alfa Romeo [also partly defensive against Ford who wanted the same company];
- Ford acquired Jaguar in 1989;
- GM took a 50% interest in Saab in 1989;
- Renault and Volvo agreed cross-shareholdings in 1989 that were intended to lead to full merger in 1993; the deal collapsed because of doubts by Volvo about its long term best interests;
- BMW acquired Rover Cars in early 1994.

In addition to the problems outlined below, a major strategic difficulty facing the six

European volume car manufacturers was that they have roughly equal market share. It is therefore difficult for one to develop a dominant position, though most have leadership in their home markets.

The European market is still protected from Japanese competition until 1999. Nissan, Toyota and Honda have all built plant in Europe in the early 1990s in low-cost countries, principally the UK and Spain. This is slowly adding to the competitive pressure. With their high quality products and relatively low costs, the Japanese manufacturers may pose an increasing threat over the next few years.

But it is far too simplistic to see European car strategy in terms only of Japanese competition. There is excess production capacity and fierce rivalry. There are likely to be further casualties in the European car industry. Establishing market niches that offer some protection is one survival strategy for example, BMW and Rover both occupy up-market positions that are marginally less vulnerable to volume car pressures. Another strategy is the increased use of joint ventures to share research and development and other costs and reduce risk. But the partnership needs to be equal: Volvo evidently did not see its increasingly close relationship with Renault in the early 1990s developing in this way and broke off the merger in late 1993.

Trucks
The European truck market can be conveniently split into two parts: light trucks, led in the mid-1990s by Renault and Peugeot/Citroen, and heavy trucks dominated by Daimler Benz. Strategies are equally complex with specialist segments developing alongside the basic strategy of price/value for industrial customers. This market is certainly pan-European but hardly global.

Motor vehicle parts
With significant cost savings coming from the further development of supplier relationships, the car parts industry is being transformed. There are essentially three types of supplier:

■ Major producers who also make items for other unrelated markets, eg Bosch, Siemens, Lucas, GKN
■ Large manufacturers who specialise in the car industry, eg Valeo in France, Magneto Marinelli in Italy
■ Many smaller companies who supply directly or indirectly to the final assembler such items as car seats, steering wheels.

Fundamentally for the strategy of these companies, the European market is essentially fragmented and the major car manufacturers buy most of their supplies from locally-based companies. This results partly from the increasingly close relationship with car manufacturers outline above, but also from the supply pressures of low stock holding strategies through just-in-time techniques, etc. Thus Daimler Benz purchases 90% of supplies within Germany. The car parts market is not pan-European in this sense nor likely to move in this direction.

Keypoint on market maturity
Although the car market overall is showing signs of maturity, there are still pockets of real growth. The strength of the four-wheel drive car market right across the Continent has been notable, especially the off-road part: these can be classified as 'growing', having moved beyond 'embryonic'.

From the business strategy viewpoint, the importance of these areas is that they tend to demand investment and cash resources: high profitability may come later rather than sooner. In some industries, such support would be funded by the other lower growth areas within the same business: the difficulty at the present time in the car industry is that investment is also required here to reduce unit costs and increase reliability. How much to invest in these arguably 'mature' markets to protect profits long term is a difficult but important strategic judgement. The strategic choices facing the European car manufacturers are quite finely balanced as a result.

Case Study: Nokia Oy AB, Finland

Data
One of the two world leaders in mobile telephones.

1992 (FM million)	Turnover	Net operat-ing profit	Classified market growth*
Telecommunications	3207	427	Growing
Mobile telephones	3641	437	Embryonic/growing
Consumer electronics	5761	(783)	Growing/mature
Cables and machinery	4619	114	Growing/mature
Other	1354	93	
Inter-segment	(414)		
Total	18168	288	

*Source: Author's assessment based on published data.

Return on capital: 2.7%
% sales in home country: 20
% sales in rest of Europe: 57
% sales in home country: 23

European and global market activity
Nokia has been very active and clear-sighted, building strength in a number of areas, but becoming over-stretched in the process.

In information systems it acquired Ericsson Data Division in Spring 1988 to combine with Nokia Information Systems Division. It is claimed that this made Nokia into the largest Scandinavian information technology company, as well as providing distribution in eight west European countries. However, the company was still small by European standards. It wisely sold the group to Fujitsu/ICL in 1992.

In telecommunications, it continued to advance in mobile telephones. For example, it started manufacturing in the USA in 1993 alongside its European operations. In equipment, it began joint ventures in Russia and Estonia. In consumer electronics, its acquisitions in the late 1980s of Salora and ITT televisions, VCRs and Sound Systems was a mistake. It claimed to be 'third in Europe', rather ignoring the global nature of the industry. Even in 1992, it was still closing four factories and blaming exchange rates for its difficulties. Low cost producers in the Far East must have been quietly satisfied.

Nokia was stretched as a result of all the purchases and it reported lower profits in 1992. It therefore had to streamline its activities, selling paper-making businesses, its electrical distribution business and its flooring operation.

Keypoint on market growth
Nokia is stretched, not only because of its purchase activity but also because it has bought into growth areas which demand cash. An 'embryonic growth' area like mobile telephones will take cash on research, as well as manufacturing facilities and general trading, before it shows results. Couple this with tough conditions in the

IT market and in consumer electronics and Nokia has some major strategic problems to solve over the next few years. Arguably, if it were to sell all its mature businesses to generate cash, this would only solve the short-term problem and thus not help strategically.

Case Study: Pilkington plc, UK

Data
One of the world's top three glass companies.

		Turnover (£ million) 1993	Classified market growth*
Flat & safety glass	Europe	1199 ⎫	Growing/mature
	N. America	591 ⎬	
	Other	305 ⎭	
Vision care glass		304	Growing
Other trading		169	
Total		2568	

Source: Author's assessment based on published data.

Return on capital: 3.7
% sales in home country: 14
% sales in rest of Europe: 39
% sales in rest of world: 47

European and global activity
Much of Europe's glass is used in cars, packaging and construction. Between them, Pilkington, Glaverbel and St. Gobain have the major European stakes: Pilkington has a majority share in Flachglas AG, Germany which largely accounts for its strong German showing. It has low sales in France and Italy because of the dominance of St. Gobain in these countries. Its home sales were depressed by the severity of the UK recession in the early 1990s.

Pilkington is involved in a continuous process business with global competitors. It needs near-full capacity to earn high profits. Demand in the 1990s came mainly from the depressed car and construction industries – hence the poor profitability. Between 1987 and 1992, the company invested around £1 billion in four new glass plants: with hindsight its timing could have been better.

During 1993, Pilkington made its first investment in glass in Poland. It also attempted to acquire the Italian glass maker SIV for £87 million. At the time of writing, this was being investigated by the EC.

Chapter 24 contains a comment on Pilkington's inept handling of distribution in the UK and its 1993 strategy to recover the situation.

Keypoint on market growth
To overcome the cyclicality associated with flat glass, the company moved into the growing market for US contact lenses, purchasing VisionCare in the US. But such developments require extensive funds and rely on a buoyant economy. By early 1994, Pilkington was over-stretched elsewhere and considered selling the business.

MARKET SHARE

Here we are concerned with each product or service and its share of its market. The competitive stance of market share is captured in the definitions used, for example, weak, viable (but still small), strong and dominant. The reasons behind these assessments are summarized in *competitive advantage*. Whole books have been written on this important topic which applies equally in a European and global context. We will consider the practical aspects of this as this book progresses. For now, let us concentrate on the basic market share definitions, which again can be tailored slightly to suit the company concerned.

What is a viable share to one company may be weak to another. For Cadbury (UK), a viable share might be a minimum of 10 per cent of the European chocolate countline market because of the need to cover high salesforce overheads and the opportunity cost of selling time related to other products. For another company such as Ferrero (Italy), wanting to build its confectionery business across Europe, a viable share (at least for some years) might be only 5 per cent.

Case Study: European oil and petrol companies

Data

			1992 sales (US$ million)			
	Country	Total	Return on capital	Destination of sales		
				Home (%)	Rest of Europe (%)	Rest of world (%)
Royal Dutch Shell	Net/UK	90937	4.8%	na	40	60
BP	UK	54950	9.2%	36	27	37
Elf Aquitaine	Fra	39788	5.8%	56	28	16
ENI	Ita	37970	8.5%	62	22	16
Total	Fra	23065	8.5%	44	27	19
Petrofina	Bel	18312	7.2%	79		21
Repsol	Spa	15928	15.2%	85	5	0
Neste	Fin	9770	(0.2)%	na		
VEBA	Ger	9017	na	na		
RWE	Ger	8901*	na	na		
OeMV	Aus	6431	0.0%	58	42	
Statoil	Nor	5494	na	na		
CEPSA	Spa	4309	na	na		
Norsk Hydro	Nor	2093	na	na		

*includes some chemicals turnover

1. The above covers petrol and oil sales only and excludes chemicals, mining, etc. However, return on capital may include non-oil activities.
2. For turnover marked *, internal company sales have been estimated and excluded.
3. Some other important US companies also do not publish useful European data (eg Mobil, Esso, Texaco, Conoco).

European and global activity
The major oil companies have been active across Europe for many years. There have been differences in tax rates, attitudes to national petrol companies and other issues, which have all led to the European structure as we now see it. But overall, the international nature and branding of the oil industry means that even the largely national companies, such as Repsol and Veba have global connections [see chapters 8 and 14].

Europe does have some importance for the *international* oil companies. It is summed up in the BP *1987 Annual Report:* 'We are . . . thinking hard about our national subsidiaries, recognizing that in a more open market it may be possible to eliminate some of the overlap in national functions that is hard to avoid today'.

For the leading *national* oil companies like Veba, ENI and Elf, the same economies are not available, but it is doubtful if this is crucial to profitability. These companies are usually market leaders in their own countries (Veba and ENI trade under the brand names ARAL in Germany and AGIP in Italy respectively).

Both Texaco and Mobil in Germany in the late 1980s sold out to national companies but this is unlikely to be due to the single market as such – more because of market share weakness.

Keypoints on market share
Each of the international oil companies has varying market shares in national countries. There is no one dominant company across Europe. In some countries, there are strong national brands such as AGIP (ENI) in Italy. Their strength lies not so much in their refining capacity as in their possession of good retail petrol filling station sites.

With such a fragmented European market, competition is fierce and profit margins tend to be low. Periodically, some companies employ either product improvements or promotions to boost sales. But the lack of real product differentiation, as seen by the target group, stops major market share building once the good filling sites have been acquired and updated.

Regional national petrol companies are possible and have attained a *viable* market share in a geographical area: the key again is the well-sited petrol filling station. In this case, petrol can be bought on the spot market only, adding to the fragmental market share status.

Case Study: Gallaher Limited, UK

Data
One of Europe's largest tobacco companies and a wholly-owned subsidiary of American Brands Inc., USA [see also Chapter 4].

1991 turnover (£ million)		*Trading profit*
Tobacco	3593	289
Optics	240	11
Distribution	871	16
Distilled spirits	166	13
Housewares	57	(17)
Other	4	0.5
Inter-company	(252)	—
Total	4678	312

Return on capital: 44.8
% sales in home country: na
% sales in rest of Europe: 98
% sales in rest of world: 2

European and global market activity
Tobacco dominates both the turnover and profits of Gallaher. It also has companies in some major European markets, e.g. Tabak GmbH (Germany) and Niemeyer (Holland), with others also in Ireland and Spain. See also chapter 5.

The second largest area of turnover is in UK retailing with two chains of newsagent shops: Forbuoys and NSS. It also has a chain of opticians which is more European in nature: in the UK (Dolland & Aitchison), Italy (Filotecnica Salmoiraghi) and Spain (General Optica SA). Housewares operates under the Prestige brand name with operations in the UK, Belgium, France, Germany and Ireland.

In 1990, Gallaher acquired the scotch whisky distillery Whyte & Mackay. This complemented Jim Beam bourbon whisky owned by American Brands in the USA. Later in 1990, Vladivar vodka was acquired and in 1993, Invergordon Whisky. But distilled spirits operate in global markets against global companies – Guinness, Seagram, GrandMet and Allied-Lyons. It will be necessary for Gallaher/American Brands to buy further companies or form alliances if it is to compete effectively around the world.

Keypoint on market share
Gallaher has a *strong* share position in the UK with two market leading brands (Benson & Hedges and Silk Cut). It has defended these with great skill over the last few years in a difficult market climate.

It has perhaps been helped by the diversion of its leading competitor, Imperial Tobacco, into other unprofitable product areas (US hotels) and finally into a losing takeover battle with Hanson plc, UK. This is important because it shows how clearly leading market shares are subject not just to the direct influence of other brands but also to the indirect influences of market battles taking place elsewhere. Imperial certainly has a *viable* market share in the UK with its John Player brand names: it is now owned by Hanson plc.

Directly attacking a strong market position may be necessary in the long run but softening-up tactics can be part of the war for international companies. These may take place outside home territory and can be debilitating for the defender if they are not recognized. Europe's leading household washing product companies, Unilever, Proctor & Gamble, Colgate and Henkel are all very aware of strategies and tactics in this field. Viable shares can become weak.

Case Study: Havas SA, France

Data
France's leading poster advertising contractor and free newspaper publisher.
Turnover (Ffr million)

	1988	1992
Publishing	10567	17454
Outdoor advertising	1611	3550
Tourism	3533	6989
Audiovisual	84	153
Holding & financial	1	37
Total	15796	28183
Return on capital:	31.8%	16.1%
% sales in home country:	over 90 estimated	35 estimated
% sales in rest of Europe:	10	60 estimated
% sales in rest of world:		5 estimated

European and global activity
Havas was privatized in 1987 (the French government held a blocking share until December 1992) and the chief businesses have developed since that time into the four main operational divisions shown above. Some businesses in Havas are still not consolidated into the turnover data above – the full figure is over Ffr 40 million.

Havas has been active in three areas related to the single European market: tourism, advertising agencies and outdoor advertising. In April 1989, it signed a deal with the Belgian tour company, Compagnie Internationale des Wagon-Lits et du Tourisme, to create a joint venture with 600 travel agencies and a turnover of Ffr 7 billion. In the years between 1989 and 1992, the company made a series of advertising agency acquisitions across Europe to form EuroRSCG. The outdoor advertising activity is described below.

Keypoint on market share
With a 35% dominant share of the French outdoor poster advertising market, there was no real scope for Havas to extend its business in France. With 25% of the UK poster industry through its subsidiary Mills and Allen, there was equally no possibility of the UK company MAI expanding its UK interests. In 1989, the two companies pooled their poster interests in a joint company called Europoster. Not only has MAI put in its Belgian subsidiary, Benaerts, but the joint company has made purchases of leading poster contractors in Spain and Portugal. It has also acquired 75% of Italy's leading poster contractor, GIG. Subsequently, Havas acquired MAI.

The enlarged company is also looking to expand its interests in free newspapers, with the French papers already being put into the venture. When coming together, the two companies said that they were contributing different areas of skill and experience to the joint venture, this being important to its success.

Overall, this was a clever way for two companies to both overcome growth problems arising from *dominant* positions in their home markets and to create a single cross-Europe company that has real market power. The key factor will be whether strong branded European companies will want cross-European media: this remains to be proven but posters with their simple and visual message could be a useful marketing weapon.

Case Study: Courtaulds plc, UK

Data
Formerly one of Europe's largest textiles, fibres and paint-coatings companies. It was split into two companies in 1989: textiles and chemicals. Courtaulds plc now trades only in chemical products.

1993 turnover (£ million)

Coatings	729
Performance materials	214
Packaging	260
Chemicals	216
Fibres and films	667
Inter-group	(37)
Discontinued	25
Total	2074

Return on capital: 23.9%
% sales in home country: 41
% sales in rest of Europe: 20
% sales in rest of world: 39 (mainly USA)

European and global activity

Within the packaging and chemicals side, it has developed strongly in coatings, particularly in specialized paints described below. It is a major world producer of some items (eg coloured acrylic fibre and Cellophane packaging), but others are mainly UK based. It has some manufacturing facilities in Europe but made no major new moves especially for the single European market. It was more concerned with its global markets in fibres and coatings.

Keypoint on market share

When Courtaulds decided to extend its interests in paint and coatings some years ago, it chose to specialize. There were many manufacturers involved in basic paint products and the market was crowded: it would have struggled to avoid a *weak* share position.

By a combination of acquisition and internal development, it has now built world leadership in paint-coatings with operations in 34 countries. Its brand names include International Paints (world), Porter (US) and Taubmann (Australia). It also leads in heavy-duty coatings for the marine and steel industries with other major products for industrial and building use. During the 1990s, it extended this further into environmentally-friendly powder paints and into specialist paints for the aerospace sector.

Importantly, it did not compete head-on against existing paint manufacturers. It has therefore built itself a *strong* but not dominant brand share in world industrial paint-coatings. This is a valuable strategic position consistent with long-term profitability against the global market leaders: AKZO, ICI, RPG and BASF.

CLASSIFYING YOUR COMPANY USING MARKET DATA

Without any doubt, there is a strong connection between market competitive position and business profits and cash flow. It is not always easy to analyse but it is worth the effort for international markets, because it highlights important strategic issues.

As mentioned at the beginning of this chapter, the key to the subject is not the numerical share or market growth data but *what this means for strategy*. The classification in Table 17.1 needs to be undertaken for each geographical market in which a company operates.

At the risk of grossly oversimplifying, table 17.1 presents some typical numbers for international markets: your own company market growth and share data can be compared with the table to see what it means for classification. Then, the implications for company profits and cash can be assessed. The table is only a rough guide. Moreover for many international markets, analysis will probably need to be undertaken on a country-by-country basis because of the variations in company strength around the world.

It should be emphasized that the table shows *typical values* only, on a three year time-scale. They are incorrect for many industries but may help to give some feel for what is needed. It is also equally possible to mismanage a perfectly good business: for example, there are unfortunately a number of strong market share businesses making a loss!

Table 17.1 Market data classification

Typical market (% growth pa)	Market growth classification	Company impact	
		Cash flow	Profits
+20% to +200%	Embryonic	Negative	Loss
+10% to +30%	Growing	Negative	Possible profit
+1% to +5%	Mature	Positive	Good
−2% to −10%	Ageing	Should be positive	Should be in profit
Rate and length of cycle varies	Cyclical	Varies (Positive and profitable in good years)	Varies
(% market share)	Market share classification		
1% to 4%	Weak	Possibly positive short term	Possibly profit short term
5% to 10%	Viable	Positive	Profit
15% to 25%	Strong	Positive	Good
30% to 60%	Dominant	Positive	Attractive

USING MARKET DATA TO DEVELOP BUSINESS STRATEGY OPTIONS

In practice, markets are dynamic: share will vary with the levels of capital investment, pricing and marketing investment. What, therefore, is usually done is to take various levels of total possible company investment over several years (or longer for some industries) and build detailed *business scenarios* which project in sequence market growth, capital and revenue investment, company sales and costs, market shares, cash flow and profits for international markets. Assets common to several parts of a company need either to be allocated or the market reassessed: are there really separate sets of customers? Best and worst case situations are also projected.

Importantly, the objective is to estimate the *broad sweep* of the data correctly rather than agonize over the last accounting detail. Arguments over decimal points and whether trivial expenditures have been included or not are totally sterile. They need to be considered but then the minutiae stamped on mercilessly! Once the scenarios have been drawn up, the strategic debate that follows is about whether they are:

(a) Logical and reasonable;
(b) Consistent with company objectives; and
(c) Attractive at acceptable risk.

In practice, this is only part of the picture since it oversimplifies the competitive situation (what will others do; what can they do?). We will explore competitive costs in the next chapter and other responses later.

Moreover, market maturity and market share say little about the practical why and how of building a long term business: they are simply results and measures of this process. We will explore ways of achieving this through *sustainable competitive advantage* after looking at relative costs.

CONCLUSIONS

Overall, with our examples drawn from Europe's Top 400 companies, there are more than a fair share of market leaders amongst this group. Whilst there are some powerful positions, Courtalds shows what companies can do when they move outside areas of existing strength.

Equally, Gallaher shows the profits deriving from the skilful protection of a strong brand share, and Havas how to extend strength further in the new single Europe. Pilkington and Nokia illustrate that the path to sales growth is smoother than that to profits growth, with significant strategic issues to be resolved.

Building business scenarios of likely outcomes for single market expansion is a major part of the process of tackling European and global markets.

CHAPTER 18

Competitor Strategy: Competitive Relative Costs

Ideally, the company tackling international markets wants to seek and hold cost leadership. Certainly, it needs to be a low-cost producer consistent with the quality and service that the target group of customers wants.

Most companies will come with an existing product or service as a starting point. Some will come with a totally open brief but, even here, they will be constrained by what the company does now and the cost experience that it has: it is unlikely that a banker will want to consider coal mining – and if he or she does, then this book will be of little value!

The questions can therefore be more limited than might be required for a full-blown strategic analysis:

1. How do company costs compare with the competition?
2. Is the company a low cost producer in the new larger market? If not, what has to be done, at what cost, to achieve this position?
3. Are there new opportunities for differentiation from competitors by completely reassessing the cost position? Might this lead, over time, to a totally new strategy, perhaps even in the home market as well?
4. Where does the company stand on the learning and experience cost curves with regard to competition?
5. Where and how is value added? What part of our own process? How does this compare with competition?

While it is beyond the scope of this book to explore in detail competitive cost strategy, (4) above deserves some explanation because it is the source of confusion. As companies become more experienced with the means of production, they find that they are often (but not exclusively) able to reduce unit costs by economies of scale: the *experience cost curve* should go down over time.

The *learning cost curve* is often confused with this but it is separate: learning is concerned not with taking the existing unit costs and, by experience, reducing them, but with analysis of customers, markets, suppliers and outside factors over time to understand the factors that really drive the costs in the company. Both curves are important.

Let us take each of the questions and look at what needs to be done.

COST COMPARISON WITH THE COMPETITION

The starting point has to be an analysis of the company's own costs and value added. Here it is useful to follow a conventional analysis of raw materials, direct costs, indirect costs and overheads etc. It will be quite difficult to determine what competitor costs really are in these areas. More importantly from a strategy viewpoint, it will not necessarily get at what is important competitively and how value is added by the company.

For strategy it is more useful to know what really *influences* costs and profits in the marketplace. Much of this can be done within the company by analyzing each of the stages of the product or service (see Table 18.1) and assessing where value is added.

The logic covered by the questions in the table is intended to relate to the product or service before contact with the company and then follow it through as a sale is made. No attempt is made to be fully comprehensive but it should be possible for the reader to follow the same logic for other situations (eg banking or retailing). The aim is partly to explore how value is added by us and our competitors: the value chain. The other purpose is to identify our costs relative to competitiveness as a starting point for reducing them.

No case study is quoted in this area because the published detail is rarely available. But in every case, the company will have access to its own cost profile and can use it to determine answers to many of the questions posed.

Table 18.1 Cost comparisons and value added

Product or service	How does our product or service compare with the competition as assessed by the target customer? What benefits does it offer? At what price?
Purchasing	Could we buy-in product rather than make it? What do our competitors do? Do we have economies of scale in purchasing?
Labour costs	How do our labour costs compare? Is labour an important total part of our costs? What happens if the process is more mechanized? Is our company more or less unionized than the competitors? What about incentives compared to competition and other benefits?
Research costs	Is this important for company development? How much does the competition spend? More or less effectively and why?
Raw materials	Do we use the same quality of raw materials as the competition? Does this have a major effect on cost? How does our mix of products compare with competitors? What would happen if the mix changed? Are there any special tie-ups between our competitors and their suppliers, eg on technical standards or quality standards? How do our own arrangements compare? Does our competitor share purchasing with another business area that could reduce costs? Do we, or could we?

Processing	Do we use the same processes as the competition? At the same cost?
	In production? Do we have the same volume from the same plant of the same age as our competitors?
Distribution	What dealers would we use to distribute our products? At what cost? What does our competition do? Special linkages?
	What means of distribution would we use? How does this compare with the competition? What extra will it cost to distribute from the home country? What tariffs? Other barriers?
Customers	What level of service do we currently offer customers? In delivery time? In salesforce calling? How would this compare to competition both actual and potential?
	What do we expect to invest in marketing funds? How does this compare with the competition? Would we outspend the competition? Has this ever happened to them before? How did they react?
	What tie-ups are we seeking with customers in the home country? Are they important? Do we sell a lot to a few or do we have many customers? How do our competitors serve their customers? Do they have tie-ups and, if so, what would it cost to break them?

IS THE COMPANY A LOW-COST PRODUCER?

From analysis of the questions in Table 18.1, it should be possible to determine whether the company is a low-cost producer. It may also be possible to establish whether it is the *lowest*-cost producer, but this needs to be treated with some caution: competitors have a habit of changing the rules!

Case Study: Peugeot Citroën SA, France

Data
One of Europe's top six car producers.
Turnover (Ffr million)

	1988	1992
Peugeot holdings	486	–
Peugeot cars	87358	88250
Citroën cars	56894	59827
Other	1800	423
Mechanical/services	13562	6931
Inter-company	(21648)	–
Total	138452	155431
Return on capital:	11.2%	7.9%
% sales in home country:	75 approx.	42
% sales in rest of Europe:		50
% sales in rest of world:		8

European and global activity

Peugeot rescued the UK former Chrysler plant in 1979. Subsequently, it has embarked on a programme of new models and plant investment to match any other company in the EC. It has had some considerable success but still relies on France for its major sales, which makes it vulnerable in the single Europe as barriers are reduced by 1999.

It is still investing in plant to reduce costs and obtain higher quality.

Keypoint on lower costs

Along with the other major European producers, Peugeot, in its Annual Report, produces detailed sales and production statistics for each model. It also quotes its levels of capital investment (eg for 1992 these were Peugeot Ffr 6815 million and Citroën Ffr 6209 million with some detail on the nature of expenditure. It also gives details of employees:

	1988 ('000)	1992 ('000)
Citroën	58	48
Peugeot	83	78
Other	2	9
Mechanical services	15	16
Total	158	151
of which France	126	123
Other	32	28

Now there is no point in pretending that as a result of this limited data all is now clear about Peugeot Citroën costs. But using available additional information on production of individual models and some reasonable estimates of raw material input costs, it should be possible to arrive at some idea of how the car company's costs break down.

Similarly, by using the sales force 'grapevine', it should be possible to estimate what pricing levels are actually being offered to car dealers and what other support is being supplied.

The same will apply to the other car companies. This is the beginning of the cost analysis to answer the questions posed above.

COST REASSESSMENT LEADING TO NEW COMPETITIVE STRATEGY

The really interesting aspect of cost analysis is that it can lead to a total reassessment of the advantages a company has versus its competitors. This may in turn lead to a totally new strategy. We will touch on this again in the next chapter on competitive advantage. The starting point is to further develop the cost analysis. There are four keys to this work:

1. Understanding what costs really have an effect on the profit line, both for the company and its competition.
2. Exploring how and where value is added in the company as raw materials are turned into a finished product or service.
3. Understanding the linkages between cost areas, both for your company and your competitors. A classic linkage is that between quality and customer satisfaction: it may actually pay to insert extra quality checks to improve

performance reliability even if this puts up the production cost. Nissan and Toyota have taught some European car manufacturers here.

4. Radical thinking on what customers really want in terms of product and service and how best to achieve this, perhaps even cutting some customers or reaching them by a new route.

In tackling European and global markets, it is not really possible in the abstract to state categorically the single best solution: it will depend on the individual circumstances.

It may be most efficient just to launch the existing product into other international markets – for example, if it is unique. However, it may be essential to spend some time thoroughly investigating competitors' cost profiles if there is strong competition in other countries. On balance, it is probably better to be cautious and seek answers in two main areas: (1) Where does our company stand versus competition on low cost production? Are we the lowest cost producer?; and (2) What are the cost linkages in our industry? What can we leverage better?

Case Study: Bertelsmann AG, Germany

Data
One of the world's top publishers.
1992 turnover (DM million)

	Germany	International	Total
Books: German language	1283	288	1571
Publishing: international	481	1254	1735
International book and record clubs	–	2313	2313
Printing & manufacturing	1599	1469	3068
Music & video	885	3033	3918
Electronic media	483	251	734
Magazine publishing*	1891	1714	3605
Total	6052	9903	15955

* Gruener & Jahr

Return on capital: 23.1%
% sales in home country: 38
% sales in rest of Europe: 35
% sales in rest of world: 27

European and global activity
Bertelsmann is one of Europe's great media companies. In addition to the above, it also has interests in Radio Television Luxembourg and Swiss and German telephone books. It has extensive world media operations, many of which have been acquired in the last few years. For example – *Books & record clubs:* Germany; Austria; Switzerland; France; Canada; and Belgium. *Publishing:* Doubleday (USA); Bantam/Transworld (USA/Europe); and Siedler (Germany). *Printing:* interests in Germany, Italy, Spain, Portugal, Austria, USA. *Music and video:* Acquired RCA and Ariola (No. 1 in USA, No. 2 in UK), plus a joint venture with JVC in Japan. *Magazines:* strong German editions plus France, UK, Spain and USA.

Bertelsmann is not only large but also profitable. In the 1990s it has identified electronic media as a major growth area.

Keypoint on low cost advantage
Bertelsmann was under-presented in the UK in the late 1980s. It then launched two magazines (based on similar names in Germany) for female readers: Best and Prima. Both were aggressively priced, well researched and presented. Essentially, they used the cost experience and skills the company had acquired over the years in Germany. They have proved formidable competition to the well established UK women's magazines (dominated by Reed Elsevier: see Part III) and have been successful. Average sales in 1992 were 587,000 for Best and 643,000 for Prima.

Here, the company used its printing and publishing cost experience, first to analyze every aspect of UK and German comparative costs. Thus it was able to establish the lowest cost means of production. Then Bertelsmann was able to probe the issue of cost linkages with its German parent and choose the lowest-cost route.

COMPARISON WITH COMPETITION ON LEARNING AND EXPERIENCE COST CURVES

Using existing knowledge can shorten the *learning curve* and produce cost advantage quickly, as Bertelsmann has shown all over Europe and the USA.

The Japanese have also not hesitated in buying experienced management and using this knowledge to move fast along the cost route. In 1989, Sony wanted a share of the growing telecommunications market in Europe. It therefore recruited the head of the European Commission on Telecommunications, Professor Tjakka Schuringa, to start a new company called Sony Telecom based in The Netherlands. This significantly shortened the learning process surrounding the minefield of European telecommunications standardization. However, it should be said that Sony Telecom was still relatively small in Europe in 1992.

The learning curve would be even steeper for competitors if a company was able to introduce to this process some form of technical development that was proprietary to itself. IBM attempted to do this with its second generation personal computers in the PS/2 series, containing proprietary hardware and software. This followed the declining market share of its previous version which was 'cloned' by market competitors to such an extent that they were able to produce a better machine more cheaply.

Similarly, the experience curve on production costs can also be shortened by buying-in expertise, as well as by straightforward investment in plant and equipment. It is reasonably well established that for on-going manufacturing processes it should be possible to reduce costs by 20–30 per cent each time production experience doubles for the industry (not for the company). Examining both where your own company is, and estimating where competitors should be, will provide useful evidence to evaluate this.

Case Study: MAN AG, Germany

Data
One of Europe's leading groups in truck manufacture, printing presses and steel trading.
1992 turnover (DM million)

Trucks	7901	MAN Trucks
Steel trading & construction	3208	Ferrostaal

Industrial plant & steel	1720	MAN GHH
Printing presses	2369	MAN Roland
Diesel	1442	MAN B&W Diesel
Space and energy technology	346	MAN Technologie
Steelmaking equipment	2049	SMS
Engineering	391	Renk
Other	371	
Inter-company	(626)	
Total	19171	

Return on capital: 3.7%
% sales in home country: 42
% sales in rest of Europe: 26
% sales in rest of world: 32

European and global activity
During the late 1980s, MAN concentrated on internal reorganization to bring the company back into profit. Its main initiative across Europe was to gain control, in co-operation with Daimler Benz, of the Spanish truck maker ENASA. However, it did not complete the deal.

In 1989, MAN acquired the Steyr truck operations of Steyr-Daimler-Puch in Austria. This made MAN one of the world's leading truck makers with a European market share of 15%: classic strategy to establish a strong share in a market segment.

During 1989, the company agreed to purchase the diesel engine business of the large Swiss firm, Sulzer, but this was blocked by the German Federal Cartel Office. The deal would have made MAN the sole supplier of large two-stroke engines to world shipyards: such machines account for 10% of the cost of large cargo ships. MAN had licensees for its engines but restricted sales from such suppliers to third parties, and would not loosen these. During the early 1990s it consolidated its main acquisitions against a background of depressed world markets.

Keypoint on cost advantage
MAN's biggest single business is trucks. In its peak year of 1984, it sold 26,500 units and had a break-even of 25,000 units. This made the company vulnerable if the market declined. Substantial measures were undertaken to bring the break-even down to below 20,000 units (new models, a cost overhaul and streamlining of production, distribution and servicing). This involved heavy capital expenditure but, in the relatively high labour cost German economy, this was essential. By installing the latest equipment, MAN gained not only from newer machinery but also by moving up the learning curve: taking advantage of newer methodology across a number of fields.

More difficult (but not impossible) to estimate for MAN Trucks is the cost advantage gained from having its own supply of steel products. Here is a cost-link that could provide real strategic advantage to the company, if steel costs are a large part of total truck costs. The same may also be true of diesel engines for installation in vehicles. In practice, a competitor is likely to have sufficient knowledge of comparative costs to be able to assess the advantage to be gained here.

CONCLUSIONS

The key questions raised in Table 18.1 need answers if European and global expansion is to be successful. The case studies show how published information, plus some intelligent speculation, can suggest answers sufficient to establish what needs to be done. Specifically, it should establish whether more investment to reduce costs will be required.

CHAPTER 19

Competitor Strategy: Sustainable Competitive Advantage

Competitive advantage is the winning attribute not possessed by competitors. Fundamentally, the lowering of international boundaries brings together into one market companies supplying products or services that are essentially the same and no longer protected by national borders: suddenly there will be new winners and losers.

Clearly, European and global companies will want to act but the problem is not just the uncertainty of what barriers will come down and when this will happen but, most importantly, how can a company win in this new situation?

The answer is by developing competitive advantage. How is this done? It is usually based on some combination of the following:

1. Lowest competitive relative costs: for example, through economies of scale, tight cost control and better sourcing of products. We looked at some of these areas in the previous chapter.
2. Product or service differentiation: for example, this might be based on superior performance, strong branding or better value for money. We discussed this topic under 'Customer strategy'.
3. Customer targeting: for example, a customer group seeking superior quality and reliability. We looked at this under 'Customer strategy', particularly in terms of *broad and narrow target groups*.

It is important in tackling the new Europe that a *sustainable* advantage is achieved: there would be little point in securing an advantage that could be easily countered by competitors.

SOURCES OF COMPETITIVE ADVANTAGE

Where do these advantages come from? They essentially derive from *company strengths*, as we saw earlier:

- Superior skills from areas the company is particularly good at (eg design expertise, fast service response and specialized segment knowledge); and
- Superior resources achieved by the company over time (eg low-cost production, finance, distribution and production capacity).
- Superior or even unique value added via low costs and/or special linkages with suppliers, customers and across the company itself.

In developing competitive advantage, every company will therefore want to look at its own skills and resources in relation to international competitors. Clearly, this could potentially be a vast task, so many companies will probably select out a few competitors to look at in depth.

It should be evident that much of the book has been designed to develop aspects of competitive advantage, along with other facets of strategy. There is, therefore, no need to repeat these elements here. What we will do is to examine three industries that illustrate various relevant aspects for international industries.

Case Study: European aerospace and defence companies

Data

	Country	1992 sales (US$ million)			
		Total	Destination of sales		
			Home	Rest of Europe	Rest of world
			(%)	(%)	(%)
European companies					
*Deutsche Aerospace	Ger	11262			
Aerospatiale	Fra	10367	32		68
**British Aerospace	UK	9069	21		79
Thomson-CSF	Fra	6758	42	20	38
SNECMA	Fra	4531	40		60
**GEC	UK	4460	34		66
**Rolls Royce	UK	3542	30	12	58
Dassault	Fra	3214	52		48
GIAT	Fra	2200	na		
**Matra	Fra	2186	na		
Celsius	Swe	1871	na		
Oerlikon	Swi	1074	na		

* wholly owned subsidiary of Daimler Benz
** only part of total turnover of company

Selected US aerospace and defence companies					
Boeing	USA	30414	42	24***	34
McDonnell Douglas	USA	17314	71	13***	16
Raytheon	USA	6230	90 est.		10
Rockwell	USA	3169	na		

*** % sales for the whole of Europe

Note:
1. In general, the return on capital is either misleading or not available for most of the companies above. However, most were undergoing a period of profound change and therefore showing losses or only small profits in 1992.
2. Italian aerospace interests, including the company Alenia, were concentrated in Finnmechanica with a turnover of around US$ 4 billion in 1990: another subsidiary of IRI (see chapter 8).

European and global activity
Many companies manufacture items both for civil and military use but do not provide separate sales data. However, strategies for the two groups differ in degree and are therefore worth examining separately.

Military aerospace and defence has been governed by a substantial contraction in defence business from the early 1990s with the end of confrontation between the West and the USSR. However, there are still important sales orders to be obtained, eg new military strike aircraft for NATO and continued purchases by Middle Eastern countries. Clearly, this is a global industry.

Development costs for such items are substantial and cannot be justified by sales in one country alone. Hence in Europe there has been extensive cross-border cooperation as a fundamental part of strategy. Defence links with national governments are another essential element of strategy. Beyond this, high levels of R&D and manufacturing skills are also important.

Civil aerospace markets can usefully be segmented into large and small aircraft. In the large category, three manufacturers dominate global markets: Boeing, McDonnell Douglas and the Airbus Consortium (which includes Deutsche Aerospace, Aerospatiale and British Aerospace). In medium and small aircraft, there are many companies along with overcapacity in the industry.

The civil aircraft market was marked by world-wide recession in the early 1990s. It was also affected by the Gulf War and its aftermath. The levels of R&D costs, technical skills and basic investment are not dissimilar to military developments. Clearly, national government involvement is not necessarily so direct as in the military market, but it can be important in practice for some sales orders.

For both sectors, European aerospace and defence companies will be more likely to survive in new alliances. The European Airbus is an example of the cooperative strategy required. But plenty of others have developed over the last few years:

- Thomson-CSF bought the defence business of Philips NV in France (more details, see Part III).
- Thomson-CSF and Aerospatiale combined their defence electronics and avionics operations.
- GEC bought the defence interests (amongst other parts) of Plessey in a joint bid with Siemens AG.
- GEC acquired the radar interests of another smaller British supplier, Ferranti, to become the dominant supplier in the British defence market.
- British Aerospace purchased the armament business of the British government known as the Royal Ordnance.
- Daimler Benz bought the troubled Germany company Messerschmitt Bolkow Blohm (MBB), now renamed Deutsche Aerospace, which is chiefly involved in defence.
- Aerospatiale and Deutsche Aerospace merged their helicopter interests in 1992.
- GIAT, the French national armaments company, has development deals with Aerospatiale and Renault and acquired the Belgian arms company FN in 1991.
- British Aerospace and Thompson-CSF planned to merge their missile businesses into 1989. They abandoned the link in 1991. In 1993, BAe tried again but this time with Matra.
- Four German and French companies agreed to combine their rocket motor interests in 1992.
- Deutsche Aerospace took over Fokker (Net) in 1992.

None of these new European groupings can yet be said to have proved itself: there will be integration problems that will take several years to resolve. In addition, the changes in eastern Europe make it likely that there will be a further decline in the size of the defence market over the next five years which will add to pressures. The civil airline market will only recover slowly.

In spite of the search for size, none of the companies listed above is as large as the top five US defence companies in terms of sales. Thus unit costs are likely to be significantly higher than for US competitors. Because defence procurement is a partially global market, this means that defence companies in Europe will have a tough time over the next few years. They will need to rely on technical innovation for success.

Keypoint on competitive advantage
This needs to be examined for the various *markets* in which each company is involved rather than for the whole defence industry (eg fighters for British Aerospace, missiles for Aerospatiale, etc). Using the categories from earlier in the chapter, we can identify the following as examples for British Aerospace plc:

1. *Broad group customers:* national governments agreeing to purchase the Tornado military aircraft from British Aerospace.
2. *Narrow group customers:* individual airforces requiring the Hawk jet trainer. (Here we have a narrow specialized requirement within an overall industry.)
3. *Product differentiation:* Harrier vertical take-off jet fighters from British Aerospace. These are quite unique in their technical ability. Clearly, they sell beyond Europe.
4. *Cost leadership:* British Aerospace is part of the 'Airbus Industrie' consortium. As a consequence of building one part – the wings – the company should be able to reduce costs in this area substantially.

More generally, customer targeting in the defence business, along with product differentiation and cost leadership, means considering the relevant political alliances. Thus to achieve sales, European governmental contacts are vital but only as a starting point to global activity – competing companies may well be outside Europe. Hence, competitive advantage cannot just be developed by comparison with other European companies.

While much of the development in Europe during the 1980s has led to some pan-European links, the declining market, higher development costs and global customers all suggest that cross-Atlantic alliances may even be needed in the late 1990s, eg on a replacement for Concorde.

Case Study: European banks

Data
September 1993 market capitalisation (US$ million)

Hong Kong and Shanghai Bank	UK	27352
Deutsche Bank	Ger	22586
Union Bank of Switzerland	Swi	20321
National Westminster Bank	UK	12788
Barclays Bank	UK	12750
Credit Suisse Holding	Swi	11874
Swiss Bank Corporation	Swi	11782
Lloyds Bank	UK	11283
Dresdner Bank	Ger	10566
ABN Amro Bank	Net	9707
Banque de Suez	Fra	9099
Societe General	Fra	8984
Abbey National	UK	8219
Paribas	Fra	7790
Banco Bilbao Vizcaya	Spa	6060
Bayerische VereinsBank	Ger	6042
Bayerische Hypotheke Bank	Ger	5888
Banco de Santander	Spa	5723

CommerzBank	Ger	5500
Argentaria	Spa	5249
TSB Group	UK	55089

Note: some leading European banks do not appear above because they are still owned by their national governments and not quoted on a stock exchange. Banque Nationale de Paris and the banks controlled by IRI, Italy, are examples. Some were in the process of being privatised at the time of writing.

Source: 'Top 500 European Companies' *Financial Times*, January 1994. Quoted with permission.

European and global activity
Because the large national banks are so coy about revealing even the simplest details of their activities, it is difficult to obtain the base data in a comparable form: hence the above, more limited information. It is less difficult to understand what is happening across European *retail banking*: only some minor ventures beyond national boundaries.

With Europe's largest retail banks in place for many years and managing large resources, it would be very difficult for a bank to expand in Europe outside its home base without acquiring an existing banking network. For example, Dresdner and Banque Nationale de Paris were reported to be interested in purchasing the regional British bank, Yorkshire Bank, when it was for sale early in 1990. In the event, it was sold to an Australian banking group.

Nevertheless, Banco Santander in 1989 bought a 10% share in the Royal Bank of Scotland, which in turn bought 2.5% of the Spanish bank. It will be some time before any major business emerges from this link-up, with a 'strong element of self-defence' having been reported as a possible reason for the move. By 1994, nothing significant appeared to have emerged.

For many years, there was an informal understanding between European banks that they would not do business in each others' territories. This broke down in commercial banking first and, more recently, in retail banking.

In *commercial banking*, Deutsche Bank in 1989 acquired the British merchant bank, Morgan Grenfell for around US$1.6 billion. This followed the German bank's purchase of a 99-branch Italian bank in 1986.

In 1993, it acquired a Spanish retail bank. Credit Lyonnais is also reported to be developing pan-European ambitions in commercial banking. It bought an Italian bank and a Belgian bank during 1989. In 1990, it moved into retail banking in Spain and, in 1993, into German banking. In 1994, it became over-extended and needed bailing out by the French government. From the UK, Nat West, Barclays and TSB have all made cautious moves into other European countries. But they faced the problem outlined above of competing with the existing national networks.

In the longer term, the trend to larger industrial world-wide corporations and to large US and Japanese banks may put increased pressure on some of Europe's largest banks to amalgamate, simply to keep business from going elsewhere. But it would need a major upheaval to make this happen quickly. Although some commercial banking is clearly global, most retail banking is not even pan-European.

Keypoint on competitive advantage
European retail banks have been chosen deliberately in this chapter because they ostensibly are so similar. In one sense, there is very limited competitive advantage between them, particularly in high street retail banking: they are all much the same. However, one of the reasons the industry is so stable right across Europe is that the banks arguably have, for the reasons described earlier, used their considerable advantage with skill to keep out unwanted new entrants. The retail bankers' competitive skill has been used to put together a stable market of banks, all content with their respective market shares. This market situation maximizes long-term profit.

> The destabilizing influence has come in the shape of other sources of lending finance: the US banks and, more recently, the UK building societies have used this as their entry point. A couple of UK building societies have now moved in a very limited way into Europe.
>
> Once such lenders establish a retail network, then the existing retail banks have little competitive advantage. Moreover, the market equilibrium is destabilized and profit margins come under pressure. This is precisely what has happened in the UK over the years leading up to 1990. It may happen elsewhere in Europe in the late 1990s.

Competitive advantage is more likely to be sustainable where some element of differentiation, or low costs are involved. This is associated with the flexibility that comes from high value-added activities. For example, it is difficult to develop sustainable advantage in sugar commodity trading and easier in patented drug manufacture. An area such as mining and metals with relatively low value-added does not lend itself easily to sustainable competitive advantage.

Case Study: Selected European metals and mining companies

Data
1992 turnover (US$ million)

ˣRTZ	UK	5368	includes aluminium and mining activities
*Degussa	Ger	4316	includes metals trading and precious metals
***Union Miniere	Bel	3945	non-ferrous metals
Trelleborg	Swe	3700	non-ferrous metals
**VAW	Ger	3548	aluminium
*Pechiney	Fra	3464	aluminium
*Alusuisse Lonza	Swi	2713	aluminium
SMI	Ita	2500 est	non-ferrous metals
*Outukumpu	Fin	2000 est	non-ferrous metals, government owned at 1992
*Johnson Matthey	UK	1686	precious metals
*Austrian Industries	Aus	1535	aluminium and non-ferrous metals
****Nord Deutsche Affinerie	Ger	1354	non-ferrous metals
*Hoogevens	Net	1251	aluminium
*Preussag	Ger	1016	non-ferrous metals
*MetalEurop	Fra	950	non-ferrous metals

* only part of total turnover of company
** subsidiary of Viag, Germany
*** wholly owned company of Societé Generale de Belgique
**** linked with Metallgesellschaft, Germany

Note: iron and steel activities are excluded from the above.

European and global activity
While all the companies are involved in global industries, it is useful to divide them into three groups for business strategy purposes:

■ aluminium

- precious metals, eg gold, silver and platinum
- other non-ferrous metals, eg zinc, copper and lead.

It is also important to distinguish between those companies that mine the ore and those that smelt and refine it.

Aluminium is used in building construction and general fabrication. There is also a large and growing market in aluminium containers and cans. Strategies in this area rely on cheap electricity sources and economies of scale in the production process. They have also increasingly employed ever-widening and specialised technical treatments and manufacture of the basic metal to produce more specialist uses. A major strategic problem of the mid-1990s has been small quantities of cheap imports from Eastern Europe.

Precious metals are used in small quantities for specialist purposes. They have higher prices than some metals but are still subject to commodity fluctuations. They rely on specialist manufacturing processes.

Other non-ferrous metals have many engineering uses, such as in piping and electrical cabling. They are produced by fairly basic processes that are not always environment-friendly. Metallgesellschaft spent much of the early 1990s investing around 1 billion DM in new plant. By 1993, it was reporting major losses and said it was likely to shut down the new plant as it had proved unprofitable. There were still too many companies around Europe smelting non-ferrous metals in cheaper, if cruder, factories.

The largest company, RTZ, had a clear strategy in the mid-1990s: to seek and secure the strongest position in whichever mining market it chose to enter. Within this, it recognised across the world the strong national feelings of ownership of some mines and therefore gave its plant managers significant autonomy. It was also quite willing to consider joint ventures if this assisted this process.

RTZ judged that a fundamental aspect of its strategy was to be the lowest cost producer, essential in a low value-added business. Hence it sought high grade mining deposits that could be mined cheaply with the best equipment. It had only limited involvement in smelting.

Union Miniere and NordDeutsche Affinerie are essentially refiners of non-ferrous metals. Because such products are commodities and difficult to differentiate, both companies reported much lower profits during the weak economic activity of the early 1990s, having 2.7% and 1.25% returns on capital respectively. The two companies, along with others in the industry, were primarily involved in retrenchment strategies during this period; plant closures, redundancies, regrouping to improve responsiveness to markets and further definition of the individual responsibility of managers.

Keypoint on competitive advantage
How does a mining and metals company build competitive advantage? Several methods are being used: quality of assets; investment in mining and processing techniques to reduce costs; downstream market linkages into metals production, packaging, etc.; and political and economic links with producer countries. There are no universal solutions but all these techniques have been used to strengthen company market competitiveness.

DEALING WITH UNCERTAINTY

One of the major difficulties in dealing with European and global markets in the mid 1990s is that much still remains to be resolved: there is still a great deal of uncertainty over tariffs, taxes, timing and so on. Couple this with predicting what competitors might do and the task can be very complex. It is my own belief that this is another reason why some companies have so far been reluctant to act. There are many problems.

But business is always full of uncertainties: that is what gives it some spice. The important aspect is how to work in this situation. There are three basic steps:

1. The development of industry scenarios;
2. The establishment within these of the best and worst case for the company concerned; and
3. The assessment of probability outcome and selection of the action to be taken (eg hedging, influencing, maintaining flexibility, etc.).

The development of *industry scenarios* is the first step: these show the current picture in the international market and make some attempt to predict how it will change. This book has constructed some of these for a wide range of industries, though in much less detail than most companies would require in practice.

Best and worst case outcomes can be derived from the background industry work and predictions of competitor activity: what would happen if, for example, we launch in France and there is no response so we obtain large numbers of new customers (best) case; or we launch in France and we make no headway, while at the same time our French competitor has made major sales gains in our home territory (worst case)?

On the unique circumstances surrounding the new European and global trade agreements and, especially, strategies just to gain distribution for products, we will come back to the *action required* at the end of Part II.

CHAPTER 20

Competitor Strategy: Competitor Response to New Entrants

If a company is really committed to a market then aggressive entry from outside can cause a major battle to take place, with lower profit margins all round. Equally, this could even provoke retaliation in the home country. But let us for the moment concentrate on entry into other international markets.

In assessing competitive response to entry, it is important to establish what rules the existing market will set: for example, the same margins and same degree of service might be over-restrictive to newcomers but any variation might so upset the existing market that retaliation would be swift and very painful.

If the competitor will admit other companies, then it may also feel happier with those that are closer to its existing objectives: a European company with a high earnings per share objective may be preferable to a Japanese company with a bottomless purse and long time horizon.

In assessing competitive response, we need, therefore, to probe two areas:

1. What share of the target market is it right to aim for? What share might an existing company allow to an entrant?
2. Given the share objective, what would it be worthwhile trying to signal to companies already in the marketplace that would satisfy them?

SHARE OBJECTIVE

For most companies, wiping competition out completely is both strategically naive and extraordinarily expensive. It may even prove completely useless if the market changes and allows entry to another tranche of competitors. Moreover, in the European Union it may be contrary to the law.

In the early 1970s in part of the UK consumer goods industry, there were three competitors in a semi-commodity market. One of the three was clear market leader with a follower and a third rather weaker competitor whose profits could be manipulated by the leader. The leader decided that the third competitor needed to be removed. After a 10-year war of attrition this duly happened in the early 1980s. Unfortunately for the leader, consumer tastes then changed towards more healthy products that could be better supplied by smaller companies: the hard-won market concentration was lost and profitability was no higher than in the earlier much stronger strategic position with a compliant third competitor.

This was of absolutely no consolation to the competitor squeezed out. Also, having removed this albatross, the third competitor then became a takeover target and was duly swallowed up by another company.

Whilst this might be regarded as an extreme case, it does show the importance of not taking on an unwinnable battle. It also illustrates the need to assess what the competition will allow a new entrant to achieve. Some companies will defend their European market positions with vigour. For example, in UK instant coffee, Nestlé is the market leader with Nescafé, followed by General Foods with Maxwell House and other brands. A new entrant with a cut-price strongly-branded product invites retaliation from the leaders, as a result of which no company will win. Similarly in German supermarket retailing, Aldi has a strong share of low-price, value for money food retailing in Germany. A new entrant coming in on a strong price platform would invite a powerful and vigorous response from Aldi. There would only be one winner and it would not be the new entrant. In both these cases, the share objective would have to be very modest to avoid competitive retaliation. It would clearly be better to differentiate the product or service, but if the existing companies see the entrant as a threat then this will not help.

Some companies may feel they need to protect their share particularly strongly. Let us look at a couple of examples.

Case Study: Oerlikon Buhrle AG, Switzerland

Data
Defence, engineering and consumer products company.
1992 turnover (Sfr million)

Military	1417
Bally shoes, etc	1046
Mechanical engineering products	439
Other	472
Total	3374

Return on capital: 7.9%
% sales in Europe: na
% sales in home country: na

European and global activity
The company, control of which still remains in the Buhrle family, is built on the famous Oerlikon gun designs and skills. As these products have become more mature, the company has moved into related areas of technology with air defence systems, training aircraft, etc. Essentially, these are global markets, as we have seen.

In 1988, the company finally completed its withdrawal from machine tools having 'misread' the market over many years. The company believed it was fortunate to have bought into consumer shoe manufacture with the up-market Bally range which sells well around the world: it is better protected than others against cheap imports.

With its Bally shoe range and its involvement in defence systems (including Leopard tank systems with Germany), Oerlikon Buhrle is already operating across European and global markets.

Keypoint on protecting basic market share
In the 1980s, the company invested over US$ 650 million to develop the Adats anti-aircraft guided missile system. By late 1990, it had sold 36 units to the Canadian army and 4 units to the US army. The US army had repeatedly put off ordering another 250 units.

Apart from the US arms manufacturer Martin Marietta, Oerlikon Buhrle was by itself. For years it pinned all its hopes on entering the US market. It reported major losses for six years in order to pursue this dream. Eventually, in late 1990, the Swiss banks forced the resignation of the chairman and started massive restructuring. By 1992 the company was back in profit. However good the technology, market protection can sometimes prove costly to the new entrant.

Case Study: Alusuisse Lonza, Switzerland and Pechiney, France

Data
Amongst other areas, both companies have strong business interests in the European aluminium industry.
1992 turnover (US$ million)

Pechiney SA		Alusuisse Lonza SA	
Aluminium	3464	Aluminium	2713
Packaging	5963	Chemicals	1150
Engineered products	969	Packaging	1033
Other products	1376	Other	67
International trade	1197		
Total	12969	Total	4963
Return on capital:	6.8%		8.6%
% sales in home country:	37		11
% sales in rest of Europe:	32		71
% sales in rest of world:	31		18

European and global activity: Pechiney
Pechiney concentrated on its packaging activity in the late 1980s, rather than focusing on aluminium. Principally, it acquired a subsidiary of American Can to make it one of the largest packaging companies in the world.

More recently, it has acquired a series of electrical and plastics companies around the world. There is no connection with packaging.

European and global activity: Alusuisse
As well as Switzerland, the company has plant in the UK, USA, Germany and Italy. Although it has continued to invest heavily in existing plant both in Switzerland and other parts of Europe, it now believes that metal production is no longer financially viable in high-cost Switzerland. It has therefore changed strategy, reducing the emphasis on aluminium. It describes its strategy as seeking higher added value in chemicals and packaging.

Keypoint on protecting basic market share
Here we have a market that is already international. We also have two companies that have involvement in other areas besides the market in question. Both companies are concentrating in the basic area by vertical integration from aluminium into packaging: they are protecting market share by buying up users of their products.

Pechiney has entered a new geographic market, without a major response from existing competitors, by acquiring one of them. This is the classic tactic for avoiding share protection problems but it takes substantial resources.

Both Alusuisse Lonza and Pechiney might be affected by a new entrant to the European aluminium market. Outside a takeover, they would both have some warning of the event: aluminium capacity cannot be set up overnight. They would therefore be in a position to take action: the level of action would depend on the threat seen, the aggression of the new company and the differentiation of its new product.

NEW ENTRY SIGNALS TO EXISTING COMPANIES

Let us turn to the matter of what the new entrant tries to signal to existing companies in various international markets to ensure that entry is smoother than might otherwise be the case. It should be noted that this needs to be done with some care or regulatory authorities such as the European Commission might take the view that there is collusion, even if this is not the case at all. Public means of announcing intentions are therefore required rather than private meetings with potential competitors: for example, public relations releases, newspaper and magazine articles and trade association meetings.

What might be signalled clearly depends on the precise circumstances, but here are some general points that might be considered as a public statement of intentions:

- A strategy that enhances the industry and expands the market is much more likely to be acceptable;
- Similar objectives for profitability and cash generation are much more likely to re-assure existing companies that their margins will not be cut;
- A strategy that reinforces market segmentation in a supportive fashion might be more acceptable. For example, a strategy seeking small sales from the higher-priced end of the market might allay suspicion. There are several European examples of where this is happening now.
- Satisfaction with small market share with limited risk and a desire not to upset the market: there are also several examples of this.

There is no point in saying something that is untrue. Apart from the ethics of such a statement, existing competitors will not be without some business judgement: an oil company in the early 1980s stating that it had little cash and its establishment of a large petrochemical complex was no threat to anyone would have had limited credibility. Similarly a Japanese electronics company stating that it had only limited share objectives and no real long-term commitment to a market would be similarly incredible. The converse of this is why such companies are powerful competitors.

Case Study: Rheinisch-Westfalisches Elektrizitätswerk, Germany

Data

Germany's fifth largest electricity company and largest company overall; voting shares controlled by municipalities.

Turnover (DM million)

	1988	1992
Electricity	16517	16729
Gas	418	743
Water	53	48
Other	898	1076
Sub-total	17886	18596
Mining and raw materials	852	2319
Petroleum & chemicals	3461*	12996*
Other plant construction & services	3388	5597
Waste management		706
Civil engineering		7517
Total	25585*	53094*

*Excludes petroleum tax of DM1272 million 1988 and DM7892 million 1992

Return on capital:	6.4%	2.1%
% sales in home country:	85	83
% sales in rest of Europe:	9	6
% sales in rest of world:	6	11

Single market activity

RWE's main activity is the supply of electricity to large parts of northern Germany and industrial units elsewhere in the country. It also has coal (lignite) mines and distributes petrol and chemicals: in June 1988, the company acquired Deutsche Texaco for DM 2.2 billion.

In late 1988, the company also bought a US rotary print manufacturing company for US$300 million and, subject to German federal cartel approval, a German waste disposal company. In 1989, it made its first single market move as outlined below. In the early 1990s, it acquired German construction companies, including Hochtief.

There seems to be little consistency to RWE's acquisition policy in terms of product areas: oil, construction and waste disposal companies do not fit obviously together. For good European strategy, this might even be said to be a wasted opportunity. Here is a case for a company to make its business logic more public.

Keypoint on new market entry signals

RWE announced in September 1989 that it was negotiating to take a 5% share in Union Electrica-Fenosa, Spain's fourth largest electrical utility. The cost was likely to be in the region of Ptas 5 billion and the shareholding would be similar to that held by Endesa, the largest Spanish electricity company. Other shares in Union Electrica-Fenosa were widely held.

Importantly, RWE signalled during the talks (and to the market afterwards) that it was 'powerful and privately owned'. This was in sharp contrast to the nationalized Electricité de France (EDF) which had also been reported as interested in Spain: extreme caution is said to have been the principal response of Spain's electricity companies to the informal EDF approaches.

As a result of its careful public statements, RWE's approach was not rebuffed, unlike the EDF soundings. RWE had correctly assessed the competitive situation and sent out the right market signals. For some days, the deal looked as if it was going to be successful. Subsequently, the Spanish energy ministry put an effective block on the RWE move for policy reasons. But the company put its case as well as it could in the circumstances and its risk was low. Moreover, the Spanish authorities subsequently permitted RWE and Fenosa to conclude an agreement in 1992 that 'anticipates the formation of joint ventures in Spain and Germany'.

CONCLUSION

It is essential to plot entry strategy very carefully and to signal this to existing companies: leaving it to chance is asking for trouble and will impact on profits.

CHAPTER 21

Competitor Strategy: Assess Likely Market Changes Over Five Years

With all the uncertainties over tariffs and other barriers plus the unresolved negotiations in so many markets, it may seem extraordinary to recommend trying to predict the five-year picture as a final part of competitive assessment. Have we taken leave of our senses?

There are two basic reasons for recommending this last step:

1. The difficulty is that the pace of change is fast with some companies active for several years in tackling international markets. Companies cannot afford to wait for final clarity before acting. We will look at three examples shortly.
2. It is only by taking a bold approach that some of the real opportunities will be identified. There is a real danger that the overall opportunity will be lost in a wealth of detail. Our examples will show how this breadth of vision can highlight the opportunity.

We have previously undertaken considerable background research in Part I: this is where we use this material.

AREAS OF ASSESSMENT

Prediction is intended to highlight such areas and it is therefore concerned with the broad shape in five years rather than the detail. It might therefore cover: market size and growth prospects; main competitors in each country with a rough market share; main products or services on sale with differentiation highlighted; location of plant across the market; customer trends; distribution trends; cost trends and value added; currency and economic trends.

Now this might only cover two sides of paper: indeed, it might be a better document if it did. It will avoid some of the worst problems that arise from some obvious factors simply not having been foreseen.

Case Study: Stora Kopparbergs Berslags AB, Sweden

Data
Europe's biggest pulp and paper producer.
Turnover (Skr million)

	1992	1988	1986
Power	1560	921	994
Forestry	5225	551	120
Chemicals	—	870	606
Woodpulp	3411	5422	2488
Printing paper	14158	3960	1811
Packaging paper & board	8768	4971	2700
Fine papers	11326	3621	1082
Floorings	5301	5878	—
Joinery & building materials	3431	3914	1833
Packaging	1940	1704	658
Matches & lighters	—	2801	—
Paper products	—	2002	—
Other/intersegment	(8225)	3253	704
Total	46895	39868	12996

Note: The data shows sales as they would have been if acquisitions had been made from the beginning of 1988. *Actual sales* were Skr 34256 million for 1988: Stora's Annual Report and Accounts are quite confusing on this point. Equivalent 1986 product sales data has been estimated by the author based on published numbers.

	1992	1988
Return on capital:	1.6%	12.8%
% sales in home country:	19	27
% sales in rest of Europe:	69	53
% sales in rest of world:	12	20

European and global activity
The company set itself the objective of becoming Europe's largest pulp and paper company. It therefore acquired (outright or bought out minority interests) a series of companies over the last three years. Some of these were in Sweden and others had a wider European base. The companies brought under full Stora control were: Papyrus AB (January 1987); and Swedish Match (May 1988). Feldmuhle Nobel (1990) Swedish Match not only has pulp and paper interests but also products in other areas that were then sold.

Since this time, the company has been consolidating its position. It has not been helped by the strength of the Swedish krone and the downturn in Europe. By the mid-1990s, its strategies were to rationalise in order to reduce costs and to divest non-core business.

Keypoint on five-year view
Stora had a clear objective over five years: it has taken some time to integrate all its activities and sell off others. At the end of this period, it should be a stronger company if the demand for forestry based products holds.

It might be argued that the developments are fine for a Swedish company but would not be possible outside that country because the base industry is not available. But what matters here is not the actual course Stora has taken but rather the *clarity of objective* based on the resources and skills it has available in its markets. The objective is not achieved by sales in one country alone: Stora needs *Europe as a base* and its 88% sales from this source (69% outside the home country) shows that it is on course.

Case Study: Svenska Cellulosa, AB, Sweden

Data
Europe's largest purchaser of pulp products.
Turnover (Skr million)

	1988	1992
Forest & timber	8836	3518
Disposable hygiene & baby products	10419	12554
Corrugated board & packaging	1727	8984
Hydroelectric power	900	1361
Inter-company	(1032)	—
Graphic paper		5067
Other		653
Total	20850	32137

	1988	1992
Return on capital:	14.4%	7.2%
% sales in home country:	34	20
% sales in rest of Europe:	61	78
% sales in rest of world:	5	2

European and global activity
The company has been active in acquisitions across Europe to meet its objective of becoming Europe's largest user of pulp products. During the period 1988–92, it acquired the following:

- Peaudouce disposable baby nappies from Agache SA, France;
- Italcarte SpA (Italy's largest manufacturer of corrugated board and recycled paper);
- Laakirchen AG (Austrian printing, paper and hygiene products manufacturer); and
- The Belgian and French corrugated board operations of Bowater plc, UK;
- Paper and packaging interests of Reed Elsevier.

Keypoint on five-year view
Again, this company had a clear mid-1990s objective which it was working towards. The company's president stated in 1992, 'Customer-driven product development is our future – fibre technology is our base'. It is now concentrating on products with substantial value added, and increasing its focus on strong brand names, even in industrial marketing.

Case Study: Electrolux AB, Sweden

Data
Europe's largest suppliers of household electrical appliances.
Turnover (Skr million)

	1986	1988	1990	1992
Household appliances	31378	41088	44890	46540
Commercial appliances	4250	6695	8699	8898
Commercial services	2504	3336	4343	772
Outdoor products	2909	4960	8680	9333
Industrial products	9087	14107	15822	14893
Building components	2962	3774	—	—
Total	53090	73960	82434	80436

Return on capital:	14.3%	6.6%
% sales in home country:	17	10
% sales in rest of Europe:	46	54
% sales in rest of world:	37	36
		(especially USA)

European and global activity

Electrolux is probably one of Europe's better known examples of companies with a clear vision and a plan to achieve it over a period of years.

The company has grown fast over the last few years as a result of a series of acquisitions elsewhere in Europe and in other parts of the world. Arguably, the result has been too demanding for the Swedish management to handle: we will consider this in Part III. Certainly, the objective of becoming the world's largest domestic and industrial appliance supplier is still possible.

Amongst the acquisitions made are the following: Zanussi (Italy, 1984); White (USA, 1986); Thorn/EMI (UK, 1987); Corbero/Domar (Spain, 1988); and Buderus (the West German interests of this Swedish company, 1989); Hungarian company (1991). In 1993, it agreed a development deal with AEG household appliances (Germany).

Interestingly, given this clear and well-publicized objective, the company's other activities amount to quite a substantial part of total sales. They include forestry products, industrial aluminium equipment and agricultural implements. Perhaps the company's vision is not so clear or, rather like Volvo, it has other interests which it is difficult to divest.

Keypoint on five-year view

Electrolux is benefiting from its clear longer-term perspective. It is important to see the way the company has drawn this not just in terms of household appliances, but with industrial appliances doing much the same job in a different environment.

CONCLUSIONS

For international markets, this vision is essential to give clarity to short-term actions involving customers and competitors. This chapter has examined acquisitions as a means of achieving this result. Arguably, this route was more appropriate in the late 1980s and other methods now apply in the mid-1990s: joint ventures, alliances and other forms of cooperation are being increasingly employed. They may be cheaper, more flexible and better suited to the increased ease of sharing information.

One further area of change that may have long-term repercussions is that of distribution for our product or service. We will consider this next.

CHAPTER 22

Channel Strategy: Assessing Existing Distribution Methods

CHANNEL STRATEGY: AN INTRODUCTION

Without doubt, one of the most important questions for the aspiring international company will be how to resolve its product or service channel strategy. Yet this is a difficult area to research well and it is also one that can produce significant profit opportunities.

For some purist business strategists, this question should have been considered and resolved elsewhere in Part II on strategy for tackling international expansion. It has been separated out here because, for some companies, it can be one of the more difficult problems to resolve and it is often (rightly or wrongly) the immediate response to the subject: how can we sell our products in other countries?

We need to be clear what is meant by channel strategy: essentially it covers physical distribution, the salesforce and the trade: what happens beyond the theoretical factory gate, including the technical discussions and negotiations that usually precede actual delivery. There are two types of customer that need to be covered by channel strategy:

1. *Direct end-users* who buy and consume the product that is purchased. They do not buy for stock and do not sell to third parties: they are not distributors.
2. *Distributors* who buy a product for stock and then sell it to the consumer. They may be agents, stockholders or other trade combinations. What distinguishes this group is that a 'sale' is not really made until they sell out and re-order.

We will deal with *both* of these customer types because the majority of companies tackling international expansion may sell to both within the same company organization. But it does require clarity of analysis as to who exactly is the target group in a specific situation – otherwise, some extremely muddled strategy will emerge.

As before, consideration of channel strategy is based on the assumption that most firms will want to sell a product or service that bears some relation to what they have now: electronics engineers will not want to become builders merchants (or vice versa).

There are three basic steps to establishing channel strategy for European and global markets: assess the existing methods (examined in this chapter); probe the distributor channels (Chapter 23); and secure the means of distribution (Chapter 24).

ASSESS EXISTING METHODS

For all products and services, there will be a channel of distribution to deliver the product or service to customers. The first task is to assess this. The most striking opportunity may well be to distribute differently but this will stand more chance of success if the current methods are properly understood. As Len Hardy says in his excellent book, *Business Strategy*: 'For those who are skilled in forecasting [channel] development accurately, and who follow through and exploit it to the full, it can provide a significant competitive advantage.' The key to forecasting is to understand the present.

It is beyond the scope of this book (and probably the patience of the reader) to detail every possible combination of distribution channel used by Europe's top companies. But the basic subject areas for the assessment of channels are clear: overall objective, distributor* needs, service levels, technical and quality specifications, distributor pricing and discounts, distributor support for the product or service and distributor profitability. Let us deal with each in turn.

Overall objective
The aim of the process must be to end up with a distributor marketing strategy. This may well mean revisiting some of the earlier Part I concepts concerned with establishing market data for key buyers but, this time, *from the distributor's point of view*: who is the retailer's competitor; who is the steel stockholder's competitor; what market is this company in?

Distributor needs
We have already discussed the need to establish who really makes the immediate purchasing decision. This is one of the crucial areas in establishing channel strategy so we will explore it separately in Chapter 23.

Service levels
This area needs to cover not only the immediate requirements for timetables and delivery but also what happens when things go wrong, regular order-taking policies and general after-sales service.

Given the physical distances involved in international markets, what might previously have been a cheap service may now need some rethinking: what level of sales back-up can be supplied between, for example, Copenhagen and the south of France? Do we need to use a local agent? How do we replace faulty product? What level of service is available now from local competition?

What happens over debt collection? What happens when an irate customer calls and we need to respond in the national language? Do customers really have to make international telephone calls to obtain service? Do we regularly take orders over the telephone in the home country? Can this be done in other

---

* For many branded food companies, 'trade' will be used to describe 'distributor': the latter is used here simply because it is easier to understand in the context of the single Europe. For other companies, 'export channel' will be the preferred description. Substitute either if you wish.

countries? If not, how might we provide the same level of service, or are we prepared to accept a lower level of sales?

Suddenly, things could become rather less profitable for the supplying company if these questions are not carefully considered. US companies will have experience of the much greater distances involved and European companies may well want to tap this. But for example, Europe, with greater language and cultural differences than the USA, will push many companies into having at least national and possibly local representation to deal with all these practical issues.

Technical and quality specifications

This topic can also be more difficult if the home country is used to standardized methods of undertaking work which are not common elsewhere. Are these normally subject to contractual agreement? Will contracts be acceptable elsewhere and, if so, under which country's law? What special national regulations apply? How are they enforced? What documentation is needed?

This is an important area to clarify but, for any company regularly involved in exporting to the country concerned, it will be less difficult.

Distributor pricing and discounts

The problem here is not so much one of agreeing the basic price as dealing with the other issues often surrounding it. It is quite likely that for some products and services there will be a discount on price for volume. There may even be an annual target for a distributor which merits an extra payment once achieved. How do you organize for this, if at all?

The matter may be handled nationally by country, but how can you be sure that the buyer (the distributor or end-user) will not shop around internationally to find other sources of your own product with greater discounts? Any company thinking this will not happen reckons without the ingenuity of buyers and the drive of separate national sales teams to make sales: it can be a real problem to balance the need for local service and decision making with the need to keep discounting under centralized control.

Are there any legal restrictions on working outside the published price list? Apart from legal restrictions, what is the current competitive practice? How might a competitor respond to a sudden major price reduction from elsewhere in its markets? What is company policy on a trade price war?

Distributor support for the product or service

In most cases involving channels, the product or service has not really been 'sold' until the distributor has sold it out of his warehouse, supermarket shelf or service centre. Trade support from the distributor is required to achieve this.

Support becomes even more vital in some capital goods markets, where it is far too simplistic to think only of the 'sale'. Design support, commissioning of the new machinery and continued technical advice are often required. This may be undertaken by a distributor or directly by the manufacturer.

What level of support is the channel currently offering the competition? What level of support is the distributor prepared to offer to the new product or service? What will be most beneficial to the customer? And most cost effective for us?

Distributor profitability

Distributors can be notoriously demanding on price, service and support, especially if they have some buying power. It is normal national practice for the supplier to occasionally undertake a study of just how profitable some customers are.

With the extra costs involved in international markets, it will be wise to undertake this task for customer accounts. It may be difficult but should be attempted for selected accounts where possible. The results are usually illuminating and can lead to markedly different treatment of an account: invest, hold or even downgrade.

Assessment of channels

These last three issues come back to the matter of distributor needs which we will tackle in the next chapter. They are included here as practical matters born out of experience rather than as fundamental to the issue of looking at the buyer's needs from basic analysis. But let no one dismiss them as merely matters of tactics: they can have a profound effect on the company's profit line and the motivation of its sales team. Let us look at some examples.

Case Study: European iron and steel industry

Data

	Country	Turnover 1992 (US$ m)	Return on capital	Destination of sales Home (%)	Rest of Europe (%)	Rest of world (%)
Usinor Sacilor	Fra	15405	loss	69*	26*	5*
Thyssen	Ger	8730**	na	na		
Ilva	Ita	8295	loss	64	36	
***Krupp/Hoesch	Ger	7805**	loss	na		
British Steel	UK	7111	(2.8)%	51	34	15
Arbed	Lux	5300 est	na	na		
Ensidesa & AHV	Spa	4500 est	na			
Voest Alpine	Aus	4456**	na	na		
Cockerill Sambre	Bel	4094**	0.25%	26	70	4****
Hoogevens	Net	2512**	na	na		
SSAB	Swe	2119	2.3%	56	37	7
*****Klockner	Ger	1656**	loss	na		

* 1990 data
** indicates that only part of total turnover of company shown.
*** Krupp and Hoesch merged in late 1992: proforma data above.
**** all % data is for group but dominated by steel.
***** Klockner Werke filed for restructuring in 1992 but then reported a profit in 1993. The company also has interests in plastics and mechanical engineering and has no connection with Klockner Humboldt Deutz.

European and global activity
Although the European Coal and Steel Community has been operating since 1952 and there are some benefits from economies of scale, the main European companies still rely heavily on home demand for their products. Moreover, when steel companies have attempted to move into other EU countries, the target country

has reacted against such incursions. Thus British Steel's attempts to acquire German and Spanish steel companies in the early 1990s were largely stopped; only Usinor Sacilor's acquisition of SaarStahl in 1991 was successful (but see chapter 24).

The strength of national interest is perhaps not surprising given that 15 of the top 20 steel producers in the EU are government-owned or have government connections. The restructuring of the European steel industry has thus largely been nationally-based:

- Usinor combined with Sacilor in France
- Ilva brought together several Italian steel companies
- British Steel was privatised and rationalised at a national level
- Krupp merged with Hoesch in Germany alone.

There have been real strategic problems in the European steel industry for at least 20 years. They have arisen because high capital investment has produced an industry needing steady 80–85% capacity utilisation to break even, while at the same time selling into markets that are cyclical and compete largely on price. In the early 1990s, this was made even worse by:

- downturn in demand for steel
- small amounts of low-price steel from Eastern Europe
- overcapacity in every sector versus likely demand
- inability in the industry to take out the least cost-efficient plants because they were government subsidised (especially in Spain and Italy)
- strong political interests to preserve national steel production.

The result is a mess that still remains unresolved at the time of writing. Although ther has been major investment in some countries to modernise plant, it does not follow that this is the 'best' European strategy. Through all the above upheavals, some small steel companies have remained profitable using a completely different strategy based on small-scale production and different, cheaper technology.

Keypoint on channel strategy
All the leading European steel companies have, or are acquiring, strong trading distributor companies: these can sell steel through local stockholders or trade nationally or internationally to sell steel to third parties which will then sell-on to the end-user. Activity here is significant:

1. Usinor-Sacilor acquired the UK's second largest steel stockholder in March 1991. It has also bought distributors in France, Italy and the USA.
2. Krupp has a trading company which sells and recycles, amongst other products, steel.
3. Hoesch also has a trading and services subsidiary with substantial sales.
4. Cockerill Sambre: 'Technical and commercial progress mean that activities which could formerly be exercised in a small geographic area must now be given a European dimension. Accordingly, while maintaining our previous agreements with the Arbed group, we have established new accords in one activity after another with, amongst others: Usinor-Sacilor (merchant bars and mill rolls); Stiness/Veba (distribution in Germany); and Bouygues in Spain (sections for the building industry).' (1987 *Annual Report*.)
5. British Steel made an agreed bid for the leading British stockholder, C. Walker, for £330 million in 1990.

By the early 1990s, over 80% of the steel stockholders in France and Germany were owned by steel mills. British Steel was partly excluded from these markets as a result.

We will return to Europe's iron and steel industry in Chapter 25.

Case Study: Thyssen AG, Germany

Data
Europe's top capital goods and steel group.
1992 turnover (DM million)

Steel	9903
Special steels	3071
Capital and manufactured goods	11977
Trading and other services	14411
Intergroup	(3606)
Total	35756

Return on capital: 4.9%
% sales in home country: 56
% sales in rest of Europe: 26
% sales in rest of world: 18

European and global activity
Thyssen has acted as the holding company for individual sectors outlined above since 1983. The company has made several acquisitions over the last few years including the Budd Company (USA) in 1987 and Birmid (UK) in 1990.

Like some other leading German companies, Thyssen has important sales to other German companies. Many of its products operate on a world-wide rather than a purely European basis. Other companies might consider making acquisitions in the single Europe as a base for global expansion but Thyssen is already of such a size that this is not the prime consideration. However, Thyssen is hardly global in terms of the destination of its sales.

Keypoint on channel strategy
Because of its vast size, Thyssen is organized into many sales teams related to the various companies within the group. Even the major headings above give little idea of the range and complexity of the channel task facing the companies. For example, within the capital goods and manufactured products group, there is Thyssen Industrie AG, comprising as follows:

1992 turnover (DM million)

Castings	1352
Forging	1171
Pumps, lathes	1225
Lifts	1714
Locomotives	841
Shipbuilding	737
Plastics	220
Engineering	437
Blohm & Voss	963
Other	46
Total	8706

Return on capital: 9.7%
% sales in home country: 50
% sales in rest of Europe: 37
% sales in rest of world: 13

Each of the above is an important company in its own right, dealing with its own range of customers which are mainly organized on a product rather than an industry basis. So, developing channel strategy in Thyssen will involve selection of customers and specification of their requirements.

Typically with such work (but not necessarily true of Thyssen where the information is not published), customers can be subdivided into:

■ Very large orders requiring *one-off central design* and manufacturing with a high individual development, design and technical content. Channels and distributor decisions are handled by head office only;

■ Industry customers requiring special *industry knowledge* on the part of the supplier, selling a balance between one-off designs and some industry design standardization: channels are handled by specialized industry teams working out of head office and across country boundaries;

■ Smaller customers taking a *standard product* and not requiring customized design skills from the supplier. Channels are typically conducted by national sales teams and often involve distributors.

For companies like Thyssen, with its involvement in markets ranging from plant design to lift manufacture, it is essential to identify just how large the individual design element will be in the product it is selling. The more the individual design, the greater the central control so that the greatest expertise can be employed. This then defines the channel to distribution.

Case Study: BICC plc, UK

Data
Major European company in construction and electrical cable manufacture.
Turnover (£ million)

	1988		*1992*
Balfour Beatty	1359	(construction)	1848
BICC Cables	583	(cables)	946
Australasia	618	(cables)	437
North American Cables	257	(cables)	320
Inter-group	(36)		(163)
Total	2781		3388
Return on capital:	28.4%		13.3%
% sales in home country:	56		64
% sales in rest of Europe:	6		14
% sales in rest of world:	38		22

European and global activity
Balfour Beatty is one of the UK's largest construction companies with road building, homes, and civil and electrical engineering contracting amongst its activities, via a host of subsidiary companies: hence the strong home country sales. During the early 1990s, it has been affected by the severe recession in UK construction. Its high financial gearing from its acquisitions in earlier years (see below) also had an impact on profitability.

BICC cables business has been restructured in the UK resulting in substantial increases in efficiency. The Australian cables subsidiary has been simplified and is now the largest of its kind in that country. BICC Technologies sold some subsidiaries and in 1989 bought Andover Controls in the US for US$44 million: the company specializes in electronic controls for buildings and will complement the construction and cable businesses at the core of BICC.

In European cable, BICC has been active with two major steps: in July 1988 it acquired Ceat Calvi, Italy's second largest cable manufacturer with customers in the Italian electrical and telephone utilities; and in December 1988 it bought 20% of Grupo Espagnol General Cables with the possibility of raising this stake at least to 49% by 1992. The company is Spain's leading cable maker. BICC is also reported to control Portugal's largest cable maker. Overall, the company will be the third largest in the EC behind Pirelli (Italy) and Cable de Lyons (France).

In addition, the company has been seeking global market share in cables: it has also purchased Cablec, a US cable maker and owns Phillips Cables in Canada. It had joint venture agreements in China, Turkey and Malaysia.

Keypoint on channel strategy
With its European and global expansion, BICC will face two types of channel problem:

1. Cable technology: how to deal with sophisticated contractual requirements from experienced and knowledgeable buyers. These could be handled centrally where the best expertise might be organized. However, knowledge of customers' specific needs will be much more precise in each country. Obtaining the right balance may not be easy.
2. Exports from national sales companies: how to handle the situation where, for example, the Spanish subsidiary identifies a sales opportunity in France that has also been noted by the UK company. In other companies (but *not* BICC), it has not been unknown for two subsidiaries to bid against each other on price and contractual terms. Companies need to lay down rules to cover this in the single Europe and monitor the results.

Case Study: AKZO NV, Netherlands

Data
The largest chemicals company in The Netherlands.
1988 turnover (Dfl million)

	1988	1992
Chemical products	6020	5679
Fibres & polymers	4678	3802
Coatings	2794	4141
Healthcare	2412	3255
Textile machinery	784	–
Other	104	–
Inter-group	(211)	(27)
Total	16581	16850

	1988	1992
Return on capital:	16.3%	14.3%
% sales in home country:	36	9
% sales in rest of Europe:	41	52
% sales in rest of world:	23	39

European and global activity
AKZO's activities have for many years been concentrated in Holland and Germany, which account respectively for 32% and 22% of the company's total of 71,000 employees. Thus the company is already experienced in some cross-border European issues.

Over the last few years, AKZO made determined moves towards global leadership. It acquired the Goodyear (US) tyre yarn business to become the world's second largest polyester yarn producer. In 1991 and 1992, it acquired Dutch and UK coatings companies to add to its US acquisitions of the 1980s. In 1993, it bought Nobel (Sweden) for its coatings business to become the largest in Europe and a global force in this market.

The company's coatings range includes DIY paints, car finishes and industrial coatings. There is plant in Mexico and Brazil, amongst other countries, plus a joint venture in Spain: international rather than European. What precise benefits are to be derived from operating on a global scale remain unclear.

Both basic chemicals and fibres and polymers operations are subject to cyclical and mature-market forces. AKZO is also a world leader in some areas of fibre production, with textile and carpet fibres and industrial yarns being the main ones. It has developed joint ventures in Turkey, Hungary and China to pursue this goal.

Keypoints on channel activity
The company's customers will be very different in its various markets: for example, pharmaceutical sales are totally unlike textile fibres. Consequently, it will not be possible to have a series of basic approaches that are substantially based around similar products adapted for different industries (unlike computer companies for example). The AKZO channel task must therefore be approached in detail on an individual market basis: this will come out of an analysis of the current customer list, size, location and profitability.

Case Study: Daimler Benz AG, Germany

Data
Germany's largest car and truck company with strong interests in defence and consumer appliances.
1992 turnover (DM million)

| | | | Destination of sales (%) | |
		Home	Rest of Europe	Rest of world
Cars	39601	45	40	15
Trucks, buses	26879	39	26	35
AEG (80%-owned)	11595	58	25	17
Deutsche Aerospace	17276	37	44	19
Debis	7341	49	12	40
Intergroup	(4143)			
Total	98549			

Return on capital: 2.6%
% sales in home country: 44
% sales in rest of Europe: 27
% sales in rest of world: 29

Single market activity
Daimler Benz has a high concentration of sales in Germany with a strong export emphasis: 80% of all employees are in Germany. Over the last few years, it has been heavily involved in the turn round of other German companies (principally AEG and Deutsche Aerospace), rather than moving out into Europe.

For the basic car, bus and truck companies Daimler Benz places heavy emphasis on export-led growth. This is its biggest area of business and is much more global. It has truck factories in the USA, Mexico, Argentina and Turkey. It has new engine developments in Korea for the south east Asian market. It has announced a new car factory in the USA (see BMW in chapter 3 for the likely reasons).

For AEG, it has been supportive in allowing the company to sort out its problems and concentrate on its strengths. The company is involved in electrical engineering, computers and household appliances which are now performing satisfactorily in Germany, though foreign earnings are weak. In late 1993 it agreed a deal with Electrolux on its domestic appliances that may lead to the sale of this particular product area. AEG is also involved in office products and power generation equipment, both of which are unprofitable. The company has sold much of its turbine interests to ASEA Brown Boveri: it could not compete against this company and the new GEC/Alsthom consortium. The office products situation remains to be resolved.

Daimler Benz acquired the troubled German aerospace company MBB in 1990. To these it added its own air engine and aerospace activities to form Deutsche Aerospace. Global activity here has come from the company's participation in the European Airbus consortium. The company is sometimes called DASA.

Daimler will have its hands full over the next few years coping with this extensive reorganization.

Keypoints on channel activity
One of Daimler's problems will be to manage the essentials along with all the activity described above. It still generates very substantial profits from its cars and trucks, trading under the Mercedes Benz name.

With such an up-market and prestigious mark, it is essential that it controls its channels carefully. Over the years, it has developed a series of exclusive dealerships with all the related matters of service levels, dealer training and branding at individual locations. This has proved very successful and represents a clear channel route for certain types of product, not just cars: arguably, for example, more computer companies could follow this route.

CONCLUSIONS AND CHECKLIST

For new companies tackling European and global markets, it will be essential to begin by assessing how other companies undertake their business. Set out below is a checklist of factors that need to be considered: *pricing* is also included here because it is (or should be) linked directly with the means of distribution (distributors need a price discount to make a profit). We looked at basic pricing in Chapter 19.

The checklist is as follows:

- The main channels to reach the end-users: direct and indirect via distributors, agents, etc. A diagram plotting this out is helpful.
- The existing physical means of delivering the product or service: national and international physical location of deliveries and outline schedules. This needs a summary of delivery points, carriers used, stock held, competitor usage, etc.
- The pricing structure offered to distributors and directly to the end-user. Competitor price lists, if available, are invaluable as a first step.
- The main discounts offered on price: included under this heading will be all forms of credit, financial deals, export guarantees, etc. More difficult to obtain, but friendly buyers and experienced sales personnel will have no difficulty in producing useful data.

- The main forms of salesforce support and sales promotion both by competitor suppliers and by the distributors: everything from free holidays in Mexico to specialized technical design teams. Examples of offers or levels of support are usually the best way to produce this rather than some detailed classification. In material collected, the distinction needs to be drawn between selling to a distributor and selling to the end-user through the distributor.

- The competitive sales team: background on individual senior people plus structure, location across each market and numbers in sales teams is essential. And it is *vital* to include the salesforce technical back-up where relevant. Also any other form of direct or indirect selling such as the telephone.

- For third-party distributors, the stock levels held, the stock turn expected and the range of stock covered. Also the level of service.

- For direct end-users, the level and quality of service (which will need to be defined carefully): included here must be the means used to tackle end-user queries and complaints.

Armed with all this information, it should now be possible to put together an assessment of the existing channel supply. But to achieve a breakthrough, it is often better to look at totally new ways of tackling the task. The starting point for this is to examine buyer needs: our next step.

CHAPTER 23

Channel Strategy: Distributor Relationships

In developing international channel strategy, the distributor is one of the key elements. 'Distributor' here means the intermediate distributor purchasing for onward sale to the target group of ultimate buyers of the product or service.

Our objective now is to explore beyond the existing channels of distribution and into new areas. There are countless examples amongst *national* businesses of new distributor relationships providing a real breakthrough in sales and profits, though there are rather fewer internationally. But the national experience suggests it is worth probing the European and global situation.

To explore international distribution, companies need to answer the following questions for each major market:

1. Who are the really important distributors?
2. What is important to them?
3. What are the actual and potential sources of differentiation that our company can offer to each distributor?
4. If we are asking a price premium for the differentiation in our product or service, is this too high for the distributor?
5. How can my company signal value to the distributor?
6. How might we change the product to make it more attractive to the distributor?
7. What changes are taking place in the patterns of distribution across each national country?
8. What changes are likely in the means used to communicate with the target group and how will this affect buying relationships?

Let us go through each of these in turn and explore their significance for European and global markets. For our case studies in this chapter, we will use examples from consumer and branded goods areas.

WHO ARE THE REALLY IMPORTANT DISTRIBUTORS?

In some markets, this is well documented while in others it is a difficult job to unearth the information, yet it is essential to strategy. It is vital to discover who will have the largest immediate impact on sales effort, even if other factors then suggest that other distributors are to be preferred.

To answer the question, it is necessary to establish who distributes the product and to estimate what share of the total market each distributor is responsible for. In practice, because a national distributor may actually purchase through more than one point around the country, it is worth adding data on buying points. Let us look at European grocery markets and identify not only the share of turnover taken by the leaders but also the number of decision buying points.

Table 23.1   Concentration of grocery buying (share of top 10 buying organizations in each country), 1986 and 1992

	% turnover		Number of key decision points: 1986
	1986	1992	
Switzerland	90	92	14
Sweden	89	90	9
Germany*	81	82	308
Netherlands	79	80	25
Belgium	66	75	—
Great Britain	66	74	12
France	62	76	145
Italy	35	39	304
Spain	26	30	10

*Excludes Aldi in Germany
Source: A.C. Nielsen Company for 1986 and author's estimates for 1992

In some countries, it will be no great task to establish who are the important distributors. In others, it will not only take longer but will involve a carefully thought out strategy as to how they are to be contacted.

WHAT IS IMPORTANT TO DISTRIBUTORS?

Having established which distributors are vital for a market, it is essential to discover what is important to them. This is quite carefully phrased: it matters little what the selling company considers to be relevant about its products or services and rather more what the distributor cares about.

In practice, many companies will recognize that this is often easier to pose as a question than establish as an answer. Many readers will have met the professional distributor whose sole task in life seems to be to explain virtually nothing, ask aggressive questions and demand impossible levels of service and price. Greater physical distances in the single Europe will make this even more difficult for the seller to manage, let alone globally.

But looked at from the distributor's viewpoint, why should he or she take yet another product offering only marginal price advantage over existing ranges? Particularly when, for example, the real pressure is on higher stock turn and lower in-store personnel? No wonder distributors put up a wall of what they would regard as polite but bored indifference.

There are many ways through this difficulty. Here are three:

1. Undertake background research on what pressures currently affect the market. What are competing distributors offering? What growth is taking place in the market? What levels of service are currently being offered? Answers here will provide leads.
2. Meet distributors at non-selling occasions such as exhibitions and trade functions.
3. Acquire the expertise of sellers already dealing with that distributor via recruitment of local nationals, acquiring a company or undertaking a joint venture with a local company.

This last area deserves to be explored further so we will return to it in the next chapter.

Distributors often regard price as the most important factor. But competition can match this most easily, so additional solutions need to be sought. Paraphrasing Michael Porter, the ultimate aim in dealing with distributors is to create *competitive advantage for the distributor* in ways besides selling to them at lower price: this will only come about by a full understanding of the distributor's needs. The problem is more acute when dealing with more than one distributor in a country: ingenuity will also be needed.

SOURCES OF DIFFERENTIATION A COMPANY CAN OFFER DISTRIBUTORS

Differentiation only means something to the distributor when he or she is able to use it either to reduce distributor costs or to raise distributor performance. Differentiation that does not tackle at least one of these two fundamental matters is irrelevant.

Reducing distributor costs is not merely a matter of selling at a lower price than the competition: this may be the worst route to take because it is so easy for others to match it. Particularly given the higher costs associated with the greater physical distances of international markets, lower price than the local competition may be a rather weak strategy. Table 23.2 shows other ways of reducing

Table 23.2   Reducing distributor costs

Method	Example
Higher reliability of product	Easier maintenance heating
Enhanced performance	New telephone systems
Lower delivery and installation costs	Pre-assembled construction
Lower rate of usage of the product	Low-cost lighting
Specialized service that replaces in-company service	Outside laundry services
Tailor-made products that cut in-service costs	Pre-packed grocery display

distributor costs that are less open to competitor response. These are examples of a broad range of issues that need to be tackled under this heading. IBM Europe has been particularly skilled at this over the last few years.

Raising distributor performance is not mutually exclusive from lowering costs. Nevertheless, it can add a totally new dimension across international markets. We looked earlier at product differentiation so consideration now should be straightforward.

Because European and global markets are so diverse in culture, skills and experience, differentiation offers many routes for the enhancement of distributor sales. Selling products differentiated from existing local varieties may raise rather than steal sales. This argument is more likely to impress the distributor.

In this context, two pan-European and global retailing distribution trends deserve special examination: both increase the availability of differentiated products across the 12 EU countries.

Specialist retailing

Retail specialization has been one of the clearer international trends over the last five years. By segmenting markets and tackling specific target groups, retailers have been able to make significant sales. It is arguable that these have been at the expense of other outlets: some department stores have taken a particular battering in Germany and the UK.

There have been some real successes: Benneton from Italy, Body Shop and Laura Ashley from the UK, Bally from Switzerland. However, the successes seem to be mainly in higher margin, fashion items which will not suit every manufacturer. Such shops are not confined to Europe but can be seen in North America and the Far East also.

Hypermarkets

Larger stores need more products to fill them, preferably ones that are different from those currently available. Successful sales variety enhances distributor performance.

Table 23.3 Development of supermarkets and hypermarkets

	% turnover	
	1976	*1986*
France	61	85
Belgium	63	75
Netherlands	43	67
Germany*	40	58
Great Britain	—	58
Spain	11	41
Italy	19	30
Portugal	11	15

Excluding Aldi in Germany.
Source: A.C. Nielsen Company.

Larger stores offer opportunities for specialist products, reflecting Europe's diversity and range, to find wider distribution. Again, these shopping trends can be seen elsewhere in the world: North America and Brazil, for example, had them rather earlier.

PRICE PREMIUM

If we are asking a price premium for the differentiation in our product or service, is this too high for the distributor? If it is too high, then either the distributor does not understand the benefits that will result from differentiation or, more likely, the distributor cannot obtain sufficient resulting benefits. Either way, it is the supplier's fault, not the distributor's.

The best way to tackle this issue is to quantify the benefits to the distributor. For example, what precisely will be the lower resulting costs? What will be the increase in sales? Sometimes this is more difficult where an intangible benefit is involved (eg business sponsorship of a cultural event), but it still needs to be attempted.

Ultimately, if the premium is too high, then the distributor will go elsewhere. International markets are the same as national ones in this respect.

HOW CAN A COMPANY SIGNAL VALUE TO THE DISTRIBUTOR?

Many distributors will need to learn about the increased range of suppliers available as trade barriers come down. Selling companies need to recognize this as an important part of their task and signal value to the distributor. Here are some ways it can be done:

- Size of installed base of customer users;
- Existing customer list;
- Results of customer research;
- Advertising and marketing support for the product or service;
- Financial status and time in business of the company;
- Parent company details;
- Quality of brochures and offices, particularly for service industries;
- Representation on industry technical bodies and international institutions;
- Published technical and other papers; and
- Factory visits to the home country.

There is no universal list of methods for undertaking this task but this does not mean it should be underestimated. Whether the aim is to gain distribution or, more fundamentally, joint venture or acquisition, this whole area deserves careful study. It may be the courtship prior to the marriage!

CHANGING THE PRODUCT TO MAKE IT MORE ATTRACTIVE TO THE DISTRIBUTOR

Superficially, once distributors' needs have been determined, this question has some attractions. But it also has great danger: it can really be the top of the slippery slope of profit decline if products are changed to suit the distributor rather than the ultimate purchaser.

It depends what change is needed: a change in pallet size or distribution service levels will be entirely appropriate. Similarly, new trade advertising and promotion relevant to the particular country may be equally acceptable. But fundamental change in the product or service itself may require a more careful analysis. The ultimate purchaser is a consumer, not the distributor near a motorway service area in West London or an industrial district of Naples where the product may simply gather dust.

This does not mean it should be ignored: every business proposition merits consideration if sufficient and continuing sales and long-term profits result. For example, if the distributor offers the opportunity of large volume sales from relabelling the product as a distributor own-brand (called 'private label' in some companies), then it would be unwise to turn this down automatically unless it is against company policy internationally.

Indeed, it is *because* it is policy for some companies to reject this approach that others have a means of entry across international markets: Mars confectionery and Kelloggs breakfast cereals are well-known examples of companies that will not make private label products. There has been some growth in own-brand products globally in the last ten years, particularly during the recession of the early 1990s.

Ultimately, outside own-branding and some limited changes associated with distribution, this question probably deserves rejecting.

CHANGES IN NATIONAL DISTRIBUTION ACROSS EACH COUNTRY

To establish channel strategy, any changes taking place in the patterns of such distribution need to be researched in the context of the product or service. Often the best opportunities emerge from picking up new trends rather than relying on the existing scenario.

Clearly, in the context of the vast size of international markets, this book cannot comprehensively wade through the whole of this issue: it can only provide some clues for deeper consideration. If more detailed work is required, then outside consultancy may provide a useful additional resource.

Nevertheless, there have been plenty of examples over the last few years of new distribution channels giving a significant boost to sales: clothing and cookery items, repackaged for presentation in grocery hypermarkets, are the obvious examples. More recent cases across Europe include DIY superstores selling central heating systems and petrol stations selling food items.

Frankly, for the single European market and grocery outlets, there is not much scope in looking for new channel presentation ideas in northern Europe: they are all largely in place now. In the southern European states, the possibilities are limited by the absence of large grocery outlets rather than any lack of ideas. In North America, many of the opportunities have also been adopted.

Ultimately, a leap of imagination rather than market research may be needed, coupled with some business risk-taking: no book can provide this. Essentially, companies need to explore what has recently happened and what new areas are available.

TARGET GROUP COMMUNICATIONS

What changes are likely in the means used to communicate with the international target group and how will this affect buying relationships? Like all generalizations, the comments below run the risk of missing a key area for an individual company and should therefore be taken only as a starting point.

Possible new channel trends for international development include mail order developments, cable and satellite television and telephone network developments.

Mail order

In the early 1990s mail order amounted to 3–6% of total retail turnover in Germany, France and the UK. Elsewhere in Europe it was rather smaller, but showing some growth in Italy and Spain.

Case Study: Selected European mail order companies

Data
1992 turnover (US$ million)

Otto Versand	Ger	9678
Quelle	Ger	6000 (est.)
GUS	UK	4644
Neckermann (subsidiary of Karstadt)	Ger	2301
Bertelsmann	Ger	1556
La Redoute	Fra	900 (est.)
Sears	UK	826

European and global activity
Clearly, Quelle is a major European company. The only reason it has been left out of Europe's Top 250 is that, due to private ownership, it has not proved possible to obtain full financial details. In addition to mail order, Quelle also has substantial high street sales in Germany: for example, it is the country's largest electrical goods trader.

This is not a full list of all European mail order: for example, the UK retailer W.H. Smith is also involved in this area but does not break out its sales. Nevertheless, the above represents most major European leaders.

Probably Otto Versand is the most interesting company for international expansion. It has been extending out of Germany for some years by a well-tried route:

■ Acquire a small mail order company or joint venture;
■ Find a new market niche in mail order;
■ Use the company's international expertise in mail order to build the business;
■ Avoid tackling leading companies head-on; and
■ Choose countries with well-developed postal systems and high population density.

In 1992, Otto purchased Grattan, the UK mail order company. Around the same time, La Redoute acquired Empire mail order (UK).

Quelle has larger sales in Germany but Otto Versand is second in France, Belgium and The Netherlands where Quelle is largely unrepresented. Otto Versand has also started in Japan. There are some real lessons from this company in international expansion.

Keypoint on communications channels
Mail order has been showing only low growth across Europe over the last few years – however there has been some scope in southern Europe. Whilst they are unlikely to represent a major distribution breakthrough, there are real opportunities to be investigated. Home shopping via television may represent a new extension of this area in the 1990s.

Cable and satellite television

Cable TV is available only in around 10 per cent of European homes. Satellite TV can potentially reach a much larger number without the massive cabling investment but is currently more of a prospect for the mid-1990s. Cable and satellite TV are extensively available in the USA and Canada. They also represent a new and existing means of reaching new audiences in the Far and Middle East and elsewhere.

The advantage of both lies not only in TV-spot advertising opportunities but also in the possibility of special channels devoted to selling consumer products: this is still largely underdeveloped in Europe compared to the USA. Direct selling via TV shopping channels would, of course, undermine existing distributors but it may be worthy of consideration.

For a more complete discussion of the media trends in Europe over the next few years, you may like to consult chapter 11 of my book *European Marketing*, also published by Kogan Page.

Depending on the pace of growth, cable and satellite could represent real opportunities for both target groups and distributors. But the risk is high and the rewards unclear: many companies do not have Mr. Rupert Murdoch's deep pockets – nor his business courage.

Telephone and computer network developments

Potentially, this represents one of the most interesting areas for channel opportunities in the 1990s. For business customers: information exchange, video conferencing, interactive computer/television demonstrations, links inside companies. The possibilities are there to be explored at a relatively modest cost. Although this area is being explored under 'distributor relationships', the strategy options are much broader.

Case Study: Europe's top telephone companies

Data

	Country	Turnover 1992 (US$ million)	Return on capital
*Deutsche Bundespost Telekom	Ger	36956	10.5%
**France Telecom	Fra	23005	na
British Telecom	UK	20645	14.6%

*STET	Ita	17500	na
*Telefonica de Espagna	Spa	11430	10.0%
Cable & Wireless	UK	9647	15.1%
**PTT Schwiez	Swi	6500 est	na
*Televerket	Swe	6251	10.7%
*PTT Nederlands	Net	6050 est	na

*Likely to be privatised in the 1990s.
**Likely to remain state-owned or controlled into the late 1990s.

Notes:
1. Although the company SIP (Italy) is publicly quoted, it is 60% owned by STET and is therefore not listed separately above.
2. The above excludes revenue from postal services.

European and global activity
Although full data is not available for most of the companies shown above, it has been reliably estimated that around 90% of their revenue is generated within the home country. The proportion of international calls is slowly rising and will continue to do so. However, strategy must therefore first address *national* issues.

In addition, strategy in telecommunications services also needs to tackle the high fixed investment by the companies in switching equipment and lines. Hence, one of the prime purposes of strategy has been to encourage the maximum usage of the equipment through price and promotional deals at times when the usage tends to drop.

Another strategy has been to charge the maximum socially acceptable price since the companies have been providing a monopoly service. For example, European international call prices are much higher than in the USA, mainly because there is greater competition in North America. We will return to the implications of this shortly.

The virtual monopoly held by many European national telephone operators has another implication: the European Union has already introduced competition on *data* transmission but around 90% of all telephone traffic is *voice* only. The real breakthrough will come when telephone companies are allowed to compete from 1998 on voice traffic. For example, British Telecom set up a Spanish network data transmission service with Banco Santander in 1992 and will be able to add voice circuits from 1998.

In the intervening period, several of the leading national operators are gearing up both for increased internal competition and for expansion elsewhere in Europe and globally. In practice, there is one small voice market already potentially available on a pan-European basis: mobile telecommunication services. This is described further in my book *Cases in European Marketing*, Kogan Page, 1994.

Currently most national operators in the EU are owned by their governments, but the majority will either be privatised or converted into semi-independent corporations over the next few years. Business strategy for these companies consists partly in preparing for these important changes: STET, Deutsche Bundespost Telekom (DB Telekom) and PTT Nederlands are amongst the leaders here. British Telecom (BT) went through this process in the early 1980s. However, in terms of productivity (measured as telephone lines managed per employee) BT was not as efficient in 1991 as France and the Netherlands, which were still under state control. Hence privatisation in itself does not necessarily lead to greater efficiency.

Because of the current restriction on European voice operations, many European telecommunications companies have been seeking to develop globally, ie where voice entry is possible. Thus BT has linked with the second largest international operator in the USA, MCI, to form a global network service called 'Syncordia'. It has also attempted to involve German and Japanese operators in the network service but without success so far. This is partly because the French and German national operators see their room for global expansion as being better served by offering a combined alternative service, possibly also linked with the largest US operator, AT&T.

Another global grouping that is underway involves the Japanese operator KDD with the Netherlands, Swedish and Swiss companies. The US company Sprint is also reported to be involved. Singapore Telecom and Telecom Australia may also link with this network or one of the others.

Several European operators have also moved into Eastern Europe, eg:

- Cable & Wireless (C&W) is investing in the Russian 'golden ring' of major cities from Moscow to St Petersburg
- C&W is also working with DB Telekom and Ameritech (USA) in Hungary
- DB Telekom is itself engaged in a massive programme to upgrade networks in the former East German Laender.

However, Cable & Wireless, which has extensive interests in the Far East (eg 50% of Hong Kong Telecom), has claimed to be less interested in global alliances. It has said its strategy was to seek partners in specific markets only because global alliances would mean attacking all the other telecommunications companies head-on: the resources required were too high.

There is an additional problem for global network building: the target group for such a venture is principally the world's 2500 multinational companies. However, many of these already employ sophisticated telecommunications engineers. The likely offering from the service providers – a complete package of globally managed telecomms services – may already be in place within the multinationals. Hence, any new global service might need to compete principally on price. Such an offering would rely heavily on being a low-cost producer, which in such a new technology area would have clear risks.

Some predict that mobile telephones linked to a new system of global satellites may represent the future (see for example *The Economist*, 28th March 1992, p. 89). We would no longer rely on fixed links at all. For myself, I believe that the prices of the telephone operators will come down so fast over the next ten years that it will be difficult to justify the competing investment in satellite services. The price pressure will intensify as television cable operators move increasingly into telephone voice services. Mobile will therefore remain premium-priced but will be valuable in remote corners of our planet where cabling would be uneconomic: for example, Siberia and the Gobi Desert. A truly global market.

Keypoints on channel strategy
General telecommunications developments: This field will have profound effects on every European company over the next 20 years. This is based on technology change but the demands of single Europe communication will make it happen more quickly and help to shrink the boundaries of the new Europe. New technology will make faster, cheaper and more reliable communications possible. Essentially, it will become much easier and cheaper to move information around Europe. Three examples will illustrate the point:

1. By the year 2000, it will no longer be necessary for a manufacturer on a pan-European basis to wait two months for a distributor to say what sales have been made and what stock remains. Daily data is highly likely.
2. After despatch of product, it will be possible to track distribution in detail right across Europe at any time to any location. Better service levels must result.
3. There will be a complete European mobile telephone network so key personnel can always be contacted.

No company should underestimate the profound effects this will have on the way business is conducted. It will actually make European integration much more of a practical reality than would have been possible when it was conceived by some in the late 1940s.

CHAPTER 24

Channel Strategy: Securing the Means of Distribution

THE THREAT AND OPPORTUNITY

Among Europe's Top 400 companies, one aspect of strategy that stands out is how many firms already own the means of distribution to the ultimate customer. This is a powerful strategic stance.

Retailers form the largest single segment in the Top 400, but this is not simply because the list uses turnover as the means of ranking the companies. It is also because many companies have great strategic stability from owning the means of distribution: the utilities, postal and telephone companies also deal direct with customers. Equally, transport companies, oil and petrol concerns and steel have all featured in these pages as having at least partially grabbed a share of direct distribution.

It is hard to quantify precisely but it is likely that there has been a shift in profits over the last 20 years, right across Europe, from manufacturing to distribution. Evidence for this can be seen in: the higher profitability of European retailers compared to various manufacturing sectors; rapid sales growth of large retail companies in Europe (20 years ago, this sector would have formed a smaller share of the total); and increasing store size (eg hypermarket growth).

This trend is neither 'good' nor 'bad': for example, companies such as Marks & Spencer (UK) and Ahold (Holland) have surely raised consumer quality standards in their own countries. Moreover, competition is certainly fierce in most European retailing so consumers have plenty of choice: perhaps the UK brewers who controlled their retail outlets are the exception here and showed what could happen to prices when other factors had to be considered.

The problem and the opportunity is that the process is not finished. Indeed, it is taking an international dimensions as distributors on both sides of the Atlantic, from pharmaceuticals to grocery, seek to put further pressure on manufacturers. Some distributors are quoted as saying that they want some share of the extra profits derived from the economies of scale of centralized manufacture.

THE ACTION TO BE TAKEN

Distributors will no doubt understand if manufacturers make the cynical judgement that the extra pressure will be applied whether economies are achieved or not: large buying groups have a tendency to gain a momentum of their own. Manufacturers might be protected by an investigation of new consortia by the European Commission, if this were to be undertaken: the EC laws on competition derive partly from the reasonably strict US anti-trust legislation. However, companies would be unwise to rely on this happening quickly.

For many firms, securing the means of distribution has therefore to figure strongly as a consideration in the development of international strategy. The most obvious solution is to buy distribution outlets. There are usually three difficulties associated with this approach:

1. Buying enough outlets to take a significant proportion of turnover cannot always be sufficiently profitable. The author has experience of analyzing the acquisition of a chain of butchers' shops to take part of the output of a large modern abattoir and reduce some of the price uncertainty in a commodity market. It was just not possible to buy sufficient outlets at a reasonable price to make this worthwhile. However, more generally, the prospects will vary with profit margins in the industry being analyzed: 'high fashion' may prove more attractive than 'meat'.
2. Distributor skills are very different to manufacturing skills. It can be a long, expensive learning process. The only way to shorten it is to buy a ready-formed chain but this will be more expensive.
3. Distributors become upset when manufacturers set up in competition with them. This is not a powerful argument but needs to be handled carefully.

SECURING DISTRIBUTION: THE OPTIONS

Despite these problems, some companies have taken action to protect themselves from competitive pressure and to exploit identified opportunities. Here are some options that firms might wish to consider:

■ Buy an existing distribution chain;
■ Buy sites and build a distribution chain;
■ Buy a manufacturing company with well-developed distribution arrangements;
■ Negotiate a long-term contract with a retailer or other distributor;
■ Franchising; or
■ Set up an exclusive arrangement and shareholding in a regional or national distributor.

Let us examine each of these in turn to see what they can offer for international distribution. All of them are examples of what might be undertaken rather than some 'magic formula' that will suit all strategic circumstances.

Buy an existing distribution chain

This is often the most expensive solution because a premium has to be paid for the existing business. Just because it is not cheap does not mean that it cannot be profitable in the long term: it just makes it more difficult. We have already examined St. Gobain glass. In 1990, the company acquired Solaglass, the UK's second largest glass distributors. This immediately increased access for the French company's products in the UK. It was not until 1993 that Pilkington awoke from its strategic obsession with low cost leadership and acquired the UK's largest glass distributors in order to defend its position.

Case Study: Usinor Sacilor SA, France

Data
Europe's largest steel company: French government owned.
1990 turnover (Ffr million)

Flat products	38181
Long products	24770
Stainless steels	14373
Metallurgy	4228
Processing	8985
Distribution	13618
Other	903
Intersegment	(9005)
Total	96053

Return on capital: 9.7% (see comment below)
% sales in home country: 69
% sales in rest of Europe: 26
% sales in rest of world: 5

European and global activity
Like all Europe's major steel producers, over the few years Usinor-Sacilor has been engaged in trying to sort out its national situation as well as the single Europe. The pressures that have brought this about result at least partly from a single market already existing in European steel.

Indeed, up to 1987, the situation across the continent was so bad that there was a cross-Europe legal agreement to fix the price of stainless sheet steel: market regulation via a crisis cartel is allowed in a slump (Article 58). In 1994, this was challenged by the European Commission.

The two French companies, Usinor and Sacilor, were brought together in 1986–87 to create a rationalized new combined company. Major investment and cuts were undertaken by the new group: the return on capital shown above is slightly misleading in view of various grants received. Moreover, the company was reported to have made a loss in 1991 and 1992, but I have been unable to obtain the details.

The objective has been to create a company capable of competing on a world-scale but with strong European connections: thus Usinor-Sacilor has taken a share of an Italian coated steel producer, La Mayone, bought 70% of the German company, Saarstahl and acquired the USA's second largest producer of stainless steel, Jones & Laughlin, for US$50 million. But building is not without difficulty: Saarstahl virtually collapsed in 1993 with German economic recession.

Keypoint on distribution channels
Among other purchases, Usinor-Sacilor acquired the major UK steel distributor, ASD, in 1991. It has said it will use this to sell more steel in the UK. This is not a cheap solution but may be essential for the French company to make progress in the UK. It followed the purchase by British Steel of the UK's leading distributor, Walker Brothers.

Buy sites and build a distribution chain

This is a slower process and cheaper in that no bid premium is paid. However, it is not necessarily more profitable because central distribution overhead costs cannot be spread over sufficient outlets while the chain is being built to make a profit.

Case Study: Petrofina SA, Belgium

Data
Europe's sixth largest oil and petrol refiner and distributor.
1992 turnover (Bfr million)

Exploration and production	50283
Refining, marketing and transportation	450671
Chemicals and paints	89027
Other	4864
Intersegment	(39087)*
Total	555758*

*Before duties and taxes of Bfr 161759 million

Return on capital: 7.1%
% sales in home country: na
% sales in Europe: 79
% sales in rest of world: 21

European and global market activity
Like many other oil companies, Petrofina is involved across Europe and North America. Over the last few years it has followed a strategy of concentrating on its strengths. Specifically, it has focused on geographical areas where it has competitive advantage, either due to the proximity of its refineries or due to efficient transport systems and logistics. As a result of this strategy, Fina Europe has recently sold part of its distribution network in France, Norway and Italy and built up its facilities elsewhere. Outlets have fallen in number of 17% over the five years 1987 to 1992, whilst volume per outlet has risen by 38%, resulting in steady overall sales and higher profitability. It has followed a similar policy in the USA.

Petrofina has a clearer concept of its company size and role than some European oil concerns: it has not become involved in agriculture, mining or other outside ventures. Perhaps because it has confined itself to what it does best, it has higher profitability than some other oil companies.

Keypoint on channel distribution
In addition to its major strength in Belgium, Petrofina has around 400 'Fina' petrol filling sites in the UK, plus others selling its petrol under franchise. In virtually every European country, filling stations only sell one brand of petrol so the only way to obtain distribution is to own or manage sites.

Petrofina has built up its UK sites over a number of years: securing distribution has been a steady process. It has meant that the company has a viable, cost-effective UK market share but has perhaps not achieved the sales of some of its rivals. Its effectiveness has partly come from linking distribution with refining.

Buy a manufacturing company with well-developed distribution

As described elsewhere in this book, in 1989 the French food company, BSN, acquired a significant share in the Italian cheese company, Galbani. At a stroke, BSN not only acquired additional dairy sales but also found a way of obtaining distribution in the fragmented Italian system. It is not necessary to buy a company outright: BSN took only a minority share in the early years, which it has subsequently increased.

Case Study: Lyonnaise des Eaux-Dumez SA, France

Data
In 1990, France's second leading water and public services company merged with the construction company Dumez by way of a share exchange.

1992 turnover (Ffr million)

Water and holding company	17395
Waste	4870
Energy	7408
Other services	3230
Building and civil engineering	26729
Road building	8828
Other construction	10348
Industrial property, financial services	11549
Total	90357

Return on capital: 2.2%
% sales in home country: 57
% sales in rest of Europe: 18
% sales in rest of world: 25 (especially USA)

Single market activity
The two French companies. Générale des Eaux and Lyonnaise des Eaux, hold major stakes in French water supply but both are engaged in a broader range of activities. During the late 1980s, Lyonnaise des Eaux has taken advantage of the more liberal UK regime to acquire: East Anglian Water Company; Essex Water Company; Newcastle and Gateshead Water Company; Sunderland and South Shields Water Company; and Bristol Water Company (18%). Its merger with Dumez in 1990 was because of common involvement in France with the same customers.

It has obtained cross holdings with Sociedad General de Aguas de Barcelona to obtain a presence in the Spanish water industry and it is also reported to have 'affiliates' in West Germany, Belgium, Italy and Switzerland. In addition, based on its experience in France, Lyonnaise has successfully bid for privatised cleaning services in the UK.

Dumez involvement in construction includes USA, Mexico, Chile, Thailand. But its deep reliance on the French market has meant it suffered with the economic downturn in the early 1990s.

Keypoint on channel distribution
Lyonnaise is also involved in funeral direction. During 1989 it has successfully bid for two large companies in this area in the UK: Kenyon and Hodgson. As the UK *Financial Times* said when the acquisition was announced: 'Funeral directing may not have been what the European Commission had in mind when it set about developing a single market in services but the three-way link between two modest

British undertakers and a French one creates a good approximation of the ideal European company of the future.'

With a high level of fixed costs in funeral directing and a fragmented market, Lyonnaise sees real opportunities for economies of scale. Importantly, by taking over the two UK companies, the French firm has acquired well-developed funeral distribution arrangements in Britain.

While some may smile at the specialist nature of this business, there is no denying its strategic usefulness: whether Lyonnaise makes real profits will depend both on the price paid and on subsequent earnings. It now claims to be the foremost operator in this area across Europe.

Negotiate a long-term contract with a retailer or other distributor

Merely making a sale to a retailer will not guarantee long-term distribution. But a sales contract with a distributor, in operation for several years, can be very worthwhile: it is often entered into under a distributor's own-brand but can offer real benefits to a manufacturer. Keen prices are often negotiated by retailers but usually there is also an emphasis on quality standards. Most of Europe's leading retailers are involved in this area.

With strong brands, some companies are reluctant to enter this sort of arrangement: Mars and Kelloggs are well-known examples. Others question the profitability of such deals and there is no point in denying that they will only suit manufacturers with modern machinery able to make product in volume on low profit margins. But retailers gain nothing by making the deal unprofitable to manufacturers, and useful high volume output can be obtained. This type of contracting exists all over Europe and 'guarantees' distribution.

It is not only retailers who are involved in such contracts and it is not only a question of obtaining volume sales. Car manufacturers seek long-term distribution arrangements because their customers need strong after-sales service.

Case Study: Volkswagen AG, Germany

Data
One of Europe's top six car manufacturers.
Turnover (DM million)

	1988	1992
Germany	22653	39508
Rest of Europe	22642	31540
North America	5828	3774
Latin America	4689	6345
Other areas	3409	4236
Total	59221	85403
Return on capital:	6.1%	(0.1%) loss
% sales in home country:	38	46
% sales in rest of Europe:	38	37
% sales in rest of world:	24	17

European and global activity
Volkswagen has been the market leader in Europe for some years but suffers from being a high-cost producer with its main plant in Germany. It moved some production to SEAT, Spain, which is lower cost. It also invested in Skoda, Czech Republic, in 1991 along with ventures in China, Portugal and East Germany. By 1993 it was beginning to realise that all these strategic moves failed to tackle the fundamental issue of high costs back home. It has now started a strategic programme of cost cutting and retrenchment in Germany.

Keypoint on channel distribution
Volkswagen has spent years and much resource building exclusive arrangements with car retail chains across Europe. The objective has been to secure both the best display arrangements at the point of sale and top quality after-sales service subsequently for VW and its subsidiary AUDI.

The results are shown in the sales levels achieved: while these vary from year to year, the company, along with Fiat, has been one of the top two volume car companies in Europe. A key part of this successful company is its powerful distribution strategy.

Franchising

Because most franchises involve an exclusive arrangement for a geographical area, they also give distribution protection as well as branding and other support. There are plenty of international franchise arrangements providing opportunities for smaller companies to obtain strategic benefit. Larger companies have also taken up the advantages as the retailer case study shows.

Case Study: Koninklijke Ahold NV, Netherlands and GIB, Belgium

Data

Ahold:		GIB:	
Holland's largest retailer.		Belgium's largest retailer.	

1992 turnover (Dfl million)		*1992 turnover (Bfr million)*	
Retail: Netherlands	10267	Retail: EC	192148
Retail: rest of Europe	209	Retail: USA	35790
Retail: USA	11118		

Return on capital:	15.4%	*Return on capital:*	8.7%
% sales in home country:	47	*% sales in home country:*	not available but mainly Belgium
% sales in rest of Europe:	1	*% sales in Europe:*	84
% sales in rest of world:	52	*% sales in rest of world:*	16

European and global activity: Ahold
Ahold trades partly in The Netherlands with a range of grocery hypermarkets (Miro) and supermarkets (Albert Heijn). It dominates Dutch retailing. As well as grocery sales, there are also other subsidiaries including a wine and spirits chain (Alberto) and a health and beauty chain (Etos).

Some years ago, the company took the view that further major growth inside the home country would be slow. Rather than expand across Europe where retailing was considered to hold few opportunities, the company selected the USA. It now has three supermarket chains in that country: First National Supermarkets; Bi-Lo; and Giant Food Stores. It has none elsewhere in Europe. However, Ahold is part of one of the new European buying retail consortia announced in 1989–90.

European and global activity: GIB

The company dominates Belgian retailing with a vast range of shop names, GB Hypermarkets and Supermarkets being the biggest single contributors to sales. There are also restaurant chains, clothing shops, toy chains and DIY chains.

With the scope for growth in Belgium being finite, GIB has expanded like Ahold into the US, where it has a 29% share in Scotty's in Florida and 65% of A-OK and Handy Andy around Chicago. However, it is not as well represented in that country as Ahold with the latter's range of wholly-owned subsidiaries.

GB has, however, expanded more than Ahold into Europe: it has acquired the French OBI Do-It-Yourself (DIY) store chain and an interest in a new Spanish chain. Its 25% interest in the UK's Sainsbury Homebase DIY subsidiary arose out of contacts in the early 1980s. Sainsbury is the UK's largest grocery retailer. It had identified DIY as a new growth area but did not have the expertise to start in the market by itself. GIB had made a great success of DIY in Belgium and came in to advise Sainsbury on its UK start-up in the early 1980s. There are now some 50 stores operating very successfully in the UK. GIB's main role in the 1990s in DIY outside Belgium is to operate a retail buying consortium on behalf of itself, Sainsbury and several other large European retail store groups. Because GIB's shareholding in these ventures is below 50%, it is not consolidated into its sales data.

Keypoint on channel distribution: GIB

Seeking other areas of growth in Belgium, the company identified restaurants. As a result of this analysis, it has taken up the franchise for Pizza Hut rather than developing a totally new concept. This has been done with Pepsico (US).

As a result of franchising, GIB secured expertise, branding and practical management experience in a new area. This reduces the risk to the company.

This book cannot provide a full discussion on the merits and problems of franchising. But it is relevant to international expansion: McDonalds (US) and Burger King (part of Grand Met) demonstrate clearly the global potential with that franchise operations around the world.

Exclusive arrangement and shareholding in a regional or national distributor

It is not necessary to take control in order to secure distribution: no grocery retailer anywhere in Europe can be without the top brands. Nevertheless, in some markets, there is little loyalty to individual brands. Here, there is a case for securing the distributor's commitment to a particular company by taking a shareholding. It may be expensive but it may also be the only way to secure the situation.

Case Study: Michelin SA, France

Data

World's largest tyre products company.

Turnover (Ffr million)

	1988	1992
Tyres and wheels	51287	64106
Tourist guides	2360	66847
Total	53647	66847

Return on capital:	14.7%	10.4%
% sales in home country:	22	18
% sales in rest of Europe:	47	40
% sales in rest of world:	31	41

European and global activity
Michelin has been highly successful at sales development world-wide: many other companies can learn from its single-minded skills in branding, technical development and company acquisition. In early 1990, it also completed the acquisition of Goodrich (US) to make it the world's largest tyre company.

As the above sales statistics also show, it is well established across Europe with strong shares in many leading markets. The single market may offer economies of production but is unlikely to produce further major sales opportunities.

Keypoint on channel distribution
In July 1989, Michelin outbid Japan's Bridgestone company and paid £140 million for the UK tyre distribution company, National Tyre Service. It was purchased from another of Europe's Top 400 – the UK company, BTR plc.

Because Michelin already owned another, even larger, tyre chain called ATS, it subsequently decided to sell NTS. In 1990, Continental acquired NTS from Michelin for £143 million and saved Michelin from the wrath of the UK Monopolies and Mergers Commission. There is not much brand loyalty in tyres, and availability to the customer through distribution is vital.

CONCLUSIONS

During 1993 and 1994, the strategic importance of controlling distribution channels was demonstrated in the world's largest pharmaceutical market: the global leader, Merck (US), acquired a leading US distributor in 1993 for US$ 6 billion. SmithKline Beecham (US/UK) then bought another leading US distributor in 1994 for US$ 2.3 billion.

Some companies will argue perfectly correctly that it is possible to obtain distribution for their products internationally through the traditional channels, such as export distributors. There is no denying that in the short term this must be true, but there may be little long-term security of distribution by this means.

The objectives of this chapter have been to demonstrate that there are other *more secure ways* of achieving the same objective. In the long term, it will be essential to explore these or be prepared to face real problems.

CHAPTER 25

Successful European and Global Strategy: The Action to be Taken

After all the definition and analysis, the time has come to boil these down to the essential strategies for the business: where possible, they need to be short, sharp and quantified. We will tackle this subject under the following headings:

1. Identifying the essentials;
2. Refining the company objectives;
3. Some words of caution on four important international issues;
4. Defending the home market;
5. Tackling production overcapacity arising from the removal of trade barriers;
6. Seeking lower costs from economies of scale and innovation;
7. Achieving larger sales from European and global markets; and
8. Excellence in one area.

To summarize all the areas we have examined so far, and to point the way forward on the issues above, Figure 25.1 shows the main steps we have followed in our development of strategies for European and global markets.

IDENTIFYING THE ESSENTIALS

One of the real dangers with strategy development is undertaking so much analysis that the company loses its sense of what is really important. Nevertheless, it is vital to investigate thoroughly the major options. So, how is the balance of what really matters obtained?

This is a question unique to each company. Unfortunately, neither this book nor any other can provide a 'formula' for the answer: it is not only Europe's Top 400 companies that are all different. However, here are four suggestions that may help:

1. Try summarizing the main conclusions on two or three sides of paper: possibly difficult, but easier if some clear management viewpoint has been reached.
2. Compare back to the original company objectives and cut conclusions that have only limited influence on what the company is setting out to achieve. This means using some managerial judgement on selecting the items that are really important.

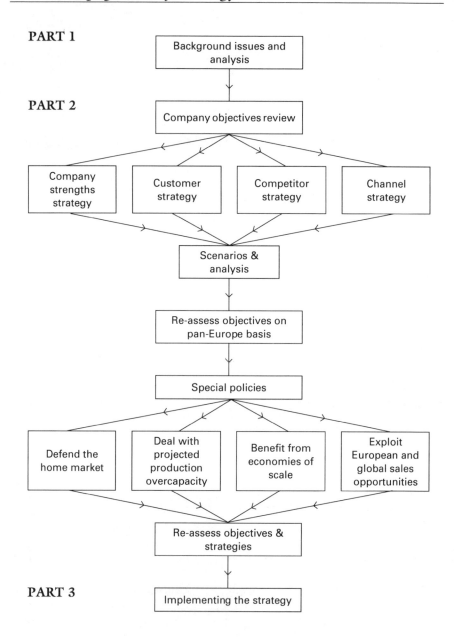

PART 1

Background issues and analysis

PART 2

Company objectives review

Company strengths strategy

Customer strategy

Competitor strategy

Channel strategy

Scenarios & analysis

Re-assess objectives on pan-Europe basis

Special policies

Defend the home market

Deal with projected production overcapacity

Benefit from economies of scale

Exploit European and global sales opportunities

Re-assess objectives & strategies

PART 3

Implementing the strategy

Figure 25.1 Overall strategic analysis

3. Quantify all items as much as possible and only retain those that will have a major impact on long-term profit. Estimating the impact in numbers is often difficult. But a *range of outcomes* may still be enough to show that, even in the best or worst case, a specific item is still unlikely to have much influence on the total and should be discarded.
4. Use the company's existing experience and knowledge as a starting point for future development. With caution, there is nothing wrong with drawing on existing knowledge: for example, if market branding and close control of labour costs is crucial in one country, then it may well be important internationally.

After all these activities have been undertaken, it will still be necessary to synthesize the outcome. Most companies have their own investment criteria (such as payback, discounted rate of return, etc.) to apply in estimating this. The difficulty with international analysis is to reduce the complex data sufficiently to calculate the results with confidence.

There are various other methods of deriving the outcome: eg cost/benefit analyses, rankings and decision trees. Companies can decide what suits them best: one that should be considered is *scenario building* as mentioned previously. *Best and worse cases* can also be built: the advantage is that they lend themselves to tackling the uncertainties that surround international markets. Figure 25.1 shows where these fit into the overall strategic analysis.

REFINING THE COMPANY OBJECTIVES

Ultimately, the reduction to essentials outlined above is assisted by the clarity of purpose of the business. What is the company really good at? What skills and resources does it fundamentally have? How can these be applied to European and global markets? And what are the critical success factors that apply internationally? Can the company do this by itself or does it need partners, a larger base of activity or skills in other countries? What are the company's objectives for international expansion? Is the market European or merely a staging post to a world market?

Perhaps this only means refining existing objectives – for example 'maintaining a viable share' might be applied to the larger market. This may be relatively undemanding and entirely consistent with the company's ambitions and identified threats. International markets may hold little scope and few problems. For other companies (possibly the majority), a thorough reappraisal will lead to a totally new set of objectives, including the need to build a new scale of operation under new rules. These will come from a detailed consideration of the opportunities and threats of international expansion, which need to be set out clearly.

We have been tackling these issues during the course of this book. But they are difficult to resolve outside the context of individual companies: the solutions are as unique as the firms themselves. They need to be summarized in the general analysis recommended above to arrive at best and worst cases and build scenarios.

In the absence of an individual company's situation, we can pursue our analysis by taking as our starting point the broad issues of European and world markets identified in the Introduction:

- The need to defend the home market;
- Tackling production overcapacity arising from the removal of barriers;
- Seeking lower costs from economies of scale and innovation; and
- Growth opportunities from larger market size.

We will use these as a template to judge what the company is good at and where it needs to develop, recognising that they may not be appropriate for every company. However, some companies may well regard these as a useful checklist for action in international markets.

WORDS OF CAUTION ON FOUR IMPORTANT INTERNATIONAL ISSUES

Let us see what our four major single market issues might mean for a company and start with some words of caution. Because companies are unique, this book has followed a straightforward path in developing strategy rather than concentrating solely on the four areas: not all companies will find all of them useful.

Defending the home market is totally meaningless to Europe's largest company, Royal Dutch Shell: it operates on such an international scale that a 'home market' is irrelevant. This is not to suggest that European and global markets have no meaning for Shell; for example, there may well be economies of scale in production that are difficult to achieve now because of cross-border barriers. Over time, they will become attainable.

Tackling production overcapacity from the removal of barriers is irrelevant in a rapidly growing European market such as mobile telecommunications. It simply does not apply.

Larger market size is meaningless to companies such as Volkswagen and Ford that are already operating essentially in global markets. There will be changes that will have a significant effect on these two companies, for example in European car type approval regulations. However, they may be nothing like as dramatic as outlined in the Cecchini Report, *1992: The Benefits of the Single Europe*, funded by the European Commission.

Lower costs from economies of scale may also be more difficult to achieve than the European Commission would have us believe, for at least two major reasons. First, Europe is too culturally diverse: just look at the cultural differences between Bavaria and northern Germany or between northern and southern England, let alone between Greece and Denmark. Second, Europe is too widely different in its ownership of wealth: compare, for example, the income per head in northern Italy with much of Ireland.

Different cultures and different levels of wealth across Europe will lead to great differences in demand across the Community. Thus it will be difficult to find easy common ground in products and services, let alone the economies of scale that might result. If there are to be such large cost savings, why are there still so many car plants in the USA? The reason is, partly at least, the diversity of demand.

The European Commission's Cecchini Report estimates major savings amounting to billions of US dollars in this area. However, it makes the simplistic assumption that, in the European car industry for example, all 12 countries will all want just a few basic models from a few massive car plants: the variety of European tastes and wealth make this unlikely. Essentially, the European Commission relies too heavily on simplistic economic price and cost arguments and not enough on the Community as a collection of diverse Europeans. The London Business School's excellent book, *1992: Myths and Realities*, explains this in detail.

Yet for some companies, there patently are cost economies of scale. Moreover, there are real cost savings from *innovation* in design and technology. Examples from confectionery to chemicals have been quoted throughout this book. Similarly, there are sales opportunities from international markets and there will be a threat to the home markets of some companies. Moreover, there will be production overcapacity in some industries. Hence, with all the words of caution outlined above, the four specific areas identified at the outset are worth addressing and exploring in the context of European and global markets. We will do this now and our specific aim will be to identify the strategies needed to tackle them.

DEFENDING THE HOME MARKET

Before we look in detail at this, let us quickly dispose of one myth: there is nothing 'anti-European' or xenophobic about a company defending what it already has. The firm's first responsibility is to its shareholders, management and employees and not to some vague concept of 'one Europe' or 'global brotherhood', however politically important these may be at a broader level. It should also be noted that 'home market' might actually be more than one country: back to our regional companies outlined at the beginning of the book.

Under this heading, a company needs to produce answers to the following questions:

1. What precisely are we defending?
2. Why are we undertaking the defence?
3. Will we defend everything we own?
4. How will we mount the defence?
5. Are there longer-term solutions that we need to examine, beyond mere defence?

What precisely are we defending?

In essence, we are defending the company business built up over time: satisfied customers; distribution networks; plant and assets; workforce, skills, etc. It is important to spell some of these out in detail, because that is the route to defending them: for example, important customers can be better retained if we know who they are.

Case Study: Tarmac plc, UK

Data
One of Europe's larger building and construction companies.
Turnover (£ million)

	1988		1992
Quarry products	486		506
Housing	786		651
Construction	683		978
Building materials	137		106
Industrial products	370		303
Properties	70		–
Tarmac America	304		247
Inter-company	(82)		–
		Business sold	145
Total	2754		2935
Return on capital:	29.4%		(1.4%)*
% sales in home country:	85		78
% sales in rest of Europe:	3		7
% sales in rest of world:	12		15

* Profit *before* major asset write-downs.

European and global activity
As will be evident from the sales data, Tarmac has hardly any European activity outside the UK. During 1990 and 1991 it made some acquisitions in France in quarrying and construction. But it has been badly affected by the economic downturn in both the UK and the USA. It has simply had no funds for expansion.

Keypoint on home defence
Arguably, with so much of its activity in one country, Tarmac has more to defend than most. It is no business of this book to build the company's defences but Tarmac will no doubt be examining such matters as:

- Customer base and the extent to which it needs defending;
- Rival UK companies and their vulnerability to takeover by, or joint venture with, other European companies; and
- Pricing and promotion policies versus other European companies.

Why are we undertaking the defence?

There are two clear responses common to most companies in this area: (a) because the home country is the bedrock of our international expansion; and (b) because the home country provides profits now.

But defence may cost profits and resources. (Indeed, as we will see below, some areas cannot be defended profitably at all.) There is therefore a balance between the costs of defence and the cost of losing some business. It may not be the most profitable strategy to defend at all costs and the responses above need some caution.

By far the best way forward is to calculate, however roughly, the *costs of defending the company* or part of it. If the cost is very high, then other solutions such as sale or joint venture may be more profitable: we will examine these shortly. Costs will obviously differ for each company but, purely as examples, they might include: loss of profit from operating at lower margins to match new competition; the cost of higher quality or service required; and higher promotional or advertising costs. Formidable competition from some Japanese companies has shown just what it can cost to mount a defence.

Will we defend everything we own?

Smaller companies with only one product range may have no choice, but larger companies with a portfolio of products or services must ask this question. There are clearly circumstances where a weak but viable national market share will turn rapidly into a disaster in larger markets.

This applies particularly where the company is currently protected by national barriers or possibly by public procurement policies that must change in the mid-1990s (if not 1992). There are plenty of examples in the defence sector, public building work, telecommunications and public health where a small viable business will no longer be able to survive without some major changes. Straight defence is not a solution in these circumstances.

Case Study: Philips NV, Netherlands

Data
Europe's largest electronics company.
1992 turnover (Dfl million)

Lighting	7351	Netherlands	3135
Consumer electronics	21588	Other Europe	32133
Other consumer products	10369	USA & Canada	12806
Professional products & systems	10530	Latin America	2939
Components and semi-conductors	6220	Africa	648
Miscellaneous	2469	Asia	5892
		Australia/New Zealand	974
Total	58527		
		Total	58527

Return on capital: 9.5% (before major restructuring costs)
% sales in home country: 5%
% sales in rest of Europe: 55
% sales in rest of world: 40%

European and global activity
Philips is already heavily involved across Europe and around the world. The company's major activity in the late 1980s has been the acquisition of three record companies with world-wide interests: Polygram, Island Records and A&M Records. The combined interests confirmed Philips as one of the top three recorded music companies in the world. In the 1990s, it has concentrated on restructuring to reduce costs.

Because of the lack of profitability in Philips' basic business, the company has had to cut back its excellent research and engineering design. It has faced severe marketing competition from the major Japanese companies over the last 10 years: cheaper Far Eastern production of some items is only one example in this world wide battle. Philips now manufactures some products in these countries for sale in the West.

Keypoint on home defence

During 1989, Philips announced that it was selling its defence companies in France, Belgium and Holland to Thomson-CSF of France. It has also sold its Swedish defence company to Bofors and is planning to sell its German interests as well. In 1990, it sold its domestic appliances business to Whirlpool (US).

The company has indicated that it is selling these interests because of growing concentration in increasingly competitive industries and the steep cost escalation and speed required in developing new products. There comes a time when businesses are no longer defendable at reasonable cost.

Two years earlier, Philips sold its telecommunications interests to Alcatel, the French telecommunications company. Again, the company said that defence was best served by withdrawal rather than a prolonged battle. However, it has to be said that, with Philips' overall funds being so low, the company may make more money from selling assets regardless of defensive tactics, so the motivation may not be just simple defence.

More broadly, company tradition can produce an emotional attachment to a business area although long-term company interests may be better served by its disposal. It may not be wise to defend everything owned.

How will we mount the defence?

Let us make the assumption that we are not going to withdraw and will defend our sales. What do we do? It depends on the nature and quality of the attack. There is no 'magic formula' but here are some pointers based on logic and experience:

- Be very clear on objectives. Do we want the other company to withdraw? Do we want a major battle over price and margins or would we settle for a less costly skirmish over quality of service or product?
- Sharpen up the market intelligence. Early warning (perhaps from a friendly customer) about new entrants and what they are offering is helpful in deciding what to do.
- Analyze the possible competitors. We have already discussed this: we need to predict how they will attack and then decide what we will do.
- If there is an obvious market niche to be attacked by a competitor, consider launching your own product or service to fill the demand. This may sound foolish but the best form of defence may well be to attack your own overall market share. Profits may be lower but nothing like so low as allowing competitive entry: there might even be some economies of scale.
- Look after your main customers in the new circumstances. You do not have to be IBM Europe to accept that this is at the heart of good defence. Customers make sales.
- Do not allow the competitor to become established. New entrants are most vulnerable in the early days. That is the time to hit back, not to wait for them to gain a foothold.
- Bold competitive moves need a strong response. New entrants offering something dramatic like a price reduction of 30 per cent or round-the-clock delivery can best be attacked by vigorous response. Sitting back and waiting

to see market reaction is asking for trouble, unless your objectives include allowing the new entrant to take sales.

■ Make entry difficult and unprofitable. Barriers still exist and no company has any obligation to hasten their destruction. There are plenty of people to undertake this task. Moreover, the courts exist to protect companies and employees against unfair attack, for example on patent infringement and copyright: lengthy delays, whilst perfectly legitimate legal and government matters are resolved, can provide added protection. They can even persuade potential competitors that a cheaper solution is best for all concerned.

■ Consider a counter-launch into the home territory of the new entrant. Sometimes the best form of defence is attack. The way to stop the new company may be to undermine its profitable home base elsewhere in the world. However, this can drain scarce resources so needs careful thought.

Defence also depends on one other important factor: whether or not your company holds market leadership. Actions may vary somewhat for market leaders: for example, they may wish to outspend new entrants in marketing funds. But the above principles are worth considering for every company regardless of share and type of market, industrial and consumer.

Are there longer-term solutions we need to examine beyond mere defence?

Ultimately, stopping competitive entry may win the battle but is unlikely to win the war. Most international markets will need to reach a new equilibrium over time. The mature company will therefore regard the defensive battle as only part of the process: longer-term solutions will be required.

We have already looked at the advantages of choosing the ideal competitor when considering market entry. The same principle in reverse applies here in the defensive battle: it is better to have a competitor keen to earn a reasonable return on capital than one with a bottomless pocket able to sustain the war for years. It may be necessary to *choose between competitors*, keeping some out and encouraging others.

Taken further, it may be better in the long term to form a business relationship with a new entrant, possibly by trading-off a threatened counter-launch. As long as this is not against EU or GATT competitive policy, then it can lead to new international market stability.

Over the next 10 years in world markets, it is likely that this will provide one of the more profitable solutions to any company defensive battles. The concept of 'war to the death' disappeared across most of Europe during the Middle Ages and its revival is not in the best interests of companies in European and global markets.

TACKLING OVERCAPACITY ARISING FROM TRADE BARRIER REMOVAL

As we saw in Part I, there is no doubt that some companies will go out of business as a result of this. Even those that survive will suffer to some extent. There is only limited value in looking to such bodies as the European

Commission for help since they seem quite determined to see rationalization take place.

For clarity, we are *only* concerned here with overcapacity that will arise as trade barriers come down. We will deal in the next section with problems arising as companies put up new plant and create new capacity to achieve economies of scale. Moreover, trade barriers involve more than the single Europe: for example, Far Eastern countries are already the largest global manufacturers of computer hard-discs and artificial textile fibres.

Whilst the European Commission's predictions on over-capacity were questioned in chapter 7, we have identified several industries in major difficulty: basic chemicals (chapter 14) and steel (chapter 22). There are no doubt other industries. The key strategic issue to explore is what can an individual company do to minimize the damage. There are four main questions to be answered:

- Just how much overcapacity will there really be?
- What options do we have to survive in the industry?
- What strategies can we devise to avoid overcapacity?
- Will any of these be worth more to the company than getting out at the right time?

Just how much overcapacity will there really be?

It is vital to assess this correctly, since the very survival of the company may depend on the conclusions. Some companies will find that this question will pass them by, but they are likely to be those with particular skills. The greater danger is probably to underestimate the problem.

Here are three suggested ways to clarify the extent of overcapacity in specific single market industries:

- Use the EC's own data. The European Commission regularly produces extensive statistics on European and global industries. They are available for public purchase. Contact your national EC office.
- Commission your own study from outside advisers. This may sound expensive but, compared with the potential downside of company survival, it may represent value for money.
- Conduct the study on an industry-wide basis. There is a real role here for the national trade organization representing a particular industry. For example, trade associations for the textile industry which has faced overcapacity for many years, have done excellent work in this area. They also provide the basis for a stronger negotiating stance with national governments, the EU and GATT. It is my own view that national trade unions also have much to gain by careful study and consideration in this area. Employer and employee interests largely coincide in this matter.

What options do we have to survive in the industry?

This needs to be examined from a pan-European and global viewpoint. The options will ultimately depend on the specific analysis but here are some general pointers based on logic and experience:

- Consider buying rival companies and closing down capacity. This may sound harsh but it has been successfully attempted in steel, textiles and the food industries in the past. The survivors are more sound.
- Decrease the cost base. This is a key decision but the survivors are much more likely to be those that have lower costs. It follows that, if this really is not an option at any stage, then some fundamental change is required. It should be recognized that it is much easier to write these few words and much more difficult to analyze and undertake. Nevertheless, companies need to face the issue that the objective of the whole process is to reduce the global cost base. It means that some individual companies will have to take the decision to invest to achieve this.
- Link through to customers or end-users. It may be possible to reduce the risk by securing part of the market by negotiating a contractual link of some kind. Some car industry suppliers have secured their future in this way.
- Introduce a stronger service element into the product portfolio. By providing a much higher service element, some companies, for example in the computer and boiler-making industries, have found the means of survival. This has the great strategic merit that it takes the company away from pan-European or global competition: service has to be regional or even local in many cases. For the smaller company faced with such a threat, this route has real business merit.
- Beware industries where some companies remain supported by funds from their governments. This is probably the single most important issue in steel and basic chemicals in the European Union. It probably needs tackling at government-to-government level. Hence it may be important to seek active support from a company's own national government.

What strategies can we devise to avoid overcapacity

Either in addition, or as an alternative to staying with existing markets and customers, it may be possible to develop in new areas. For example, it may be possible to *redefine the market* – look for new customers for existing products. For example, railway stock manufacture has recently been extended to become 'local area mass transit' using train systems. This takes the train transport market into a new area. Alternatively, *develop a specialist market* – new uses and new customers.

Let us examine an industry that has already had to face some significant capacity problems.

Case Study: Selected European mechanical and heavy engineering companies

	Country	1992 Turnover (US$ m)	Return on capital	Sales destination Home (%)	Rest of Europe (%)	Rest of world (%)
*Siemens	Ger	25833	na			
*Asea Brown Boveri	Swi/ Swe	23616	na			
*Mannesmann	Ger	10487	na			
*Thyssen	Ger	8060	na			
*GEC	UK	6672	na			
*Krupp	Ger	6118	na			
*MAN	Ger	5597	na			
*Alcatel Alsthom	Fra	5458	na			
Sulzer	Swi	5155	5.2%	18	45	37
Deutsche Babcock	Ger	5144	2.1%	61	18	21
Linde	Ger	5070	9.9%	50	37	13
SKF	Swe	4756	(5.7%)	5	56	39
*Trafalgar House	UK	4046	na			
Alfa Laval	Swe	3600 est	na			
*BTR	UK	3122	na			
Sandvik	Swe	3069	11.0%	7	51	42
Atlas Copco	Swe	2857	11.6%	5	52	43
Klockner Humboldt Duetz	Ger	2466	13.7%	18	31	51
Siebe	Ger	2470 est	na			
*Austrian Industries	Aus	2463	na			
FAG Group	Ger	2398	(1.1%)	39	29	32
*Rolls Royce	UK	2345	na			
*AGIV	Ger	2114	na			
TI Group	UK	1900	13.7%	18	31	51
*Klockner Werke	Ger	1357	na			
Stork	Net	1239	na	36	36	28
EFIM	Ita	622	na			
*Pechiney	Fra	465	na			
*Oerlikon Buhrle	Swi	332	na			

* Turnover is only part of total for company

Notes:
1. The above table covers plant engineering and design, mechanical engineering, shipbuilding, machine tools, diesel engines, turbines, boilers and environmental control. It does not cover electrical engineering, car components and steel but there is an expanding grey area arising from the increased sophistication of many products.
2. Because different sectors of heavy engineering have been combined together, the relative positions of companies in each sector will not necessarily be as shown above.
3. Spanish and Italian companies are largely missing. This is because most are still owned by the government or banks and data is not published.

European and global activity
Many of the listed companies are described in detail elsewhere in this book. They are therefore not covered here.

Rolls Royce acquired the British turbine makers, NEI during 1989. Also, a joint agreement has since been signed with ABB turbines to give that company access to the UK market. Without doubt, the turbine industry is global.

Sulzer and MAN attempted to form a joint company for diesel engines but this was stopped by the German cartel office. Sulzer's textile machinery-making business has been depressed, along with the rest of this global industry.

Strategies in all these industries involve close and long term cooperation with potential customers, innovation in design and, in some cases, advanced engineering skills.

Keypoint on moving into new product areas

Several of the leading companies have been developing and extending their activities in one of the potential growth markets of the 1990s: environmental control and engineering. Specifically, ABB and Deutsche Babcock both list this product area as one with substantial sales.

Companies are using their existing experience and capacity in plant design, sewage and waste disposal systems to meet demand in this rapidly growing area. While aspects of heavy engineering, such as machine tools and diesel engines, suffer from excess capacity and sophisticated competition, some companies have been able to move into new fields to more than compensate for losses elsewhere.

Will any of these strategies be worth more than getting out at the right time?

There is usually a cost and time delay involved in all new investment decisions. There may be an alternative which is to withdraw from the marketplace. Rational decision making demands that the cost of this option be considered. It is not possible in this book to predict the outcome but it is appropriate to raise the matter.

SEEKING LOWER COSTS FROM ECONOMIES OF SCALE AND INNOVATION

By now, this book will hopefully have aroused a healthy suspicion amongst most readers about projected economies of scale in European and global operations. Innovation in process design may further reduce costs radically. The whole issue is particularly difficult to pin down for the individual company because most of the analysis has been done on an industry-wide rather than for the individual firm. Moreover, the economic assumptions used at the broad level are difficult to apply to the individual company – eg the scale and pace of change and innovation cannot be considered.

Let us concentrate solely on the individual company and the seven questions it will want to ask about economies of scale and innovation:

1. Will we create overcapacity in our industry when we move to achieve economies of scale or innovate?
2. Where are cost savings likely to be obtained in our industry and company?
3. When are the cost savings likely to be achieved?
4. How will the cost savings be achieved in the competitive marketplace?
5. Will it be necessary to take a gamble on investment before the savings are obtained?
6. How will we increase sales to justify the scale or innovative investment?
7. Can Europe provide the basis for global expansion?

Will we create overcapacity when we move to achieve economies of scale or innovate?

We have already looked at overcapacity in European industries as barriers come down. We are now concerned with a different issue: *creating* excess capacity as a result of building larger plant innovation to reduce our costs. Even if international markets are largely in balance at present, it is essential to look at this crucial question because it may affect the action to be taken. Clearly, any company's decision to add capacity, however cost-effective, will have to be very brave if substantial overcapacity is created as a result. Any company which doubts that this is a real consideration has only to look at parts of the European chemical or steel industries over the last 10 years.

It may be argued that the economies to be achieved by the new capacity will be so overwhelming that they will force other companies to close. This may be true but it is also possible that other companies may fight for their survival and choose to lose money for at least a time. Even if they eventually go out of business, they could do enormous damage to the survivors and for a period, make scale economies less profitable. This is precisely what has happened in European iron and steel (see case study).

A much more profitable solution might be to spend the capital earmarked for economies of scale on doing a deal with other companies to eliminate the overcapacity in the market. The chances are that if there is a substantial problem then someone is cutting prices somewhere in order to make a sale: just eliminating this would raise margins. The difficulty is that cutting capacity will mean sacking employees and some governments find this unacceptable.

Case Study: European iron and steel industry

This case needs to be read in conjunction with the market data in Chapter 22 ('Channel strategy').

Major companies have been modernized for years without resolving the excessive capacity in the market because of national political pressures. Efficient companies have been forced into bankruptcy, while others have been kept alive by government subsidies. All this has been made worse by the partial suspension of normal free market pressures.

Until the market turned up in the late 1980s and eliminated excess capacity, price and production controls were dominant and profits were dreadful. A major national steel company actually referred to its successful modernization programme as providing survival if demand should slacken, because the company would still be profitable. When demand turned down in the early 1990s, the crisis returned.

Companies in the rest of European industry need to work hard to avoid similar difficulties in the 1990s. And companies need to be tough with the European Commission if it starts to argue the nonsense that has bedevilled the iron and steel industry over the last 30 years.

More generally, if there is likely to be overcapacity in the single market, then economies of scale are only one possible route to increased profits. It may be more profitable to remove the overcapacity first. It may also be essential to find innovative new solutions.

What cost savings are likely to be obtained in our industry and company?

With the increased scope provided by European and global markets, companies need to identify whether one of the advantages will be the opportunity to obtain scale economies or other cost savings. This means looking at the industry's and the company's cost structures.

Companies will have a good idea in their own areas of where the savings might come. The obvious ones are plant size economies, new processes and transport and warehousing logistics. Equally, there are areas where economies of scale in the larger markets will only be achieved with difficulty. For example:

- Where transport costs are a large percentage of the total cost (eg soft drinks can manufacture);
- Where market demand places a premium on individually made items (eg fashion items);
- Where market demand is varied and dislikes a standardized product (eg some textiles); and
- Where personal service forms a high proportion of total costs (eg some forms of insurance).

Ideal industries are those with standardized products produced in large plants such as chemicals, oil and petrol. But, of course, European and global markets already have the benefit of many of these, even if they are distorted by barriers, both obvious and hidden.

If you believe simple economic analysis, then some of the cost reductions will also find their way through into lower prices and increased sales. This is fine in theory but more difficult to project accurately for the individual firm: in practice, this makes it difficult to use sales increases in the assessment of economies of scale. Innovation and its effects are equally difficult to predict.

When are cost savings likely to be achieved?

Timing is just as important as type of investment in obtaining profitability: for example, there is no point in investing in new plant for 1992 if major barriers still exist until 1997. The careful analysis of open and hidden barriers will provide evidence in this area. However, it is likely that the company may have to take a calculated risk: this can be reduced if the time lag to achieve the cost saving can be reduced.

Case Study: Ford Motor Company, USA

Data
One of Europe's top six motor companies.

1992 turnover (US$ million)		Net losses
USA	59138	(582)
Europe	24739	(1283)
Other	19345	90
Intersegment	(18815)	
Total	84407	(1775)

Return on capital: (0.1%)
% sales in home country: 57
% sales in Europe: 24
% sales in rest of world: 19

European and global market activity
First, it is useful to be reminded that the USA is far more important to Ford than Europe.

In late 1989, Ford acquired the UK premium car company, Jaguar plc, with the aim of mounting a stronger challenge in that sector of the market in the late 1990s against BMW and Mercedes Benz. In spite of major investment in Jaguar, Ford had still not seen a significant return on its investment by 1994. Ford will remain a powerful player as the European car market develops during the 1990s.

Keypoint on cost savings
Ford has, of course, operated integrated production across Europe for some years. Thus, it produces various models in one location and then transports them to other countries for sale: Granadas from Germany to the UK, Escorts from Spain to Germany.

What has been noticeable, as production and logistics have been rationalized, is that the scale economies have been justified, in public statements by Ford, by lower costs not increased sales. Although Ford has no doubt identified sales benefits through higher profit margins, it has not built its public case on this basis: cost reductions are without doubt more certain than sales gains in assessing economies of scale and perhaps in justifying investment proposals to experienced Ford senior management!

In addition, as the remaining European car type approval barriers are removed, it is likely that Ford will be able to achieve further scale economies. However, the timing of these has to be uncertain and therefore it is difficult to project profit benefits.

Much larger cost savings are now being achieved by Ford from innovation, closer relationships with suppliers and plant process improvements.

How will cost savings be achieved in the competitive marketplace?

Once again, there is no 'magic formula' for companies but here are a few suggestions:

- Assess the company's cost profile and identify where increased investment would provide significant cost savings, along with the underlying assumptions. Purely as examples, the assumptions might include product range rationalization, deals with trade unions on manning levels and increased yields from new processes.
- Identify competitors, assess their capacity utilization and any future investment plans they might have announced. The proposed saving must be set in the context of competitive activity. It may be of limited value to achieve a cost reduction of 20 per cent if the competition is moving to attain 30 per cent within the following year.
- Take an early lead in achieving cost savings. The experience curve shows quite clearly that catching up is always more difficult.
- If a competitor takes an early lead on price cuts from cost savings, consider responding with an equal cut, even at some loss of profit, in order to hold

customers whilst the investment is made. Inevitably, some firms will be first. If the situation is recoverable in a reasonable time frame, then protecting customers is highly important. But recognize that this is only short term: some European computer companies seem to have seen this as a semi-permanent solution.

■ If the competitor has a major cost lead, then consider either making a major leap past this company or developing another market initiative such as a niche positioning. Running simply to catch up can only be a short-term solution. A technological jump or some other move is needed to recover the situation, or it may be better to move the company away from direct competition.

■ Lay the emphasis on cost savings rather than sales increases to justify the investment involved. This has a higher probability of being correct. Naturally, it may not be feasible to rely wholly on cost savings: some increase in sales may be required. It is a matter of emphasis rather than absolutes.

■ Investigate barriers or other structural conditions carefully to ensure that the planned saving will be achievable and on what timescale. Do not place too much hope in protesting to the European Commission if they remain: the response may be sympathetic but power still remains at least partially with national governments.

Finally, it is worth bearing in mind that cost savings are based on the rational argument that all buying decisions are made mainly on price. Even in industrial markets this is plainly only partially true: quality of service, specialized products and all the other areas outlined elsewhere in this book also sell goods and services.

The best way to overcome competitive cost reduction may be to sidestep price cuts and seek something else which will be of real benefit to customers. It is partly this that makes some Japanese companies such powerful competitors.

Will we need to take a gamble on the investment before savings are obtained?

There are some situations where it takes several years just to design and install the investment before it begins to earn anything at all. Even after this time, savings may not be achievable because, for example, barriers remain: they are expected to disappear but it is not certain. It may therefore be necessary to gamble on the investment before obtaining the economy.

While it is right to identify this question as one that some companies will need to answer, it is not possible to resolve here: there are too many issues involved. The scale of investment, the risk-taking stance of the company and the importance of any remaining structural impediments will all need to be assessed.

How will we increase sales to justify the scale or innovative investment?

Clearly, this is an essential part of the process. It is naive marketing to think that just by reducing the price it will be possible to achieve increased sales. Taking the Japanese company experience again, possible strategies might include:

- Seeking a segment of the market;
- Heavy advertising and promotion;
- Higher quality products;
- Better service levels than current products; and
- Lower prices.

And all these will be funded by lower costs from economies of scale. But this is part of the larger question of increased sales in the single market, which may be associated (but not necessarily) with cost savings.

Can Europe provide the basis for global expansion?

For companies such as GEC Alsthom turbine manufacture, European joint venture has provided the scale to assist its global activities. This may be an important consideration when assessing the cost profile arising from European-scale activity.

ACHIEVING LARGER SALES FROM EUROPEAN AND GLOBAL MARKETS

This is at the heart of the international market opportunity. We started our discussions by asking whether it was an opportunity or an irrelevance: we are now primarily concerned with those companies who see possible opportunities. Much of this book is concerned with ways of analysing and resolving this issue. Ultimately, the company will need to answer six specific questions:

1. What market are we in and what does this imply for marketing and sales strategy?
2. Are there any special selling opportunities that we need to tackle?
3. What will our company bring to potential customers?
4. Which of the four main ways will we choose for our international expansion: launch, joint venture, alliance or takeover?
5. How will we tackle existing competitors?
6. How will we gain distribution and keep it?

What market are we in and what does this imply for marketing and sales strategy?

Grizzled strategy professionals will recognize this question, which is just as relevant to European and global markets as it was when applied to other markets years ago. Companies need to resolve whether they are engaged in: world markets, European markets, regional markets within Europe, national markets or local markets inside a national boundary. If the conclusion is 'European markets', then firms also need to be clear why this has been identified: is it for the opportunities that the market offers in itself, or is it because it provides the scale to tackle world markets?

We looked earlier at issues to be examined in resolving this, so will not repeat them here. Because it will define our market size, growth prospects and competition, it will have a profound effect on strategy. There may be more than one answer to the question, so that is where *scenario building* of options comes into its own again.

It is at this early stage that marketing strategy needs to be explored. The steps to assist its development have been laid out in this book. Not all will be relevant to each company, so reject what is not wanted. There is no overall strategy that will fit all circumstances for international expansion. It will need to be developed for the situation of a European or global industry: this is why this book has presented European industry analyses, rather than a universal solution because it does not exist. As Professor John Kay says in the London Business School's book on the single Europe: 'the significance of 1992 is almost entirely to be found in measures that are industry-specific.'

Are there any special selling opportunities we need to tackle?

Companies need to probe two main areas to answer this: (1) European and global opportunities; and (2) trade barrier and structural opportunities. With regard to European and global opportunities, for a specialist product or service, it may be possible to sell this beyond existing markets. It is certainly worth examining the possibility. On trade barrier and structural opportunities, there are some specific areas where barriers will eventually come down and offer real opportunities. These include public procurement, national buying policies by semi-governmental and other agencies and heavily protected industries that will suddenly be opened up. These may be easier to identify in Europe and North America than some more distant markets.

Let us look briefly at a couple of examples in these areas.

Case Study: Robert Bosch GmbH, Germany

Data
World's largest automobile equipment manufacturer.
Turnover (DM million)

	1988	1992
Automotive equipment	14418	17225
Communications technology	6629	8172
Consumer goods	4816	7070
Capital goods	1812	1965
Total	27675	34432
Return on capital:	16.6%	6.1%
% sales in home country:	na	na
% sales in Europe:	82	85
% sales in rest of world:	18	15

European and global activity
For many years, Bosch has been managed out of Germany. Its consumer goods businesses (household appliances, power tools, etc.) still rely partly on their German sales. Similarly, communications (car radios, home electronics, etc.) also rely on the home market where the company is second to Siemens. More recently, it has developed a cooperation agreement with Maytag in the USA. It also has plant in Greece and Spain, but 64% of all employees are in Germany.

Its international business is concentrated in communications and automotive products, where the company has been active across Europe. Activities include acquiring shares in a Portuguese car parts company and setting up UK car alternator manufacturing. The company is also building more manufacturing closer to individual car plants in order to meet the needs of local customers (so much for the EC's economies of scale!).

More recently, Bosch has been developing joint ventures in the USA, Czech Republic, Japan and Turkey. It has also made great efforts to expand its distribution networks across much of Eastern Europe and into South Korea and the Philippines. Its strategy is becoming increasingly global.

Keypoint on Europe-wide opportunities
Bosch has built its reputation on technically superior products which it has sold initially in Germany and then all over Europe. For example, it was the pioneer of anti-lock braking systems for cars and is now world leader. It used Europe as the spring-board for world sales in this case.

Case Study: Ciba, Switzerland

Data
One of the world's largest chemical and pharmaceutical companies.
1992 turnover (Sfr million)

Healthcare	8662
Agriculture	4817
Industry	8725
Total	22204

Return on capital: 6.6% after tax
% sales in home country: na (but clearly low)
% sales in Europe: 43
% sales in rest of world: 57

European and global activity
With well over half its sales outside Europe, Ciba is a truly global company: 32% of total sales were made to North America alone in 1992. Throughout the period 1988–92, it has continued to develop its global businesses with acquisitions in North America, Japan and elsewhere.

It has also divested some businesses to concentrate on healthcare, which has risen from 30% to nearly 40% of sales over the period. Hence its research-based investment has also risen.

Keypoint on special selling opportunities
With the increased costs of pharmaceutical development, drug companies like Ciba benefit from access to as many markets as possible. Being Swiss-based, the company must therefore welcome all reductions in restrictions on market entry into EU and GATT markets around the world. The 1993 Uruguay Round of GATT may therefore have a special, positive effect on the company.

More generally in answer to this question, there will be opportunities in a number of national areas from cars to telecommunications. It will only be possible to identify these in the context of the specific markets: that means market analysis.

What will our company bring to potential customers?

Although nothing is impossible, it is unlikely that a similar product to those already available will attract many customers. We have explored this in detail earlier. In effect, we have looked at two aspects of the answer: (1) it needs to be relevant to what customers want; and (2) it needs to be different from what customers are being offered now. The first will emerge from customer strategy and the second from competitive strategy. It is appropriate to raise the question now, but it can best be answered by the detailed analysis previously described: as before, you can ignore parts that are irrelevant to your circumstances.

A completely different company answer to the question mght be 'essentially nothing', in which case the only solutions that make sense involve joint venture or acquisition in the target country. We discuss this next.

International expansion: launch, joint venture, alliance or takeover?

After all the analysis, there are only four ways to move internationally: one must be chosen if a move is to be made. Naturally, coupled with this, there are the questions of how existing competitors are to be tackled and distribution gained. We will come to these shortly.

To illustrate the four routes, let us take the case of a product or service to be sold more widely into international markets. *Launch* means the product or service is taken from the home country and launched into another market. It may be adapted to suit the new customers by simple changes or something more complex. It is quite likely that the product will be exported from the home country.

With *joint venture*, the product or service is still launched into a selected market but here the originating company does not do so by itself. Two companies typically combine their resources, often in the home country as well as in the selected country, to form one new enlarged company undertaking the launch. While the decisions on distribution are usually easier because they rely on the greater experience of each country's managers, other decisions on targeting, price and promotion are more difficult. Moreover, management decisions over time can also be a problem depending on the objectives of the originating companies. For example, something as straightforward as dividend payout policies to shareholders may be different and cause conflict.

With *alliances*, cross-shareholdings are sometimes undertaken. They tend to leave management decision taking to the target country. They give the new country a real incentive to succeed with the new product, but there is the loosest management control.

Finally, there is *takeover*: here a local company is acquired in order to facilitate the distribution of the home country's products as well as contribute its own sales to the new combined group. Clearly, once the takeover has been agreed, decision making can be more straightforward. In practice, matters are not always so simple. For example, a premium may well have been paid to secure the company, which means that the launch has to work harder to meet its return on capital objectives.

In addition, there are real practical problems with *hostile* takeovers in many parts of the world. For example, in Germany the banks and other institutions often hold effective controlling interests in companies. In Italy one estimate puts the number of public companies open to takeover at only three! In France many leading companies are either controlled by, or contain strong minority shareholdings from, the State and the banks. In the Benelux countries blocking vote shares often make takeover difficult. The UK has probably the most liberal regime in the EU: *friendly* takeovers, joint ventures or new launches may be more productive elsewhere. Takeovers are also relatively easy in the USA as long as sensitive national interests or anti-trust legislation is not breached.

In seeking the answer to moving internationally, the individual company and market situation is paramount: there are no general solutions. Nevertheless, it is possible to draw up a list of some of the main advantages and problems of the four routes (see Table 25.1).

Table 25.1 Some advantages and problems of routes into Europe

Advantages	*Problems*
Launch (including exporting)	
Cheaper	Slow
Lower risk: less committing	May miss opportunities through lack of knowledge
Good route for unique product	
Allows slow build-up and learning about market conditions	Allows home competitors to assess and build response
More control	Building scale economies may be high risk and expensive
Keeps economies of scale at home base	
No need to share technology	
Joint venture	
Builds scale quickly	Control lost to some extent
Obtain local knowledge and distribution	Works best where both parties contribute something different to the mix
Cheaper than takeover	Difficult to manage
Local entry where takeover not even possible	Share profits with partner
Can be used where outright takeover not feasible	
Can be used where similar product available	
Alliance (minority shareholding)	
Real incentive to new country	Loses management control
Close contact	Profit stream from new unrelated products
Locks out other competitors	
Takeover	
Can be fast	Premium paid
Useful for national expertise	High risk if wrong
Buy presence	Best targets may have already gone in some markets
	Expensive
Buy size	Not always easy to dispose of unwanted assets

Ideally, all four routes need to be assessed. Some may rule themselves out quickly. Resolving others will need scenario building and negotiations with possible partners. In examining the conclusions, they need to be set against the company's objectives and investment criteria. In addition, it is essential to calculate the cash flow implications of each of the routes: most new launches are hungry on company cash in the early years, with a payback that can be long in some cases. European and global markets will not make this easier.

To look in a practical way at the launch choices facing a company, let us examine the European electrical industry.

Case Study: Selected European electronics and electrical engineering

	Country	1992 Turnover (US$ m)	Consumer electronics	Industrial electronics	Telecomms equipment	Electrical Engineering
Alcatel Alsthom	Fra	30840	No	Yes	Yes	Yes
Philips	Net	24396	Yes	Yes	No	Yes
Siemens	Ger	18405	No	Yes	Yes	Yes
Thomson	Fra	14082	Yes	Yes	No	No
ABB	Swe/Swi	8951	No	Yes	No	Yes
Finnmechanica	Ita	8900 est	No	Yes	No	Yes
Ericsson	Swe	8047	No	Yes	Yes	Yes
GEC	UK	8271	Yes	Yes	Yes	Yes
AEG/Daimler	Ger	7802	Yes	Yes	No	No
Bosch	Ger	5499	Yes	Yes	No	No
Schneider	Fra	4230	No	No	No	Yes
Nokia	Fin	3854	Yes	Yes	Yes	Yes
Hawker/BTR	UK	2913	No	Yes	No	Yes
BICC	UK	2897	No	Yes	No	Yes
DASA/Daimler	Ger	2439	No	Yes	No	No
Aerospatiale	Fra	2219	No	Yes	No	No
Racal	UK	2104	No	Yes	Yes	No
Matra	Fra	1468	No	No	Yes	No
AGIV	Ger	1388	No	No	No	Yes
Lucas	UK	1060	No	Yes	No	No
Mannesmann	Ger	983	No	No	No	Yes

and for comparison:

	Country	1992 Turnover (US$ m)	Consumer electronics	Industrial electronics	Telecomms equipment	Electrical Engineering
Sony	Jap	22959	Yes	No	No	No
Pioneer	Jap	5084	Yes	No	No	No
Sanyo	Jap	3321	Yes	No	No	No

Note: In the case of several companies above, the product categories are only approximate.

Note: Most companies have sales outside the areas shown above; data excludes computers, information technology and electrical wholesaling and retailing.

The above general categories do not fully reflect the activities and strengths of individual companies: the markets are large enough to contain many specializations which have been simplified here for presentational reasons.

European and global activity
Many of the changes have been described in case studies on individual companies. The main trends that come out of the table are:

- Philips, Netherlands may be one of the largest companies but has not been able to obtain a dominant, profitable position: it is too small in areas such as semi conductors and some electronic components. It faces severe competition from cheaper Far East consumer electronics.

- Thomson SA, France has built a large consumer electronics base, in terms of sales, by acquisition but not yet in terms of profitability, mainly because it has chosen to compete head-on against Japanese consumer electronics.
- Asea Brown Boveri (ABB) has obtained a strong position in electrical engineering through its joint venture, though this will take some years to mature. It is still building globally.
- Alcatel has also built a strong position by joint venture which is now in the process of consolidation (see Part III for details).
- GEC, UK has moved to a series of mergers and joint ventures to consolidate its position (see Part III).
- Nokia, Finland is spread thinly across several areas: this is strategically weak as discussed in Chapter 17.

Overall, there is nothing wrong with being one of the smaller companies if there is a clear market segment and its profit margins support any lack of scale that may result. Firms like BICC have acquired companies in the European and world markets to become strong in a specialist segment (ie electrical cable). This demonstrates what can be done successfully if the management vision and objectives are clear.

Keypoint on launches, joint ventures, alliances and takeovers
Takeover has built a strong market position for Alcatel, in some sectors very quickly. But the company is not truly profitable yet and the strain on senior management as the reorganization is undertaken is significant. The route is often difficult because shareholding rules can make many companies virtually impregnable (eg in Holland, Germany and Belgium). Second, acquisitions of companies the same size (or larger) are needed to produce anything like sufficient market share in the new country: large bites are not easy to swallow (Alcatel of ITT Europe for example).

Thus many of the above companies have turned to joint ventures but these also have their problems. For example, giving up decision making to the unified company (instances include GEC and Alcatel). Also parent company interests may diverge and cause tensions. For example, Alcatel is state-owned and GEC is not. While no problems have emerged in this area at present, they might.

Interestingly, there are not many joint ventures in the data above. Asea Brown Boveri is a special case since it was a merger of two companies rather than merely a venture into a specific market area. Some companies have formed alliances with minority shareholdings (eg Ericsson has taken a shareholding in part of Matra, giving a degree of commitment and funding to the new area whilst locking out other companies).

Other companies have simply used launches of products – this is the route used by Bosch and Sony. These companies have thus kept real control of their products and are able to use home-based technology and economies of scale to advantage until overseas plant can be justified.

Clearly, the implementation of the chosen route is crucial to success. A number of companies have now gone down this road so there is evidence of the pleasures and pitfalls. We will discuss this, with examples, in Part III.

How will we tackle existing competitors?

Whatever route that is chosen to approach the single Europe, there are likely to be existing companies operating in the marketplace. Earlier in Part II we looked in detail at how we measure up to them and what this means for strategy.

Having decided on our overall approach to the market, we can now decide how we will tackle competition. There are four main possibilities for the attack, which have been developed out of military strategy: head-on, flanking, occupy totally new territory or guerrilla. We will go through each and explore what they mean for international markets.

Head-on

After careful analysis, we have decided to tackle the market leader in another country head-on. There is no question of taking a small part of the market or mounting a simple and flexible operation with low overheads.

Here are some guidelines, using the European computer industry as our example.

- Unless you have resources for a sustained campaign, it is unlikely to be profitable. A sustained campaign means several years for branded goods to well over six years for capital goods. Resources can only be judged in relation to what is currently being spent. Launching into the European computer industry in under three years without an extensive marketing campaign and distribution drive is totally unrealistic.
- Attack where the leader is weak. This means understanding the leader well in terms of product, salesforce, pricing and service. If there is an area where the leader is particularly strong then this is *not* the area to attack. Moreover, if there is an area where the leader can easily respond then this is not the area to attack: we have seen that lower price is weak because it can easily be defended. Attacking IBM Europe on price in the business minicomputer market has had only limited success. Many companies regard service and reliability as more important.
- Pick a narrow front on which to mount the campaign. Even with good resource, the chance of success will be higher if the attack area is limited. Spreading resources too thinly is unlikely to establish a bridge-head. IBM Europe has been vulnerable in minicomputers in terms of performance and lack of compatibility between models. It has been successfully attacked on these fronts with machines that, in some cases, are even higher priced.

Sony, Hitachi and Toshiba have all taken the European TV industry head on over the last 20 years. How have they done it? By technical innovation (eg Sony's Trinitron technology), by using low-cost Japanese manufacture for as long as possible, by outspending European companies on advertising and promotions, by higher reliability, by competitive pricing and by plugging away for years.

My own belief is that this route will not suit many companies moving internationally: the costs are high and many companies will be more aware of the dangers than in the past.

Flanking

Our studies show that tackling the market leader head-on is unlikely to be successful. We have decided to mount a flanking attack on a specific part of the leader's franchise.

Here are some guidelines for the flanking attack, using the European car industry as our example:

- Choose a flank that is relatively undefended. Rather than an area where there is considerable attention, it may be better to seek out one that currently holds little interest to the major companies. Obvious examples are premium sectors of markets in terms of price, service and quality, which lack the volume to attract the main companies. Whilst Fiat, Ford and Volkswagen battle it out in volume cars, some of the smaller Japanese companies have come in and taken market leadership from Land Rover in the off-road, four-wheel drive market.

- Aim to take a significant share of the flank. It does not make business sense to take a limited area of a market which be definition is small. Moreover, small footholds are more easily dislodged. Because of agreed EC quota restrictions, Japanese car makers such as Toyota have moved into up-market sports cars so restricted sales can be coupled with high margins. They have not been content with a very limited share of this market sector and are seeking significant volume.

- Expect to invest in the flank for some years. Having gained a foothold, it is vital to hold this ground. This means investing behind the new found success, not supporting weakness elsewhere. Unless Toyota continues to invest in this sector, other manufacturers such as Volkswagen will produce models that will take back the hard-won ground.

- Pricing and value for money are often the distinguishing feature of a flank. Either high price or low price can be used to pinpoint where a flank might be opened up. Similarly, performance and service can also provide indicators. Car companies such as Proton and Hyundai have shown that Far Eastern cars can take a share of the low price sector.

In international markets, flanking is likely to be more profitable for many companies than outright war against the leaders. It is lower risk and less expensive. Additionally in this case, there is nothing to stop alliances being formed with local companies, which should increase the chance of success.

Occupy totally new territory

Here, all the research indicates that the leaders are well-entrenched in the market. The only route in is to create a totally new sector: the 'niche' market. This tends to be an area that is so small that the leaders are simply not interested and not geared up to handle it. Thus Dunhill, Yves St Laurent and Gucci have been able to carve out substantial sales across global markets without threatening the major fashion and clothing companies.

Here are some guidelines, using household detergents as a European example:

- Expect to operate at premium prices. Only in this way will it be possible to survive on small volumes. One of Europe's leading detergent manufacturers has never been able to establish a presence in the UK: Henkel AG, West Germany. It has been kept out by the formidable marketing clout of Lever (Unilever) and Procter & Gamble. Henkel launched a higher price, ecologically friendly product in the UK in 1989 which was different from the existing leading products. But even this has made no significant impact.

- If volumes rise then the leaders will suddenly take notice. This is a fact of life: there is no doubt that if these types of washing powder sell well then the leaders will launch their own brands. Proctor & Gamble joined the process with Ariel Ultra.
- Consider launching on a modest scale in specialized outlets with carefully targeted promotion. With niche products, there is a sense in which the target group may seek out the product once they have heard of its existence. Health food products and high fashion items are not sold widely yet find their target groups. Henkel had real problems matching the virtual 98% coverage of Lever and P&G in the UK. It may not need to attain this if its product is available to its target group through specialist stores.
- Innovation is at the core of this route. New products, new ideas and new promotional methods are more likely to be successful here than familiar approaches. Simply improving existing washing powder brands will lead nowhere.

Although we have been looking mainly at consumer examples, the principles apply equally to industrial products and services. Technical innovation and performance, coupled with carefully targeted distribution, is a powerful combination in such markets. For example, the European telecommunications equipment market is characterized by just such a combination of products and outlets selling alongside the few major companies such as Ericsson and Alcatel. There is a vast range of specialist equipment, all unique in design, performance and price.

For many companies, this route must hold real merit for European and global markets.

Guerrilla

Research has failed to show up any clear flanking or niche opportunities in the single market but it has shown up a gap that might be short term: here is the classic guerrilla opportunity.

Large companies sometimes fail to see the gaps left by their own marketing: thus, one-off machinery designs or limited-run fashion products are launched to take advantage of market opportunities.

Guidelines for exploiting this area include the following:

- Market intelligence is important for success. Guerrilla tactics rely on reliable information to quickly identify the opportunities.
- It is vital to have a fast response to market opportunities. There is no point going back for a committee debate. If the sale is there and the factory can handle it then it is taken. Only certain types of lean company structure can handle this strategy.
- Market areas need to be where the guerrila company selects, not where large companies are entrenched. Guerrillas do not stand and fight large companies but pick their own battle ground. Thus matching a large supplier in its traditional markets on price and quality might well be wrong. Better to choose flexibility and high personal service with short product runs at higher prices. For example, selling standard clothing items to large German

department stores is less likely to be successful than high fashion, higher priced items with limited volumes.

■ Guerrilla attack may be a useful form of home defence. Referring back to our earlier discussion, even large companies have not hesitated to launch spoiling products or prices as short-term measures to divert attention from attack on the home market. The European bulk chemicals markets contains examples where special deals have been used to counter sales initiatives across Europe.

■ Be prepared to withdraw rather than stand and fight. If large companies move in, then it may be better to stand aside than tackle them on such issues as unit costs, where they are likely to win.

Guerrilla tactics have their place in international markets – for example, in some commodity markets and in some small volume fashion areas. But the infrastructure is not in place for many companies to move fast enough to fully exploit the opportunities in some parts of the world. This is unlikely to be a major area of opportunity for some years.

How will we gain distribution and keep it?

There are three main methods: acquire; negotiate a deal locally; or set up from first base.

Earlier in Part II, we looked at these issues in detail. Like other aspects of international markets, the answers are unique to each company and its circumstances.

EXCELLENCE IN ONE AREA

As a result of European and global market pressures, some companies have already increased in size. This does not mean that they will necessarily be more profitable: economies of scale are often counterbalanced by a slower response to the market. Indeed, none that have so far grown in this way show attractive returns on capital, though it is still perhaps too early to prove this.

There are US and Japanese companies that are larger than similar European companies. The key to their profitability lies not in their size but in the excellence with which they are organized and managed. As Professor John Kay says: 'It cannot be repeated frequently enough that the larger relative size of American and Japanese companies … is the *result* of their success, not the *cause* of it.' Seeking size in the European and global markets will not bring success. What is important is excellence in a specific business area. Reviewing Europe's Top 400 companies, many of the more successful are particularly skilled at one activity or in one market. For example, cement production (Holderbank), bearing manufacture (SFK), media (Bertelsmann), mining (RTZ) and tyre manufacture and distribution (Michelin).

This concept of excellence needs to be built into company objectives and then executed in strategy. Size will follow. It means answering questions like: 'What are we especially good at?'; 'What areas of excellence do we wish to be known for?'

The European Commission has laid some emphasis on the size necessary for European companies to survive in world markets. On a broad scale, there is some merit in this approach. But for the individual company developing its own strategy for international markets, it is more important to be excellent in an area than have size for its own sake.

Implementing the Strategy in European and Global Markets

Because most of the topics covered so far in this book have been illustrated with actual examples of what Europe's top companies have done, some might say that implementation should be straightforward. If only matters were so simple.

With a powerful strategy, it should be possible not only to specify the objectives but also to plot the course of the various moves that have to be made with an outline timetable. In practice, there will be gaps in knowledge that need to be filled and risks that need to be taken. For example:

- Negotiating with companies in other countries with different languages, finance and legal systems is not without its hazards (and anyone who thinks these will be harmonized by the single Europe is living in dreamland).
- Joint ventures and takeovers produce their own complications leaving aside the problems of international markets. Potential partners always seem to have difficulty in reaching agreement on the final day of the negotiations.
- The differences that exist between and within various European countries will produce difficulties over management planning and control that need to be overcome. Even simple matters like reporting across Europe on the monthly sales figures and remedial action required can be fraught with misdirected tension. Global coverage would only make this more complex.

In implementing strategies in international markets, there are unfortunately no simple rules. We will attempt to cover some of the more obvious areas in the chapters that follow. But we need to recognize that they are not management-proof against the real world. Topics covered are as follows: testing the strategy; negotiating the deal; making takeovers and joint ventures work; organization and control for European and global markets; and reducing risk and planning for the rewards.

CHAPTER 26

Testing the Strategy

Every strategy is worth testing and there are plenty of sources of help available to explore the issues *without* revealing confidential details. Most companies, both large and small, will present elements of it to immediate company advisors and other knowledgeable individuals and listen to their reactions.

POSSIBLE SOURCES OF OPINION

In addition to in-company discussions, it is also useful to meet potential customers, distributors and outside consultants, both for the information they will have and the impressions they will convey. This process is often best conducted informally outside even the hint of business negotiations.

Possible sources might include the following:

- Accountants, legal and other professional advisors and management consultants.
- Marketing and advertising consultants and market research companies.
- Governmental organizations and national export corporations. For example in the UK, these must include the Department of Trade and Industry and its export arm.
- National and local business organizations. The Confederation of British Industry and Chambers of Commerce have been doing sterling work in the UK on European and global issues. In addition, equivalent organizations exist in many European countries: they can be contacted and visited.
- Trade and industry organizations and seminars.
- International exhibitions: a particularly good source both for the industry itself and its suppliers and customers. A company's own trade buyers are valuable here.
- International research conferences, not so much during the formal papers but rather the outside discussions.
- The European Commission itself and its various subsidiary offices: there is one in each national capital of the 12 EC countries.

All these will help in the process of better understanding the customer and refining the strategy.

TIMING THE TESTING PROCESS

Some will argue that it is better to talk to the people listed above at an early stage before strategy is formulated: there is certainly a case for some early fact gathering. However, in most instances, it will be more efficient to form a preliminary view and then test this rather than drift around trying to pick up opinions while strategy remains unformed.

Ultimately, strategies are written on paper and not tablets of stone: if it is clear that the proposals need modifying, then it is essential to make the change flexibly and without delay. Once the outline is agreed then negotiations can begin.

CHAPTER 27

Negotiating the Deal

Whether the deal is to sell products into a retail shop chain in Germany and Spain or to propose a joint venture with a North American company, it will need to be negotiated.

For the really big deals, some executives will say that the main negotiations are best left to senior managers and that therefore this area does not concern them. In the better run companies, nothing could be further from the truth: many managers are involved in the decisions that need to be taken and it is only the final negotiations that usually involve senior managers. Indeed, there are sometimes good tactical negotiating reasons for saving the really senior directors for the final discussions.

Moreover, once the deal is concluded then many managers are involved in the practicality of making it work: the time to contribute and to express doubts is *before the ink is dry, not later*. Thus, all managers need to think carefully, about their roles during negotiations.

THE NEGOTIATING PROCESS

In negotiating European and global markets, there are six main areas that need to be considered:

1. Selling the company to the other side;
2. Listening and talking;
3. Pitching the price;
4. Dealing with disagreements;
5. Protecting vital interests; and
6. Concluding the deal.

Let us go through each of the above and then consider three recent case studies.

Selling the company to the other side

Whatever the precise nature of the deal, the reality of international markets for many companies is that they will know little about the company now making contact with them. It is therefore essential to *sell the company itself* as well as the particular deal under consideration.

This is not just a matter of company ownership, products and home-country experience, but rather what *benefits* the company will bring to the relationship: stability, skills, marketing standing, quality standards and relevant recent plant investment might all feature.

Just as much as its specific product or service, the company needs to persuade its potential partner of its own credentials as part of the new relationship. And proof is the best persuader.

Listening and talking

Good negotiators are good listeners. Moreover, they tend to let the other party do much of the talking. However, they also recognize that some deals are outlined quite quickly in any negotiations and that they need to know how to react to these circumstances if they arise.

One vital reason for listening hard is that it is difficult to gain sufficient reliable outside data on some companies in international markets. Thus part of the role of early negotiations has to be to obtain correct information.

A poor approach would be to enter negotiations with a stereotyped idea as to how the nationals of another country are likely to react. People and company styles are so different across nations that such attitudes are likely to be counter-productive. What the seller is listening for is the bargaining signals that come out of discussions: what problems do the buyers have; what would they like to see changed; and so on. These can then be played back in constructing the deal.

Pitching the price

However complex the negotiations, there will come a time when it will be necessary to pitch the price, service levels, etc. While the precise timing has to be left open, the basic deal must be much firmer. Negotiators really do need to go in with quite clear objectives and ideas on their final position: lack of clarity here is one of the main reasons why sellers are squeezed and poor deals are done.

This does not mean that it is always wise to state the final price at the outset of discussions: some room for manoeuvre is essential. This may mean pitching high at the start. Moreover, a concession always gives the other party satisfaction.

However, once an offer has been made, it cannot easily be withdrawn, if at all. Certainly, it is not usually credible to put the price higher later in the discussion! Hence, it is wise in most circumstances to pitch on the high side. But ultimately the best deal is one that *both sides* believe to be attractive so it is important not to go too high.

Dealing with disagreements

Negotiating is about bargaining power between two or more parties. Open flexing of muscles in negotiations may be unavoidable but it does invite a strong reaction. In European and global markets, most companies will be seeking *long-term relationships* which are not best served by difficult discussions in the early days.

Nevertheless, disagreements may well arise. Because they only store up trouble for later if ignored, they do need to be sorted out. The best way is to clarify them and then move forward: this is where it helps to be clear in advance on your objectives. In this way, it may be possible to trade away a smaller concession against another that is fundamental to the objectives.

Sometimes disagreement is introduced in order to gain extra concessions. Complete withdrawal can even be threatened (and was on one occasion to the author). The keys to responding are first to be clear in advance on the importance of the disagreement to the overall deal (it may actually be better to pull out), and second to keep real emotions out as much as possible – though some drama may be useful.

Protecting vital interests

The best way to protect vital interests is to agree them at the time and make them part of the written agreement. A meeting record is useful here. Whilst international law is there as a last resort, it should be recognized that, if it is necessary to use it, then it usually means that the deal has broken down.

Concluding the deal

Timing is a vital skill in negotiations: many deals cannot be rushed. They sometimes worth plotting in advance and it is always worth rehearsing the major points. Ultimately, after probing the situation, the final offer has to be made with every indication that this is the end.

But, in reality, it is of course only the end of the negotiations: we will deal with the next chapter with the business of making agreements work.

Case Study: Thomson SA, France

Data

One of Europe's largest companies in the aerospace and defence sector and in consumer electronics: nationalized

Turnover (Ffr million)

	1988	1992
Electronics & defence	32661 (Thomson-CSF)	34199
Consumer electronics	40035 (Thomson Grand Public)	30552
Corporated items	3427	—
Inter-company	(1289)	—
*Thomson Electroménager		6083
Miscellaneous		155
Total	74834	70989

*Sold to the Italian company Elfi in December 1992

	1988	1992
Return on capital:	8.5%	3.8%
% sales in home country:	29	32
% sales in rest of Europe:	22	23
% sales in rest of world:	49	45

European and global market activity

Thomson is a holding group for two distinct areas of activity: aerospace/defence and consumer products. It owns a controlling interest in each of the subsidiaries but not necessarily 100%. The group has been particularly vigorous at buying and exchanging parts of its empire to create large European and global companies.

Thomson–CSF had reached the following position in the period up to 1992:

- 50/50 joint venture with STET, Italy in 1987 in microelectronics (not consolidated in the data above): called SGS–Thomson. It is Europe's second largest semiconductor manufacturer;
- Acquired Inmos microelectronics from Thorn/EMI (UK) – 1988;
- Agreement to acquire Philips defence electronics business – 1989;
- New 50/50 company with British Aerospace in top-security missile systems – 1989;
- World leader in air traffic control systems: linked with Siemens Plessey;
- Joint venture with Aerospatiale, France in general avionics to create European market leadership and fourth or fifth world-ranking company.

All these developments have global rather than European perspectives. However they rely on European partners for success.

Thomson Grand Public was essentially formed by the following actions:

1. In 1988, the company exchanged its medical equipment subsidiary for General Electric's (US) consumer electronics business. This gave Thomson the RCA and GE brand names in the USA;
2. In the same year, it bought Thorn/EMI's (UK) consumer electronics business (under the Ferguson brand name).

Thomson said that the US and UK deals gave it market leadership in the United States and made it number two in Europe (after including the household appliance business it already owned). TV sales for the company are international whilst household appliances were mainly domestic and sold in late 1992.

Thomson – GP clearly has a global business which it has built by acquisition. However, in moving to a global-scale, it has taken the Japanese consumer electronics companies head-on without a clear winning strategy. Its only advantages would appear to be sheer size and subsidies from the French government; hardly long-term sustainable advantages.

Keypoints on negotiating deals
In the many deals done by Thomson over the last three years, let us highlight two features:

1. Clarity of business purpose in negotiating and completing deals. The company has identified the markets that it wishes to build and has pursued these. It has divested itself of others.
2. Some opportunism in picking up companies that others wished to sell: parts of Thorn/EMI and Philips are examples. This may have reduced the price.

Negotiations that have clearly identified objectives are much more likely to succeed. Equally, there is often a point in business dealing when an opportunity arises that it is useful to seize.

Thomson still has to make the deals work: size is not enough in itself, the danger is to mistake size for strength.

Case Study: General Electric Company plc, UK

Data
One of Europe's leading electronics and electrical engineering companies.
1992 turnover (£ million)

Electronic systems	2698
Power systems	3135
Telecommunications	1012
Consumer goods	253
Electronic metrology	413
Office equipment and printing	314
Medical equipment	568
Electronic components	314
Industrial apparatus	334
Distribution and trading	341
Other	162
Intersegment	(134)
Total	9410

Return on capital: 21.4%
% sales in home country: 32
% sales in rest of Europe: 31
% sales in rest of world: 37

European and global market activity
GEC agreed a series of international deals during recent years that have transformed its business:

- Power turbines: new 50/50 company with Alcatel Alsthom, France. It has proved successful after re-organization.
- Telecommunications: takeover of Plessey (UK) with Siemens, Germany with 60% ownership of this product area.
- Consumer: 50/50 deal with General Electric (US) in their European operations.
- Electronic systems: GEC acquired Plessey's avionics and anti-submarine warfare business.
- Joint ownership of Plessey's semiconductor business with Siemens.
- Merged its Marconi space interests with Matra, France. Has also proved successful.
- Purchase of Ferranti defence interests.
- New joint venture with Instrumentarium of Finland in medical electronics.

The reasons for the deals were essentially that GEC judged it needed to compete in European and world markets and therefore needed to be bigger, even if this meant joint ventures in some cases. The single Europe was clearly a catalyst, but global trends in electronics, turbines and aerospace markets have been the main factor.

Keypoint on negotiating deals
In reaching agreement on the above deals, GEC accepted that its partners, Matra, Alcatel, Siemens and General Electric would have powers of veto, voting rights on subsidiary boards and various forms of marketing and know-how contracts. Such arrangements are inevitable in any complex realignment of resources. It is much better to spell them out in advance than to run into confusion later.

It was claimed in some parts of the British press, that, as a result, GEC had surrendered control of important decisions. But this missed the point: in any deal of this nature, there must be a new balance of control in the new situation. Any negotiator looking to do deals in international markets and retain all existing decision making is wasting his or her time.

It is the mark of a mature negotiator to recognize that a new power balance is required at the outset and get on with the job of sorting the best deal in these circumstances. This applies both to large and small companies.

Case Study: Mannesmann AG, Germany

Data
One of Europe's largest mechanical engineering companies.

1992 turnover (DM million)		*Subsidiary*
Machinery and plant construction	12672	Demag
		Rexroth
Automotive technology	653	Fichtel & Sachs
Electrical engineering	1461	Hartmann & Braun
Mobile telecommunications	138	
Tubes and piping	4337	

Trading	3904
Other	758
Total	29801

Return on capital: 0.7%
% sales in home country: 43
% sales in rest of Europe: 31
% sales in rest of world: 26

European and global market activity
In 1975, Mannesmann derived 50% of its turnover from steel and tubing. By 1992, this had dropped to 15%. Over the intervening years, the company's strategy was to move to higher value-added products, especially in technology-led companies. It accomplished this partially by internal growth and also acquisition. In 1987, it acquired the motor components company Fichtel & Sachs.

Keypoint in negotiating deals
In September 1989, Mannesmann and the UK group, TI plc, announced, after exploratory discussions between the two companies, a strategic alliance. TI, with sales around US$1800 million, was much smaller than Mannesmann, with sales of US$11,600 million. The UK company had three main operational areas: mechanical seals, car tubing and white household goods. The deal was confirmed with the German company buying 5% of TI. In 1990, this was raised to 9.9%.

The two companies explained the agreement as being good for both parties, though concrete plans remained to be resolved. Possible areas included Mannesmann gaining access to TI's US distribution network and TI using the extensive German distribution network of Mannesmann to increase sales.

By late 1989, a senior management committee had been set by the two companies to examine areas of co-operation in sales, marketing and joint acquisitions, but these plans were still some way from fruition. Controls for heat equipment technology had been identified as a possible area for joint work.

These types of negotiation have so far been rare across the single European market. They are made more difficult because it is essential for each party to contribute to the deal, otherwise it tends to fall apart: sharing international distribution was a good starting point.

Subsequently, nothing seems to have happened. Both companies made no mention of the alliance in their 1992 Annual Reports. The early enthusiasm of 1989 does not seem to have born fruit.

TI went on to acquire Dowty (UK) in 1992. Mannesmann was coping with German recession.

AGREEMENT CONTENT

Two types of discussions are possible in international deals:

1. Supply/distribution agreements between two companies providing sales profits; and
2. Deals that lead to long-term co-operation between two companies, and thus to profits.

Neither of the two types is better than the other. Both have their place as potential structures in the new market. It is possible that the former will lead to the latter as potential partners come to know each other better.

There is an opportunity here for small as well as large companies. But *both parties* need to contribute something to the deal over time, beyond merely being a buyer or seller.

CHAPTER 28

Making Takeovers and Joint Ventures Work

Even within one country, joint ventures and takeovers are not easy to operate. Couple this with the differences across international markets and we may be looking at some real failures over the next five years. Yet enough is known to improve the chances of success.

GUIDELINES FOR TAKEOVERS AND JOINT VENTURES

Although this chapter cannot hope to cover every conceivable aspect of the problem, and there are no all-purpose solutions, there are some guidelines that will at least start matters on the right path. Let us go through them and then look at three case studies of takeovers and joint ventures in European and global markets. Finally, we will look at the special problems of joint ventures. The guidelines are as follows:

1. Deal quickly with any major closures or job losses. Uncertainty can never be good for management. In international markets where the head office can be remote and local managers may fear that they cannot communicate adequately, it makes sense to resolve such issues quickly. It may even be best to deal with the matter, if possible, on the day that the takeover is announced.
2. State the objectives and what is expected of managers. The uncertainty that persists after new management move in can be allayed by a clear statement of what is required. It is surprising how senior management occasionally fails even to say what it wants.
3. Allow time and opportunity for learning about new colleagues. Whether it is a joint venture or takeover, there does need to be time to adjust to new management guidance and requirements. This can be advanced by making occasions for meeting colleagues, but they need to be real projects, not artificial hybrids.
4. Deal with language and cultural differences by organizing exchanges and training. This is bound to arise in new joint companies across international markets. It needs to be tackled: more than one company has simply relied on nationals from the home country to take on all the senior jobs because it

takes time and resource to do anything else. This is storing up trouble for the future.

5. Make it clear where the decision making lies. Considerable time can be wasted and resentment created if this is not handled well. This is not just in the interests of the subsidiary: the centre needs to know what other parts of the company are responsible for or it will have problems holding managers responsible for actions taken.

6. Devolve responsibility to operating companies closer to the marketplace. This will not suit the management style of every company and, as outlined elsewhere in this book, national companies can compete against each other to the detriment of the group. Nevertheless, operating companies should be closer to the customer, almost by definition. That is a powerful reason for giving them some control. The case studies will emphasize this point.

7. Ensure that in joint ventures there is real contribution from both parties, and benefits to each partner. Joint ventures are not easy to operate. There is direct evidence that they are occasionally set up with high hopes which tend to smother crucial details: what will both parties contribute and how will they both benefit?

   Where these matters are not clarified in advance, there have been cases where one company has subsequently felt it was doing too much and obtaining little in return. A better joint venture would be one where skills or resources are at least partly complementary: for example, one has the research know-how and the other the distribution.

8. Accept that there will be some loss of control by the original owners in joint ventures. This type of deal will simply not work where the participating companies expect to maintain their right to all major decisions as if nothing had changed except the resources. The new combined company must be allowed to manage.

It needs to be said that there are fundamental differences between takeovers and joint ventures in terms of management control. We will come back to the special issues raised by joint ventures later.

Let us now look at two companies that have a highly successful record at managing takeovers. We will then examine a European industry where takeovers have come thick and fast over the last ten years, and brought some hard words with them.

Case Study: Hanson plc, UK

Data
One of Europe's largest companies with many takeovers in the 1980s.
1993 turnover (£ million)
Industrial

Coal mining	1012
Chemicals	609
Material handling	258
Other	821
	2700

Consumer

Tobacco	3071
Other	985
	4056

Building

Aggregates	1400
Forest and timber	321
Housebuilding	466
Other	725
	2912
	92
	9760

Return on capital: 17.3%
% sales in home country (UK): 42
% sales in rest of Europe: 6 estimate
% sales in rest of world: 52 (46% in US)

European and global market activity
During the 1970s and 1980s, Hanson grew by acquisition in both the UK and US; in many cases parts of acquired groups were then sold for significantly more than the original purchase price. In 1993, Hanson purchased Quantum Chemical for US$ 2226 million, but the pace of acquisition and disposal has slowed. This is partly because it was easier to purchase with shares in the 1980s, but also because Hanson's strategy was viewed as largely opportunistic and fortunes change. The company's strategy has now been redefined as being in basic industries.

Keypoint on joint ventures and takeovers
Hanson has grown to its present size by its skills not only in acquisition and disposal of companies, but also in its management of companies taken over. The group's profit and growth record are such that it must provide evidence of one way of operating takeovers in international markets.

Essentially, the group manages its companies by devolving responsibility back to directors and managers at company level. It makes lines of responsibility and reporting clear, and invests where required, but then allows company management to get on with it. The group does not try to direct from the centre, nor does it have trans-national product responsibility.

This will not necessarily work with all markets, especially world-wide markets. Hanson is essentially involved long term with a series of basic industries that are able to operate semi-autonomously with local economies of scale. Whilst the group is international, individual companies are more country-based. This might suit some types of international company, but not necessarily those that will gain most economic advantage from the new European and global situation. Nevertheless, its method of handling takeover management bears close examination.

Case Study: BTR plc, UK

Data
World-wide consumer and industrial products group.

1992 turnover (£ million)		*Trading companies include*
Consumer-related	1840	Dunlop Slazenger, Huyck Paper,
		Healthcare (UK & US), Puma

Construction	1434	Tilcon (UK & US), Graham Builder's Merchants, Tiles
Control & electrical	1763	BTR valves, metering and Warner
Industrial	1889	ACI (Australia & Japan), Serck, Hawker Clarkson, Apex Belling (Belgium)
Transportation	1764	Dunlop, BTR specialist automotive companies
Corporate	151	
Total	8841	

Return on capital: 25.8%
% sales in home country: 31
% sales in rest of Europe: 18
% sales in rest of world: 51

European and global market activity
BTR has followed an active acquisitions policy during the 1980s and 1990s. This has led the company world-wide rather than to the single Europe. The company's recent acquisitions record is lengthy and includes:

- Stewart Warner Corporation (USA), 1987;
- Rockware glass (UK) 1991;
- ACI International (Australia), 1988;
- Hawker Siddeley (UK) 1991; and numerous companies in Canada, US, Australia, Germany.

The company does have some subsidiaries in Europe, but only as part of its pursuit of the global opportunity. BTR believes that global markets are now developing in its primary product areas, based on standard designs, quality uniformity, predictability of automated processes and increasing consumer sophistication. It has used acquisitions to give global coverage in its chosen areas.

Keypoint to joint ventures and takeovers
The careful acquisition of Hawker Siddeley after its acquisition in 1991 included:

- 40 BTR executives chosen especially for advanced familiarization with Hawker;
- after acquisition, executives were paired with their counterparts at Hawker;
- co-ordination group at BTR HQ plus central staff functions also set up;
- co-ordinated 60-day programme of site visits, assessment of company management, conversion of financial controls, priorities agreed;
- operations evaluation recognizing the existing investment in people, plant and technology.

There are many lessons in the above on the professional integration of takeovers into the new larger company.

BTR's acquisitions stretch back over the 1980s. In all that time, it has never engaged in a joint venture on any significant scale: the ownership has always been over 50%.

This is consistent with BTR's stated view of the management of its companies which is to grant company autonomy within defined group limits: joint ventures are difficult to operate in this way because the two owners may have differing views on company objectives and management.

Companies with a different management style may find it easier to manage joint ventures. For BTR, its highly successful business record and management of subsidiaries, some of which are on the other side of the world, suggest that its judgement on joint ventures needs to be considered carefully.

Case Study: leading European insurance companies

		Market capitalization September 1993 (US$ million)
Allianz Holding	Ger	30867
Generali Assicurazione	Ita	18347
Munchener Ruchversicherungs	Ger	13976
Prudential	UK	9827
UAP	Fra	9585
Zurich Insurance	Swi	7972
AGF	Fra	7189
Alleanza	Ita	6090
Allianz Lebensversicherungs	Ger	5895
Swiss Reinsurance	Swi	5720
Fortis	Bel/Net	5026
Commercial Union	UK	5023
General Accident	UK	4819
Aegon	Net	4781
Sun Alliance	UK	4733
Lloyds Abbey Life	UK	4638
GAN	Fra	4033
Winterthur Versicherung	Swi	4003
AMB: Aachener und Munchener Beteil	Ger	3713
Legal & General	UK	3615
RAS	Ita	3442
Royal Insurance	UK	3017
Guardian Royal Exchange	UK	2818
Victoria Holding	Ger	2664
Fondiaria	Ita	2023
Royale Belge	Bel	2000
SAI	Ita	1753
Baloise Holding	Swi	1583
Wuertemburgische Versich	Ger	1538
Volksfuersorge	Ger	1506

Source: Financial Times 'Top 500' January 1994. Quoted with permission

Because assets and premiums can be misleading, stock market valuation has been used to derive Europe's top insurers. But even this is not without its weaknesses: stock markets tend to place more reliance on short-term performance and often over-react to general economic events.

There are other problems with the list:

- Some leading insurers are part of broader groups so are not even identified above: for example, Eagle Star (UK) is part of BAT (UK); the second biggest French insurer, Victoire, is controlled by the French holding company, Suez.
- Others were still under state ownership in 1994, eg INA, one of Italy's largest insurers.
- Some companies have other links, eg Allianz owns 25% of Munchener Re; AGF and AMB have a co-operation agreement.
- Reinsurance – the purchase of backup insurance by the insurers – is a specialized business in a sector by itself.

- Some are mutual funds, ie owned by the insured, and therefore not quoted on a stock exchange.

European and global activity
During recent years, the European insurance industry has seen more takeovers, alliances and joint ventures than many other areas. There appear to be three main reasons:

- *Economic downturn and some exceptional insurance disasters, eg hurricanes in 1987 and 1990.* This had the effect of reducing premium income at the same time as increasing payouts. Insurance companies need a strong capital base to underpin assets and this was undermined by such difficulties. Larger groupings may have more resilience.
- *European insurance deregulation.* Some national insurance markets have been highly competitive on types of insurance and price for years, eg the UK and US. Others have been tightly controlled but are now being liberalized by single European market directives, eg German deregulation during 1994. Companies in controlled markets have been able to earn above-average profits, which they have used to pay acquisition premium for companies in other markets.
- *Drive for European and North American expansion.* Insurance companies have had objectives that could only be satisfied by the international acquisition and merger activity described below.

In practice, the consequences have been mainly confined to Europe and North America, rather than being truly global. Moreover, the trans-Atlantic takeover traffic has largely been from Europe into the more liberal US and Canadian markets. The result has been that premium income amongst Europe's largest insurers has come increasingly from outside their domestic markets, often amounting to over 50% of the total in the 1990s.

Alianz, Germany's biggest insurer, is the giant of Europe. It controls the following: RAS, Italy's second largest insurer; Cornhill UK; 50% of Navigation Mixte, the French holding company with 40% of its business in insurance; 50% of the French insurer Via Rhin et Moselle; the former East German state insurance company; Fireman's Fund, the 15th biggest insurer in North America. It also has extensive shareholdings in German banks and industrial companies, eg 22% of Dresdner Bank, 14% of BASF, 13% of RWE, 12% of VEBA.

Generali, Italy's biggest insurer, has links with AXA-Midi, France, which in turn owns Equity & Law (UK).

Union des Assurances de Paris (UAP) was still awaiting full privatization at the time of writing. Over the last few years, it acquired Royale Belge, Allsecures (Italy, GESA (Spain), Sun Life (UK) and Colonia (Germany). The Germany acquisition is particularly significant because Colonia is Germany's second largest insurer.

Assurance Generales de France (AGF) has acquired companies in Italy, Ireland, Belgium along with 25% of Aachener Munchener (Germany).

Winterthur (Switzerland) has acquired companies in Germany, Italy and the UK.

In addition, there have been other moves: for example, four medium size insurers; Friends Provident (UK), Wasa (Sweden), Avero Centraal Behaer (Netherlands), Topdanmark (Denmark) agreed in 1992 to pool their non-home country assets into a European holding company; it could ultimately lead to a full merger. Sun Alliance (UK) signed an agreement in the same year on co-operation with Helvetia (Switzerland). Aegon (Netherlands) invested £240 million in 1993 for a minority stake in Scottish Equitable (UK).

But not all acquisitions have gone smoothly. Guardian Royal Exchange (UK) was reported to have lost £70 million buying two Italian insurance companies. Eagle Star pulled out of France in 1990 and Prudential (UK) sold its Belgian company. Probably the biggest mistake was made by Hafnia (Denmark): it attempted to build a pan-

Nordic insurance giant in 1990–91 and became totally over-stretched financially in the process. It had to be rescued in 1992.

The strategy of size for its own sake is epitomized by the unsuccessful Hafnia adventure, and the (so far) more rewarding French acquisitions. But it remains largely unproven. It has been argued that the advantages of size in insurance are:

1. Larger asset base to provide a defence against insurance market cyclicality.
2. Higher capital base needed for more rapid growth.
3. Buys expertise in new forms of insurance, such as unit-linked policies and telephone selling which are not undertaken in every European country.
4. Builds barriers to entry.

But if size is purchased via acquisition, then the premium on assets may well over-extend the company and negate the first three above. The fourth point has some ostensible validity: for example, which company could match Allianz's 60,000 insurance representatives in Germany? But new technology and careful re-appraisal of insurance risks has taken telephone/computer selling of car insurance in the UK and US to around 33% of the market, without any personal representation. It may only be a matter to time before the same technology is applied in Germany. With increased liberalization across the single Europe, new technology in computers and telecommunications needs to be built more clearly into business strategy.

Outside the genuinely global reinsurance and large commercial risk policies, there may be no clear need for a pan-European strategy. Some North American companies have even given up trying to obtain a large share of all types of insurance right across North America. They have chosen to specialize in some types of insurance in limited geographical areas because this is more profitable and easier to manage. If this were true across Europe, then some of the acquisitions and alliances described above could become a real burden over the next few years.

Keypoint on joint ventures and takeovers
Some European insurance company takeovers have aroused strong emotions, particularly in France and Belgium, often associated with power struggles in the original companies. For example, it was reported in the UK *Financial Times* that Sir Douglas Wass of the British insurer, Equity and Law, was voted down as that company's representative on the parent board of the French insurer Midi as a shareholders' meeting in 1989.

While harsh words may be the correct tactics during a takeover battle, joint ventures and acquisitions are easier to handle afterwards if passions have not been aroused. The introduction of new methods of operating, the need for job losses and new reporting procedures all benefit from a calm approach during the takeover. How were Equity and Law employees supposed to feel after this incident took place?

Strong emotions can be aroused during bids. This is not the best framework for rational decision making: certainly, the temperature needs to be reduced when the new company takes over.

LONGER-TERM CONSEQUENCES OF JOINT VENTURES

Joint ventures are fundamentally different from takeovers because ownership and partnership remains collaborative rather than one-sided. Thus there are long-term management implications for joint ventures: this is a completely different way of working for companies used to 100 per cent ownership and ultimate control of subsidiaries.

If companies cannot live with this change in management style then they should not embark on joint ventures. Let us explore this most important issue further.

Case Study: Corning, USA

Corning, the US glass multinational, has a series of joint ventures ranging from one with Dow Chemicals which is 40 years old to another with IBM that was only set up in 1988. This case is taken from an interview published in the *Financial Times* on 22 January 1990 with the group president of Corning, Mr. Richard Dulude.

'You can never afford to surprise your partner. You must treat him like a customer. That means you have to talk a lot. Things you might normally do as a reflex or routine you have to explain and be prepared to change.'

Mr. Dulude's checklist for the management of successful joint ventures is as follows:

- If the first question raised in negotiations is 'who is going to control the venture?', tidy your papers, slide back your chair and head for the door – the venture will not work. Equally, if most of the negotiations focus on how the parties will be able to escape if the venture fails, claim pressing engagements and leave.
- The venture will have to be able to grow, unless it is a purely defensive move to protect a market against incursion from competitors. If the venture gets hemmed in, either geographically or technologically, there will be constant friction between the venture and its parents.
- The venture has to develop its own culture and identity as a business. Employees and customers must be encouraged not to treat it like an airport, something they want to pass through quickly and dread getting stuck in.
- The managers of the venture have to have access to senior executives in the parent companies. If not, strategic decisions may be delayed and the venture will be relegated to the margins.
- Beware of monolithic companies with strong centralized organizations which are used to doing everything for themselves. Joint venture partners have to want to share responsibility.
- As the number of joint ventures grows, so a company's sense of itself has to change. Corning sees itself as the centre of a dense web of links. Joint ventures are only one of those links. The others include wholly-owned subsidiaries, majority stakes, minority interests and marketing agreements.

    Mr. Dulude says: 'We are neither a monolithic operating company, nor a holding company. We work more like a network. Companies will have to think much more in terms of networking rather than just controlling.'

Here is a mature view of how takeovers and mergers should work based on experience and reality. It provides valuable guidelines for all companies seeking this route for international expansion.

CHAPTER 29

Organization and Control for European and Global Markets

As we have seen in the case studies recorded here, it is important to produce an effective organization to implement decisions taken on international expansion. The chaos that can result from managers in the same company competing unnecessarily with each other across national boundaries for international contracts, the occasional confusion over who is responsible for what in matrix management, the tensions from differing cultural expectations: all of these impact on profits.

Just as European union is still some way from full achievement, some international company organizations are also still in the early stages of development. Others, like Unilever and Royal Dutch Shell, have been international for years. As described at the beginning of the book, there is plenty of market and financial company variety across Europe. This is mirrored in organizational development, but it is less well recorded: broad financial and marketing details are published at least annually, but organizational data less frequently and on an irregular basis.

Nevertheless, there is enough evidence to produce some guidelines for international organization and control. Here are seven areas a company may wish to consider in establishing its organizational structure for the new opportunities:

1. Background to the expansion: is it all resolved or is there still considerable uncertainty?
2. Company objectives and strategies.
3. National customers versus international demand.
4. Product or service range across international markets.
5. Degree and frequency of reporting and control between the individual companies and headquarters.
6. Industrial relations and employment aspects of the move to new markets.
7. Information technology strategy for the new structure.

Let us examine each of these areas for their relevance to international strategy.

Background to the expansion

If there is still considerable uncertainty, then this needs to be taken into account when building the organization. This does not mean that a company should not be bold in its moves. Rather than, for example, if it has not yet been established that an outline distribution strategy is correct, then there is a case for not recruiting large numbers for this service. Equally, if the search for local allies is still underway as a major plank of strategy, then setting up a vast European or global organization might be counter-productive.

As outlined earlier in the book, regional expansion is a perfectly viable strategy for some markets but it does require *flexibility* in the organization as the expansion takes place. In the same way, pan-European or global organizations will benefit from informal contacts in the early days as new colleagues try to get to know each other: a non-rigid structure will facilitate this.

Company objectives and strategies

In addition to the uncertainty surrounding international moves outlined above, organizations clearly need to be tailored to meet company objectives, as defined and agreed.

Within this large subject, one area does need consideration in new international organizations: the balance between central objective setting and the use of local initiatives. For some companies starting to move internationally, the overall strategy will have been derived centrally: that is how it may have been submitted for approval by its main board. But now, in implementation, there may be the real problem that national companies acquired or associated with the new moves may need to be given objectives that they have neither seen nor agreed to. One way round this is to do what some Japanese companies do and set up from scratch. Another way is to accept that the overall plans are subject to change as the national company considers the detail.

In every case, the key to the whole matter is not to expect too much too quickly. This needs to be built into the objectives along with a 'learning phase' to help managers to understand each other. We will come back to this shortly.

National customers versus international demand

Along with setting objectives, there is a need to consider the balance between international products or services and national demand, which may not match what has been developed globally. Clearly, this is unlikely to affect Coca Cola or McDonalds but it does apply to, for example, chocolate across Europe: some countries like the UK have a much higher vegetable fat content in the product than others such as France. In both cases, the product to be sold must be what the national customer wants and not what is dictated from international head office.

Similarly, in electronic household goods, there are variations in demand. The 24-hour clock is used extensively in some parts of Europe but not in others, thus affecting the design of clock digital displays. How is this variation to be handled? Just how much autonomy is to be given to local companies?

We will look shortly at what Electrolux and Sony have been doing but let us first examine some research evidence from Professor Peter Doyle and his colleagues*. They surveyed a sample of companies from the USA, Japan and the UK concerning their development of marketing strategy: 'The Japanese considered themselves significantly more autonomous than the American subsidiaries. Autonomy covered the selection of products to sell, pricing, promotion and distribution policies.'

In some markets, there is no doubt that local demand variations must be met and companies organized accordingly. It is usually best to define precisely those issues that can be decided locally.

Product or service range across international markets

In a similar way, products and services may be introduced across the world or only launched into selected countries. The author recalls being part of a project team to launch a new soft drink across Europe in the late 1970s. Whilst national countries were allowed to vary the formula to suit local tastes, as outlined above, most countries were really given little choice but to launch a product into the market. It has subsequently been withdrawn in several markets because the problem was with the *concept* imposed centrally, rather than local variations developed across Europe.

Case Study: Matra-Hachette SA, France

Data
One of Europe's top publishing and defence industry groups.
1992 turnover (Ffr million)
Matra

Defence	5500
Space	5500
Automobiles	5600
Telecommunications and CAD/CAM	7400
Transmit systems	1700
Hachette	
Book publishing	6200
Print media	8800
Distribution services	12100
Total	55100

Return on capital: 8.9%
% sales in home country: 50
% sales in rest of world: 50

European and global activity
Matra-Hachette is surely one of Europe's more curious larger companies. It consists of two quite distinct parts – Hachette publishing and Matra aerospace and defence – that only came together in 1992.

Both companies have significant global interests. Matra business strategy has centred around its French-based defence industry contacts. By contrast, Hachette

---

* P. Doyle, J. Saunders and L. Wright, 'A comparative study of US and Japanese companies in the British market', private paper, July 1987.

grew via acquisition in Spain and the USA in the late 1980s – it also publishes actively in several European countries as well as in Mexico, Argentina and Chile.

With such an obvious difference in markets and strategy, the reasons for the merger deserve examination. They stem from Hachette's interest in the French TV station, La Cinq, which collapsed in 1992 after making losses for several years. Hachette was faced with debts of US$ 1.65 billion and its very survival was at stake. Its chairman, M. Jean-Luc Largardere also held the same post at Matra.

Hachette needed a refinancing package of US$ 500 million from its French bankers. In the process of the negotiations, they also agreed to a merger with the financially stronger Matra group to provide more stability. There was no industrial logic for the merger – business strategy of the simplest kind. In practice it is likely that the French banks saw this as the cheapest way to rescue Hachette and protect some of their investment.

Keypoint on organization and control
Hachette has used its expertise and knowledge in publishing as the base for its world expansion. But publishing has obvious local requirements: encyclopaedias in the French language are unlikely to top the best selling lists in Spain.

Hence, in buying national companies, it has left a good deal of discretion to them. Hachette offers a world-wide portfolio of publishing titles but allows local management discretion in its choice and presentation of material. The resources and skills that both parties bring to the process need to complement each other and thus avoid conflict.

Reporting and control between individual companies and headquarters

Let us return to the research about US, Japanese and British companies quoted earlier in this chapter. In researching how the two groups of foreign companies operated in the UK, the researchers found that both groups of subsidiaries had their performance closely monitored by headquarters at home: 'The types of controls were, however, different. The Americans relied on much more detailed and *formal* controls ... the Japanese did not favour the detailed standardized planning systems which Western multinationals tend to use, instead they relied on continuous *informal monitoring*. All the subsidiaries indicated that reporting was a "daily" or "constant" process with the telephone as the main mode of communication with Japan. Headquarters were invariably viewed as extremely well informed of activities, problems and progress ...

'Japanese headquarter–subsidiary relations appeared to reflect, better than the Americans, the two desiderata of Peters and Waterman's excellent companies – "operational autonomy to encourage entrepreneurship" and "simultaneous loose–tight controls".'

Similar principles might be taken to apply elsewhere. The balance will depend on the stage of development, the nature of the markets and, as much as anything, the demands of the customer.

Industrial relations and employment aspects of moves to new markets

This most important topic is beyond the scope of this book. The European Commission has published extensively in this area and other books and papers cover legislation and freedom of movement of skills across the market. Appendix

3 includes some material to allow adequate consideration of this subject, which is listed here for completeness.

Let us now consider two examples of the opportunities and problems facing companies operating in the single Europe.

Case Study: Sony Inc., Japan

Data
One of the world's leading home electronics companies.
1992 turnover (US$ million)

Japan	7234	Video equipment	6739
USA	8337	Audio equipment	7126
Europe	8116	Televisions	4456
Other	5008	Other products	4637
		Total electronics	22959
		Music entertainment	3299
		Filmed entertainment	2475
		Total entertainment	5775
Total	28734	Total	28734

Return on capital: na
% sales in home country: 25
% sales in rest of Europe: 28
% sales in rest of world: 47

European and global market activity
Sony set up its first European plant in Wales in 1974. By 1990s, it was manufacturing a range of TVs, VCRs, hi-fi and CD players and tapes in six European countries. While some of the basic new technology is developed in Japan, the company is reported to be willing to consider European initiatives: both a plant for making CD players and designs for professional broadcast tape were accepted by Sony instead of Japanese recommendations.

Sony is a global company, epitomized not only by its world consumer electronics but also by its acquisition of CBS Entertainment (US) in 1990.

Keypoints on organization and control
Compared to other Japanese companies, Sony is regarded as more cosmopolitan. Without doubt this stems in part from one of its co-founders, Akio Morita, who wanted to bridge the divide between East and West. Yet there are still reported to be considerable problems, especially in the area of local autonomy. European managers have sought to make Europe into an area able to take more of its own decisions based on local needs.

Sony has retained a close interest in its European operations using a fluid style of reporting and structure broadly similar to that described above. The company has said that this assists fast response to marketplace events.

Additionally, there have been management promotion difficulties in Europe: it used to be mainly Japanese who moved around between European companies. Now, European promotion is possible. Just in case the reader might be thinking this was an exclusively Japanese problem, Electrolux has the same difficulty: see below.

Case Study: Electrolux AB, Sweden

These additional comments need to be read in conjunction with the basic case study in Chapter 21.

Keypoints on organization and control
Over the last few years, Electrolux has acquired a range of businesses in its main areas of domestic appliances across most of Europe and the USA. There has therefore been a need for product rationalization, factory rationalization, central development and local initiatives. This is a major international task by any standards. Reorganization was progressing in the early 1990s with some tension still in existence, possibly encouraged in some cases to stimulate discussion.

In many international companies, such as Unilever, there is a matrix structure: it consists essentially of national managements and international product teams both having responsibility for aspects of the same business. In Electrolux, there is a third element as well: decentralized strategic business units. This has produced a highly complex structure with its own tensions.

There are also problems for the company in international management and promotion. Informal discussions and some of the major decisions were reported to take place in the Swedish head office. Electrolux's management is mainly Swedish and arguably needs to be internationalized.

As with the Sony management, Electrolux fully acknowledges the need to change. Both managements have the maturity to discuss these difficulties openly and set in train programmes to alter the situation. The key to this development is to accept that these matters will not happen overnight, nor need they. It is better that organizations evolve rather than change by revolution because profits and long-term viability are thereby preserved. The single Europe may be a catalyst for change but is only part of a world trend in some industries, so should not be taken out of context. It was still mainly Swedish at the top in 1993. For a fuller description of the organization, see my book, *Cases in European Marketing*, Kogan Page 1994.

Information technology strategy for the new structure

Over the last few years, IT has transformed the operations of business based in a number of locations. It is essential to use this for international expansion.

Because of the greater distances involved and the increased pace of change in modern business, it is essential to develop an IT strategy for dealing with communications based on:

- The new organizational structure;
- The geographical locations;
- The computer and telecommunications equipment now in place or to be purchased; and
- The defined needs for information flows.

This cannot be left to chance and the odd telephone call when the half-yearly financial statements are due. It must be the subject of a clear resource and development study. The details are beyond the scope of this book but there are plenty of computer companies and telecommunications companies willing to advise in this field.

It is my personal belief that a well executed IT strategy will turn the most difficult task of managing across global markets into a cost-effective reality for all companies, both large and small.

CHAPTER 30

Reducing Risk and Planning for Rewards

There can be no doubt that European and global markets will provide substantial rewards to those companies which are successful in exploiting the new opportunities. But, for every winner, there will also be losers. The job of all managers across the world will be to end up among the winners.

Rewards will favour the bold: decisive international marketing entry strategies are the starting point for this. We have looked hard at these and also at the necessary protective measures throughout this book. Our final step is to assess the risk and take measures that will reduce it.

Like other aspects of European and global business strategy, many of the best ways of reducing risk will only come from analyzing the precise strategies being undertaken. However, here are some general pointers that may help:

- Consider building alliances. There is often more strength from combination with other companies. It is more profitable for potential enemies to join together than fight.
- When going for broke on a strategy, seek ways to minimize the downside exposure of the company and avoid jeopardizing all the company's activities. If the opportunity does not work out, then it is clearly preferable to have isolated the area such that the company is able to continue trading elsewhere. In this context, we will look at a German construction company and European media companies later in this chapter.
- Build shareholder protection where possible. This is difficult in the UK and easier in some other EU and Far Eastern countries: we will look at a German packaging company case study below.
- Seek ways to move out of weak areas before being pushed. If a market sector is likely to prove exceptionally vulnerable it may be wiser to withdraw while it is still profitable: we will look at the case of a French company below.
- Consider operating staged development. Many companies take a number of years to build their share in markets: the time perspective allows for development to be undertaken in stages. This clearly reduces risk and is not inconsistent with the realistic exploitation of the single market.
- Appoint good professional advisers: accountants, bankers, lawyers and consultants. Both the specialist expertise and more general advice reduce the risk and build protection.

Finally, we must accept that some risk is highly likely. We will look at how two companies accept that risk. Now let us examine the case studies mentioned above.

Case Study: Philipp Holzmann AG, Germany

Data
Germany's largest quoted construction group.

Turnover (DM million)	1987	1992
Domestic	2560	7713
Foreign	780	4759
USA	1363	see below
Affiliates (est.)	1093	–
Total	5796	12472

Return on capital:	5.4%	8.7% (estimate)
% sales home country:	44	62
% sales in rest of Europe:	6	15
% sales in rest of world:	50	23

European and global market activity
Holzmann has main branches across Germany and holdings in other German construction companies. German re-unification provided a boost for business.

Keypoint on risk
Along with other international construction companies, Holzmann had a serious decline in its Middle Eastern business during the late 1980s. But it used the profits earned in the good years to build more stable international business elsewhere.

Specifically, it built its international business over this period in the USA and Canada. It acquired the construction companies, J. Jones, North Carolina and William L. Crow, New York. These geographic areas clearly have lower risk in the world markets for construction skills. By 1992, they were no longer identified separately in the accounts.

Holzmann was therefore able to ride out the sales difficulties from the decline in its Middle Eastern business by balancing the portfolio with lower-risk North American business. In international markets, companies should explore whether high-risk developments in some parts can be balanced by lower-risk activities elsewhere.

Case Study: Europe's leading paper, board and packaging companies

	Country	Turnover 1992 (US$ m)	Return on capital (%)	Home (%)	Rest of Europe (%)	Rest of world (%)
					Destination of sales	
Glass						
*St. Gobain	Fra	4453	na			
Pilkington	UK	4242	3.7	14	39	47
*BSN packaging	Fra	1398	na			

Metal						
*Pechiney	Fra	5463	na			
CarnaudMetalBox	Fra	4925	13.5		86	14
*Alusuisse Lonza	Swi	1033	na			
Timber, paper and board						
KNP BT	Net	7030	na	25	58	17
*Stora Kopparbergs	Swe	6811	na			
SCA	Swe	5735	7.2	20	78	2
Tetrapak	Swe	5300 est	na			
Arjo Wiggins Appleton	UK	4334	12.8	18	64	18
*Repola	Fin	3049	na			
Kymmene	Fin	2887	5.2	na		
PWA	Ger	2854	3.2	52	33	15
MoDo	Swe	2813	(2.4)	16	77	7
Jefferson Smurfitt	Ire	2229	8.1	15	47	38
**Bowater	UK	2092	12.6	48	11	31
Courtaulds	UK	1090 est	na			

* only part of turnover for company
** only part of turnover for Bowater but other parts are small

For some purposes, the above companies are not in the same markets – glass windows do not normally compete with corrugated board. However, principally in the area of packaging, they can be substitutes for each other depending on precise usage requirements and cost. We have explored other areas elsewhere in this book so in this section we will concentrate primarily on packaging.

European and global activity
Within Europe, substantial consolidation and vertical integration of timber, paper and packaging companies has taken place over the past few years. The strategy reasons are not difficult to discern:

- economies of scale;
- secure sources of supply: vertical integration upstream;
- distribution strength with many leading manufacturers acquiring their distributors: vertical integration downstream;
- extension into higher added-value products such as special quality papers;
- market strength: share and geographical coverage.

Overall, the companies are fiercely competitive, not just amongst themselves but also in certain applications with glass, metal and plastic packaging companies. The strategies of some of the leading companies have been explored elsewhere in this book.

One company not mentioned elsewhere is the relatively new company KNP BT. It was a merger in late 1992 of three medium-size Dutch companies with the published objective of achieving global representation. Whether this is really beneficial and whether the new company amounts to anything more than the consolidation of three sets of company accounts, remained to be resolved at the time of writing. However, the company has begun a significant reorganization of its facilities to achieve the necessary results.

Both St. Gobain and Pilkington have extensive pan-European and global interests. They have been built over the last few years and represent a powerful position from which to exploit international markets.

European packaging markets showed sustained growth in the 1980s but the mid 1990s economic downturn had a severe impact on profitability. One of the important issues will be that of recycling packaging materials: most European multinationals are working on this.

Keypoint on risk taking
Several of the Finnish companies and Arjo Wiggins Appleton have shareholding structures that inhibit their being taken over by other companies. This reduces the risk of losing control if circumstances change.

Equally, during the 1990s in some EC countries, it was also possible for a third party to buy large share stakes without declaring the matter because there were no disclosure rules. It was even possible to keep the share price down by denying any interest in the company. Ultimately, it is when a company with a real takeover interest comes along that the third party is able to take the profits from this type of share dealing. You have been warned!

Case Study: Lafarge Coppee SA, France

Data
France's largest supplier of cement and other building materials.
1992 turnover (Ffr million)

Cement	12338
Concrete and aggregates	9202
Plaster and gypsum	2425
Speciality	5065
Biochemicals	1421
Total	30451

Return on capital: 9.1%
% sales in home country: 41
% sales in rest of Europe: 22
% sales in rest of world: 37

European and global market activity
Apart from one plant in Germany, the company's cement business is concentrated in France where it has 12 plants and is market leader with 35%. Its other main area of operation is in the USA and Canada accounting for over 30% of total turnover. During 1989, the company took control of Cementia, a Swiss cement group, for US$843 million and also acquired a majority shareholding in the leading Spanish cement producer, Asland. Through the Cementia deal, Lafarge Coppee gained entry to the Indian Ocean market. It has subsequently set up plant in Taiwan to challenge the Far East market.

With the 'Alia' brand name, the company claims to be a European leader in bathroom equipment.

Keypoint on risk
In the 1980s, Lafarge Coppee moved into biological activities: biochemicals, field seeds and vegetable and flower seeds. While there was some growth in the early years, the area was still a very minor contribution to profits in the mid 1990s.

Moreover, the company moved into the highly competitive pan-European biochemicals market: major international companies involved in agricultural seed products competed directly with Lafarge Coppee from the early 1990s. The company made no comment on prospects in the biochemicals business area, but the risk is such that it may be better to consider the sale of the business before the pressure really increases. Risk can be reduced by divesting in weak areas as well as investing in strong sectors.

Case Study: selected European media, information and entertainment groups

	Country	Turnover 1992 (US$ m)	Return on capital (%)	Destination of sales Home (%)	Rest of Europe (%)	Rest of world (%)
Time Warner	USA	13070	na	84	11	5
Bertelsmann	Ger	10737	23.1	38	35	27
News Corporation	Aust	8419	6.8	14	18	68
*Sony	Jap	5775	na			
*Hachette	Fra	5376	na			
Paramount	USA	4265	na			
Havas	Fra	4204	na			
Reed Elsevier	UK/Net	4067	17.2	na	54	46
*Thompson Corp	Can	3827	na	47	50	3
Reuters	UK	2591	34.5		61	39
Axel Springer	Ger	2400	2.1	na		
*Pearson	UK	1893	10.5	54	11	55
Mondadori	Ita	1220	16.2	na		

* only part of total turnover of company

Note: some major US entertainment groups have been excluded from the above because data was not available.

European and global strategy

Most media and publishing groups of the size of those above would regard themselves as being involved in global rather than European markets. However, there are a large number of major businesses in the European Union, that manage successful operations on a national or regional scale across Europe without global ambitions.

Global strategies were developed for five major reasons:

- world-wide and common interests and tastes of some customers;
- new communications technologies that permit inexpensive and widely available broadcasts across the world;
- advertisers with products and services available globally;
- increased wealth globally;
- computer technology that has dramatically reduced the cost of the printed and broadcast word.

News Corporation is in the process of building a global media presence with a staged expansion:

- establish a base of stable titles to provide cash flow: Australia, UK newspapers;
- expand aggressively, particularly to secure a strong position in North American and European television: Fox TV and Sky TV;
- negotiate satellite deals to extend TV coverage: Star TV in Asia and the Middle East.

Time Warner is arguably not truly global in that its main business comes from its extensive US publishing interests. Yet its worldwide music interests (Atlantic Records) and Warner Brothers film interests, all suggest other avenues for globalization. Bertelsmann has pursued a similar route (see chapter 18), based on a number of acquisitions in the USA coupled with the natural extension of existing titles. Reed (UK) and Elsevier (Net) merged to provide a similar basis for global expansion – described separately next.

Companies such as Reuter in financial data and Pearson with its interests in the *Financial Times, The Economist* and book publishing, have also extended their interests around the world, particularly as global financial markets have moved increasingly together based on a common language: English. This may explain why expansion has been global rather than pan-European, where language may be more of an obstacle.

Yet the European media market must continue to hold opportunities for national and regional development. The wealth, language and cultural differences across Europe will continue well into the next century. They will form a bedrock for continued diversity in European media and publishing. The real question is whether publishing skills are transferable from one language to another at a profit. Bertelsmann's success in the UK suggests that they are.

Keypoint on risk taking
Rupert Murdoch would hardly have built the News Corporation to its present size if he had been cautious. He took a real risk when he launched the Sky TV satellite service in Europe in the late 1980s – his company was reported to be spending US$ 3 million per week. He had similar exposure with the Fox TV channel in the USA in the 1990s.

For some years analysts feared his company would be over-stretched financially. But although the sums were significant in absolute terms, they were relatively small in comparison to the total resources and cash flow of the company. They were also capable of producing substantial rewards that justified the risk if successful. Every investment has its reward: the key is to set the payoff against the exposure involved, and then take a judgement on the acceptable level of risk for that company in that situation.

Case Study: Reed Elsevier, UK and the Netherlands

Data
One of Europe's largest publishers.
1992 turnover (£ million)

Scientific and medical	450
Professional	356
Business	859
Consumer	796
Total	2461

Return on capital: 17.2%
Destination of sales:
  UK: 31
  Netherlands: 12
  Rest of Europe: 11
  North America: 34
  Rest of world: 12

European and global activity
Back in the late 1980s, Reed (UK) was a conglomerate with a product range that included paint, DIY products, paper and packaging interests along with publishing. The company spent three years at the end of the 1980s divesting some parts and acquiring other companies to become a media and information-based company. Its purchases included Octopus Books, US Technical books and the US publishing interests of News Corporation. Most of the acquisitions were in the English-speaking world, particularly the USA. Little was done in continental Europe.

At the same time, the major Dutch publisher Elsevier was developing its relationship with the Pearson Group (UK). Both companies judged that size and geographical coverage were important in global expansion. However, the relationship was eventually and amicably terminated for reasons never wholly clear but probably due to incompatibility in management style.

Reed and Elsevier then came together during 1991–92 and formally merged at the end of 1992 – the above financial data is taken from the merger document, and shows what the company would have been like as one group if it had operated during 1992.

The two companies found that they had complementary interests: Reed wanted to move into continental Europe, Elsevier into the USA. They also both had ambitions to make a larger company through acquisitions that neither could afford as separate entities. Subsequently, the group has already had some success: it purchased the largest legal publisher in France, Editions Technique, for £77 million in 1993. This will sit alongside the Reed Elsevier ownership of the UK legal publishers, Butterworths. In late 1993, the company bought the Official Airline Guides (US) from the administrators of the Maxwell Group for over US$ 400 million.

Although the combined group has become one of the world's largest publishers, its strategy has been where possible to develop strong interests in well-differentiated and established specialist publications; for example, scientific journals and professional law books. While these are competitive markets, the highly specialist nature makes barriers high for any further new entrants, and supports high profit margins for companies already established.

Keypoint on risk taking
Not many companies have undertaken the radical restructuring undertaken at Reed before it joined with Elsevier. This brings its own risks associated with the purchase and sale of large companies for enormous cash sums.

Before further purchases were made, Reed was sitting on a large cash sum which did nothing to make it less attractive to a takeover bidder. Equally, as a strategy like this becomes clear in the market, potential sellers can either become nervous or simply demand a higher price: high risk indeed, but acceptable to the company and its shareholders for the rewards that would come on completion.

Again, the key to risk assessment is a mature balance of the projections of risk and reward from the strategy. When the details are set out, the task of senior management is to probe whether they are reasonable in all the circumstances and whether the resulting profitability justifies the exposure. This was an analysis conducted by Reed before it embarked on its divestment and acquisition strategy.

Case Study: Henkel AG, Germany

Data
Germany's fourth largest chemical company with some strong consumer brands.
Turnover (DM million)

	1988	1992
Chemical products	2818	3644
Institutional hygiene	1629	1361
Industrial adhesives & technical consumer products	1539	2266
Cosmetics & toiletries	732	1529
Detergents & household cleaners	3371	4510
Metal chemicals	–	621
Other	163	170
Total	10252	14101

Return on capital:	11.0%	9.8%
% sales in home country:	30	29
% sales in rest of Europe:	49	51
% sales in rest of world:	21	20

European and global market activity
Henkel has two main parts to its activities: it is one of the world's leading companies in the production of basic chemicals for fatty products used in natural oils, cosmetics and pharmaceuticals. Secondly, it also has a strong branded consumer product range based partly on its involvement in basic chemicals. In recent years it has sought to strengthen these activities in Europe and the USA.

Germany accounts for nearly one-third of total sales. The company was a major German advertising spender in the 1990s on detergents, cosmetics and adhesives.

In France, Henkel bought three companies in 1987: Union Générale de Savionniere; Solitaire; and Cotelle. In 1992, it purchased the Swedish company, Bärnangen, in order to expand in northern Europe.

In the UK the company bought the adhesives firm, Unibond Copydex Limited, while in Holland, Italy and Spain it has launched liquid Persil and liquid Dixan.

In the USA it has acquired a major oleochemical company Quantum Chemical for US$480 million cash. In Eastern Europe, it has commenced new ventures in the Czech and Slovak Republics and in Hungary. It has also been negotiating a joint venture in China.

Overall, Henkel is an important player in some European detergent markets and a world company in oleochemicals. The company has said that it is planning global expansion through its product range, branding, pricing and full utilization of rationalization in production and logistics.

Keypoint on risk taking
Henkel's attitude to risk and its rewards is summarized in the headline it used in its 1987 *Annual Report*. It brings home another aspect of risk taking for international expansion: risk means uncertainty but that is what makes business exciting:

'To succeed in business you need "skill, patience, money . . . and a bit of luck."''

I have deliberately put this quote last. It seems to me to sum up the tremendous challenges and rewards of international markets, while at the same time adding a touch of management maturity. And European and global strategies will need this to survive the test of time and prosper in the real world of lower trade barriers and increased international competition over the next few years.

Europe's Top 400 Companies

This appendix ranks Europe's Top 400 companies in descending order of turnover. Background on this list, for those wishing to understand more about the selection and what it means for strengths and weaknesses, is given in Appendix 2.

	Company	Country	Main products	Turnover 1991 (US$ m)
1	Royal Dutch Shell	UK/Net	Oil & petrol	131,500
2	British Petroleum	UK	Oil & petrol	57,650
3	Daimler Benz	Ger	Cars & trucks	57,234
4	IRI	Ita	Holding	54,949
5	Volkswagen	Ger	Cars & trucks	45,972
6	Fiat	Ita	Cars & trucks	45,650
7	Siemens	Ger	Telecomms equip.	43,980
8	ENI	Ita	Oil & petrol	41,121
9	Unilever	Net/UK	Consumer goods	40,985
10	VEBA	Ger	Electricity	35,846
11	Elf	Fra	Oil & petrol	36,643
12	Nestlé	Swi	Consumer goods	35,304
13	BAT	UK	Insurance/tobacco	31,306
14	Philips	Net	Elec. Eng.	30,555
15	Electricite de France	Fra	Electricity	30,448
16	RWE	Ger	Electricity	30,054
17	Renault	Fra	Cars & trucks	29,480
18	Hoechst	Ger	Chemicals	28,925
19	ASEA Brown Boveri	Swi/Swe	Heavy Eng.	28,833
20	Peugeot Citroën	Fra	Cars & trucks	28,449
21	Alcatel	Fra	Telecomms equip.	28,434
22	Deutsche B. Telekom	Ger	Tel. service	28,430
23	Tengelmann	Ger	Retail	28,130
24	BASF	Ger	Chemicals	28,087
25	Total	Fra	Oil & petrol	25,403
26	Bayer	Ger	Chemicals	24,816
27	France Telecom	Fra	Tel. service	23,500
28	British Telecom	UK	Tel. service	23,252
29	Gen des Eaux	Fra	Public service	22,904
30	REWE	Ger	Retail	22,531
31	Thyssen	Ger	Iron & steel	22,025
32	ICI	UK	Chemicals	22,004
33	ENEL	Ita	Electricity	21,756
34	Bosch	Ger	Cars & trucks	20,240
35	InterMarche	Fra	Retail	19,094

	Company	Country	Main products	Turnover 1991 (US$ m)
36	Le Clerc	Fra	Retail	18,917
37	British Aerospace	UK	Aerospace	18,670
38	STET	Ita	Tel. service	18,564
39	British Gas	UK	Gas	18,126
40	BMW	Ger	Cars & trucks	17,975
41	Carrefour	Fra	Retail	17,829
42	Petrofina	Bel	Oil & petrol	17,576
43	Usinor Sacilor	Fra	Iron & steel	17,260
44	Aldi	Ger	Retail	16,506
45	Repsol	Spa	Oil & petrol	15,733
46	Lyonnaise/Dumez	Fra	Holding	15,539
47	Grand Met	UK	Spirits/consumer	15,464
48	Rhone-Poulenc	Fra	Chemicals	14,887
49	RuhrKohle	Ger	Coal	14,879
50	Deutsche B PostDienst	Ger	Post	14,759
51	Ciba	Swi	Chemical/pharm.	14,739
52	Mannesmann	Ger	Heavy Eng.	14,647
53	Ferruzzi	Ita	Holding/consumer	14,375
54	Viag	Ger	Metals	14,209
55	Sainsbury's	UK	Retail	13,811
56	Hanson	UK	Holding	13,595
57	Promodes	Fra	Retail	13,564
58	Otto Versand	Ger	Mail order	13,526
59	St Gobain	Fra	Glass	13,333
60	Pechiney	Fra	Metals	13,219
61	Electrolux	Swe	Consumer goods	13,093
62=	SNCF	Fra	Rail	12,970
62=	Volvo	Swe	Cars & trucks	12,970
64	Metallgesellschaft	Ger	Trading	12,759
65	MontEdison	Ita	Chemicals	12,706
66	Thomson	Fra	Aerospace & elec.	12,660
67	Pinault	Fra	Retail	12,562
68	Tesco	UK	Retail	12,545
69	Michelin	Fra	Rubber	12,015
70	BTR	UK	Holding	11,917
71	BSN	Fra	Consumer goods	11,738
72	Metro	Ger	Retail	11,500
73	M.A.N.	Ger	Heavy Eng. & trucks	11,464
74	Stora	Swe	Paper	11,120
75	Bouygues	Fra	Construction	11,115
76	Statoil	Nor	Oil & petrol	11,048
77	ASKO	Ger	Retail	10,824
78	Ahold	Net	Retail	10,789
79	GEC	UK	Holding	10,682
80	SPEP	Fra	Holding	10,497
81	Schneider	Fra	Elec. Eng.	10,483
82	Haniel	Ger	Transport	10,337
83	Karstadt	Ger	Retail	10,317
84	Schickedanz	Ger	Retail	10,297
85	KF	Swe	Retail	10,219
86	Marks & Spencer	UK	Retail	10,209
87	Migros	Swi	Retail	10,162

	Company	Country	Main products	Turnover 1991 (US$ m)
88	Ned GasUnie	Net	Gas	10,137
89	Deutsch BundesBahn	Ger	Rail	9,878
90	Lufthansa	Ger	Air	9,699
91	Matra-Hachette	Fra	Holding	9,682
92	SHV	Net	Retail	9,541
93	Telefonica	Spa	Tel. services	9,500
94	Allied Lyons	UK	Consumer goods	9,475
95	Sandoz	Swi	Pharmaceuticals	9,401
96	Norsk Hydro	Nor	Chemical	9,368
97	Kaufhof	Ger	Retail	9,335
98	PTT Nederlands	Net	Tel. & post	9,300
99	British Airways	UK	Air	9,234
100	Ruhrgas	Ger	Gas	9,201
101	Krupp	Ger	Iron & steel	9,116
102	Post Office	UK	Post	9,101
103	Delhaize	Bel	Retail	9,093
104	AKZO	Net	Chemicals	9,035
105	Gaz de France	Fra	Gas	8,767
106	Finnmechanica	Ita	Elec. Eng.	8,757
107	Bertelsmann	Ger	Publishing	8,724
108	P&O	UK	Holding	8,657
109	Austrian Industries	Aus	Iron & steel	8,650
110	Aerospatiale	Fra	Aerospace	8,629
111	Assoc British Foods	UK	Consumer goods	8,612
112	TetraPak	Swe	Packaging	8,600
113	ILVA	Ita	Iron & steel	8,574
114	Argyll	UK	Retail	8,359
115	National Power	UK	Electricity	8,310
116	SK Beecham	UK/USA	Pharmaceuticals	8,282
117	Hillsdown	UK	Consumer goods	8,232
118	Neste	Fin	Oil & petrol	8,196
119	Eridiana Beghin-Say	Fra	Consumer goods	8,139
120	British Steel	UK	Iron & steel	8,127
121	Pirelli	Ita	Rubber & cable	8,103
122	Degussa	Ger	Metals	8,042
123	Hoffman la Roche	Swi	Pharmaceuticals	8,008
124	ASDA	UK	Retail	8,006
125	PTT Schweiz	Swi	Tel. & Post	8,000
126	Auchan	Fra	Retail	7,904
127=	Air France	Fra	Air	7,774
127=	Henkel	Ger	Chemicals	7,774
129	Ericsson	Swe	Telecom equip.	7,587
130	Casino	Fra	Retail	7,534
131	Solvay	Bel	Chemicals	7,479
132	Deutsche Aerospace	Ger	Aerospace	7,438
133	Edeka	Ger	Retail	7,319
134	Coop Schweiz	Swi	Retail	7,290
135	Guinness	UK	Spirits & beer	7,189
136	ICA	Swe	Retail	7,187
137	Kesko Koncernen	Fin	Retail/wholesale	7,050
138	Société Genérale de Belgique	Bel	Holding	7,019
139	British Coal	UK	Coal	6,982

	Company	Country	Main products	Turnover 1991 (US$ m)
140	Olivetti	Ita	Computers	6,958
141	Boots	UK	Retail	6,943
142	Tractabel	Bel	Electricity	6,912
143	CEA	Fra	Electricity	6,904
144	Danzas	Swi	Transport	6,752
145	Ladbroke	UK	Betting/hotels	6,693
146	Endesa	Spa	Electricity	6,604
147	Thorn EMI	UK	Consumer goods	6,470
148	Dalgety	UK	Consumer goods	6,468
149	Inchcape	UK	Trading	6,408
150	GIB	Bel	Retail	6,373
151	Procordia	Swe	Holding	6,304
152	RTZ	UK	Mining	6,279
153	Tabacalera	Spa	Tobacco	6,275
154	Rolls Royce	UK	Aerospace	6,213
155	BICC	UK	Construction	6,102
156	Glaxo	UK	Pharmaceuticals	6,004
157	Kingfisher	UK	Retail	5,990
158	OeMV	Aus	Oil & petrol	5,979
159	Trafalgar House	UK	Heavy Eng.	5,978
160	L'Oreal	Fra	Cosmetics	5,940
161	Machines Bull	Fra	Computers	5,930
162	Arbed	Lux	Iron & steel	5,817
163	Booker	UK	Wholesale	5,814
164	Preussen Elektra	Ger	Electricity	5,760
165	Cadbury Schweppes	UK	Consumer goods	5,722
166	Televerket	Swe	Tel. services	5,702
167	Tarmac	UK	Construction	5,700
168	Tate & Lyle	UK	Consumer goods	5,694
169	Air Liquide	Fra	Gases	5,652
170	Continental	Ger	Rubber	5,649
171	LaFarge Coppee	Fra	Construction	5,621
172	Cable and Wireless	UK	Tel. service	5,614
173	Electrabel	Bel	Electricity	5,585
174	Repola	Fin	Paper	5,512
175	SAS	Swe	Air	5,348
176	PowerGen	UK	Electricity	5,319
177	C&A Modes	Ger	Retail	5,311
178	Lonrho	UK	Trading	5,300
179	Docks de France	Fra	Retail	5,221
180	SAE	Fra	Construction	5,194
181	Iberdroia	Spa	Electricity	5,160
182	Sucree & Denree	Fra	Trading	5,112
183	Cockerill Sambre	Bel	Iron & steel	5,093
184	Skanska	Swe	Construction	5,037
185	DSM	Net	Chemicals	5,012
186	Saab Scania	Swe	Holding	4,972
187	RMC	UK	Cement	4,946
188	BOC Group	UK	Gases	4,805
189	Holzmann	Ger	Construction	4,765
190	United Biscuits	UK	Consumer goods	4,728
191	Havas	Fra	Media	4,706

	Company	Country	Main products	Turnover 1991 (US$ m)
192	Forte	UK	Hotels	4,706
193	SME	Ita	Consumer goods	4,699
194	Heineken	Net	Beer	4,663
195	Pilkington	UK	Glass	4,613
196	GUS	UK	Mail order	4,591
197	Sulzer	Swi	Heavy Eng.	4,458
198	Alusuisse Lonza	Swi	Metals	4,428
199	Arjo Wiggins Teape	UK	Paper	4,396
200	SKF	Swe	Heavy Eng.	4,357
201	CEPSA	Spa	Oil & petrol	4,309
202	SNECMA	Fra	Aerospace	4,250
203	KlocknerWerke	Ger	Mech. Eng.	4,224
204	Holderbank	Swi	Cement	4,173
205	Lucas	UK	Elec. Eng.	4,108
206	Linde	Ger	Heavy Eng.	4,164
207	Burmah Castrol	UK	Retail	4,158
208	Swissair	Swi	Air	4,157
209	BET	UK	Services	4,127
210	Nobel	Nor	Chemicals	4,094
211	AGIV	Ger	Heavy Eng.	4,057
212	Rothmans	Swi/UK	Tobacco	4,053
213	VEW	Ger	Electricity	4,053
214	Christian Dior	Fra	Consumer goods	4,033
215	Reed Elsevier	UK/Net	Publishing	4,000
216	Whitbread	UK	Beer	3,874
217	Schering	Ger	Pharmaceuticals	3,871
218	W.H. Smith	UK	Retail	3,760
219	Comptoirs Moderne	Fra	Retail	3,753
220	Rank Leisure	UK	Hotels/leisure	3,736
221	Bayenwerk	Ger	Electricity	3,734
222	NedLloyd	Net	Transport	3,617
223	Vattenfall	Swe	Electricity	3,563
224	Trelleborg	Swe	Metals	3,558
225	KLM	Net	Air	3,538
226	Valeo	Fra	Car parts	3,529
227	Poliet	Fra	Construction	3,509
228	Coats Viyella	UK	Textiles	3,501
229	Sears	UK	Retail	3,498
230	Elf Sanofi	Fra	Pharmaceuticals	3,482
231	Navigation Mixte	Fra	Holding	3,465
232	Courtaulds	UK	Chemicals	3,435
233	GKN	UK	Car parts	3,402
234	Unigate	UK	Consumer goods	3,348
235	Kymmene	Fin	Paper	3,329
236	Dixons	UK	Retail	3,293
237	Reckitt & Colman	UK	Consumer goods	3,279
238	Harrisons & Crossf.	UK	Trading	3,226
239	La Redoute	Fra	Retail	3,205
240=	Alfa Laval	Swe	Heavy Eng.	3,200
240=	Racal	UK	Elec. Eng.	3,200
242	Electrowatt	Swi	Electricity	3,171
243	Kwik Save	UK	Retail	3,155

	Company	Country	Main products	Turnover 1991 (US$ m)
244	Wolseley	UK	Wholesale	3,072
245	Rinscente	Ita	Retail	3,043
246	Gehe	Ger	Pharmaceuticals	3,034
247	Buhrmann Tetrode	Net	Paper	2,993
248	SudZucker	Ger	Consumer goods	2,972
249	Sandvik	Swe	Heavy Eng.	2,906
250	Kvaerner	Nor	Petrol & oil	2,883
251	Siebe	Ger	Heavy Eng.	2,877
252	Wellcome	UK	Pharmaceuticals	2,838
253	Pearson	UK	Publishing	2,828
254	Dassault	Fra	Aerospace	2,824
255	Campina MelkUnie	Net	Consumer goods	2,822
256	FENOSA	Spa	Electricity	2,794
257	Fomento de Constru.	Spa	Construction	2,790
258	Beiersdorf	Ger	Consumer goods	2,704
259	Pernod Ricard	Fra	Spirits & drinks	2,703
260	PWA	Ger	Paper	2,648
261	Scottish & Newcastle	UK	Beer & hotels	2,628
262	Reuters	UK	Information	2,593
263	Northern Foods	UK	Consumer goods	2,553
264	Accor	Fra	Hotels	2,493
265	Taylor Woodrow	UK	Construction	2,464
266	Italgas	Ita	Gas	2,452
267	Scottish Power	UK	Electricity	2,439
268	Oerlikon-Buhrle	Swi	Heavy Eng.	2,409
269	Sevillana Elec.	Spa	Electricity	2,299
270	Redland	UK	Construction	2,296
271	SSAB	Swe	Iron & steel	2,280
272	Bowater	UK	Paper	2,241
273	Axel Springer	Ger	Publishing	2,217
274=	Seita	Fra	Tobacco	2,203
274=	Hapag Lloyd	Ger	Transport	2,203
276	Atlas Copco	Swe	Heavy Eng.	2,138
277	Coop-Germany	Ger	Retail	2,136
278	AGA	Swe	Chemicals	2,109
279	Aker	Nor	Oil & petrol	2,102
280	FECSA	Spa	Electricity	2,091
281	Wessanen	Net	Consumer goods	2,085
282	Hochtief	Ger	Construction	2,034
283	Blue Circle	UK	Cement	2,031
284	Gas Natural	Spa	Gas	1,934
285	Stork	Net	Heavy Eng.	1,855
286	Chargeurs	Fra	Textiles	1,800
287	Benetton	Ita	Retail	1,781
288	LeGrand	Fra	Elec. Eng.	1,767
289	Charbonnage de Fra.	Fra	Coal	1,742
290	Sommer Alibert	Fra	Chemicals	1,693
291	Berliner Kräft & Licht	Ger	Electricity	1,645
292	Courtaulds Textiles	UK	Textiles	1,630
293	SMH	Swi	Consumer goods	1,611
294	Carlsberg	Den	Beer	1,605
295	Jefferson Smurfitt	Ire	Paper	1,601

	Company	Country	Main products	Turnover 1991 (US$ m)
296	TI Group	UK	Heavy Eng.	1,589
297	Heidelberger Zement	Ger	Cement	1,468
298	Cimentries CBR	Bel	Cement	1,361
299	Italcemente	Ita	Cement	1,333
300	Brit. Airports Auth.	UK	Transport service	1,320
301	Mondadori	Ita	Publishing	1,180

In addition to the above, there are the many North American and global companies identified in the text, many of which have major interests in Europe. In particular, the sectors covering consumer goods, computers, pharmaceuticals, aerospace and cars contain major Japanese and North American companies that are important in strategy development. They amount to another 50 companies approximately.

The major European Banks and European Insurance Companies are listed in chapters 19 and 28 respectively. There are around 20 banks and 30 insurance companies listed.

The Selection Criteria for the Top 400

This appendix provides some background information about the rankings for those wishing to understand the basis of selection and what this means for its strengths and weaknesses.

HOW EUROPE'S TOP 400 COMPANIES WERE SELECTED

Since this book is primarily concerned with European and global business strategy, the starting point must be customers and markets. For companies, sales turnover is the primary way of monitoring and recording these elements: it is consistent with strategy because when coupled with trading profits, it is a measure of trading performance.

Hence, for the majority of the Top 400, *total sales* were used to rank European Companies. However, for some companies, this would produce a wildly distorted ranking (eg large retail banks, large insurance companies, some large commodity traders and property companies). Banks handle major sums of money but it would be misleading to describe this as turnover in the same way as for a manufacturing company: the transactions simply go through the banks. Similarly, insurance companies handle vast sums in premiums but it would be unwise to compare these directly with manufacturing company sales. This also applies to some large commodity traders.

For Europe's top banks and insurance companies, assets are no better in some cases as a ranking method because they are not all recorded in the balance sheet. Stock market capitalization takes all these matters into account to some extent. Hence, it has been used as the basis for ranking banks and insurance companies and has been shown separately in order to avoid confusion with companies ranked by turnover.

Among major commodity traders, those companies *solely* concerned with this business area have been excluded: in practice, this principally means several metal and agricultural traders. Equally, companies engaged *solely* in property holding have been excluded, but construction companies are included. Both property and commodity traders are very difficult to assess.

A large number of Europe's Top 400 have some involvement in trading (eg oil companies). This is part of their normal business, so such companies' sales are included. But it does mean that the list is biased towards companies with large trading turnover, eg retailers, at the expense of measures associated with shareholders and assets. However, if stock market valuation had been used for the selection of the complete list, this would have been highly biased towards the UK, where there are many more publicly-quoted companies. The aim throughout has been to identify Europe's Top 400 whether they are public, private or government-owned, rather than concentrate solely on those with stock market listings. Moreover, stock market valuation is typically short term and thus inconsistent with strategy which is longer term in outlook. It has only been used to select banks and insurance companies.

Two arbitrary guidelines in Europe's Top 400
Because banks and insurance companies have been selected on a different basis to the majority of companies, there is no automatic process that brings the two lists together. Hence, a largely arbitrary line has been drawn: around thirty each of Europe's top banks and insurers are included. The rest are selected on turnover as outlined above.

However, this is no more arbitrary than the selection of only 400 of Europe's top companies in the first place: there is nothing special about the quantity 400. It has simply been chosen as a useful total to illustrate various aspects of strategy.

A word of caution on the market sector analyses
Because companies were chosen for their total turnover across all product area, some slightly smaller companies concentrated in one product area may have been excluded from certain specific market sector analyses. Where this is known, then an appropriate note has been included in the commentary. This is why some analyses are headed 'selected' companies: there may be an important omission.

Choice of year for ranking
The year 1991 was chosen because, at the time of compiling the list in Autumn 1992, a significant number of companies had not produced 1992 accounts. Although there will be a few dramatic changes as a result of takeovers and mergers over the period to mid 1990, many of Europe's Top 400 are large and have restrictive shareholding structures: they only change slowly. Thus the selection should remain relevant for its purpose for some years.

Geographical basis for selection
'Europe' means all of western Europe, not just companies with headquarters in the European Community.

Nevertheless, selection has concentrated on those companies with European headquarters. But it clearly made no more sense to completely exclude such great world companies as Du Pont and Sony, even though their prime trading stance relates to the USA. For such major US and Japanese companies, this would lead to a gross underestimate of their importance to Europe: IBM Europe and Esso Europe are other clear examples. As a compromise, for some major US and Japanese corporations, where possible, data on their turnover has been used and the companies included in the ranking on this basis.

Currency basis for international sales comparison
Whilst the ECU is used throughout the EC, the US dollar is employed much more widely for international trading purposes. Thus, although it may not be

very 'Community-minded', all local currencies have been translated into the ubiquitous US dollar at the rate ruling in June 1991 or June 1992. Clearly, any currency translation brings its own distortions but there is no realistic alternative.

What all this means is that the rankings should be treated with caution. Ultimately, the book is about tackling European and global markets, not about a company's precise position in a European league table.

National comparisons within Europe's Top 400

Nowhere in the book will you find any reference to the overall number of companies by country: Germany, UK, Italy or whatever. The data is largely irrelevant to any strategic analysis and I have not bothered to calculate it.

What does matter for strategy is how a company compares with others in a *particular European industry*: that is why there are 25 special comparison tables in the book. We will leave national comparisons to the political arena.

DEFINITIONS

The definitions used in the book are based on the principle that the prime point of interest is a company's *trading ability* in the marketplace, not its ability to manipulate its corporate treasury portfolio. The significance of this is that profits are measured *before* tax and interest charges.

Turnover is the total income of the company excluding Value Added Tax (TVA) and similar taxes, except where otherwise stated. It will include royalty income (often a means of remitting trading profits to a parent) but exclude inter-group sales between subsidiaries of a group.

Profit is the trading profit of the company before interest and taxes. It is calculated, where possible, before extraordinary items. Where profit is shown for a subsidiary or constituent parts of a company, this is usually on the basis as given by the company: this means that it may not be consistent with the definition used elsewhere. The problem is that the company usually does not supply sufficient detail to be able to recalculate it on a common basis. Profit is always shown after normal trading costs (eg depreciation charges, auditors' fees and employee costs).

Capital employed is the difference between the total fixed and current assets of the company after deducting depreciation and current liabilities (ie those due for settlement inside one year).

Return on capital is the trading profit divided by the capital employed, as defined above, and expressed as a percentage.

Currencies for individual companies are those quoted in their annual accounts.

APPENDIX 3
Bibliography

Two valuable books of annual statistics on the EC are *Basic Statistics of the Community, Eurostat Review 1991–92*, Statistical Office of the European Communities, and a review of some 125 EC industries (although with limited company data), *Panorama of EC Industry 1993*, Commission of the European Communities.

Two other EC reports in areas concerned with markets and competition are *European Economy: Horizontal Mergers and Competition Policy in the EC No. 40*, European Commission (1989) and the *18th Report on Competition Policy*, European Commission (1989). For more specific data on European companies, here are three sources: Extel card European service; McCarthy press cuttings service for European companies; and the companies themselves (Appendix 1 contains the names and addresses of the first 250).

The EC's case for the projected massive benefits of the single Europe is set out in the paperback *1992: the Benefits of a Single Market*, Paolo Cecchini, Wildwood House (1988) and, in more detail, in *Research on the 'Cost of non-Europe'*, European Commission, 12 volumes (1989). (Vol. 1 contains executive summaries with another 11 volumes containing the consulting reports on different industries.)

For three useful books on background aspects of the single market see: *A Common Man's Guide to the Common Market*, Hugh Arbuthnott and Geoffrey Edwards, Macmillan (1989); *The Structure of European Industry*, H. W. de Jong (editor), Kluwer Academic Publishers (1988); and *Setting Up a Company in the European Community*, Brebner & Co, Kogan Page (1989).

Two books on business strategy connected with Europe are: *1992 Myths and Realities*, Centre for Business Strategy, London Business School (1989); and *1993 and Beyond: New Strategies for the Enlarged Single Market*, James W. Dudley, Kogan Page (1993). For a more general paperback on business strategy that is useful for its breadth and insights see *Strategic Market Planning*, George S. Day, West Publishing (1984).

My own books, *European Marketing*, Kogan Page (1992) and *Cases in European Marketing*, Kogan Page (1994) also contain a wealth of additional material. I also have no hesitation in recommending my friend Chris Halliburton and his colleague, Reinhard Huenerberg's, *European Marketing: Readings and Cases*, Addison-Wesley (1993).

The two classics on business strategy, again mainly with American examples, are *Competitive Strategy*, Michael Porter, Free Press (1980) and *Competitive Advantage*, Michael Porter, Free Press (1985). For two more practical books on implementation see *Offensive Marketing*, Hugh Davidson, Penguin (1987) – packed with mainly UK examples in the marketing area – and *Bargaining for Results*, John Winkler, Pan (1987).

Finally, here are four publications on the important topic of European employment and social policy: *1992: the European Social Dimension*, Patrick Venturini, European Commission (1989); *A Guide to Working in a Europe Without Frontiers*, Jean-Claude Seche, European Commission (1989); *European Foundation for the Improvement of Living and Working Conditions: Annual Report 1988*, European Commission (1989); and *Trends in Non-wage Labour Costs and their Effects on Employment: Final Report 1988*, European Commission (1989). Colin Randlesome edited a most useful book in this area: *Business Cultures in Europe*, Heinemann (1992).

Index